STRUGGLING FOR RECOGNITION

THE UNITED STATES ARMY CHAPLAINCY

1791–1865

By

Herman A. Norton

Volume II

OFFICE OF THE CHIEF OF CHAPLAINS
DEPARTMENT OF THE ARMY
WASHINGTON, D.C. 1977

FOREWORD

This volume is one of a series of five prepared by various authors, designed to be useful and instructive regarding the long history of the United States Army Chaplaincy. The emphasis throughout is on how chaplains did their ministry in the contexts of both war and peace. The series seeks to present as full and as balanced an account as limitations of space and research time permit. The bibliography in each volume offers opportunities for further research leading to detailed studies, articles, monographs, and perhaps even volumes regarding persons, developments, and events of the periods concerned. No attempt has been made to express any specific point of view or to make policy recommendations. The contents of each volume represent the work of the individual author and do not represent the official view of the United States government.

An effort has been made to make this volume as complete and factual as possible. In the light of new informtion and developments, there may be modifications required concerning the material, interpretations, and conclusions presented. Such corrections, additions, and suggestions as readers may have are welcome for use in future revisions; they should be addressed to:

> Director of Support
> US Army Chaplain Center and School
> ATTN: Historian
> Fort Wadsworth, Staten Island, NY

10305

This volume is the work of Chaplain Herman A. Norton, a Reserve Component chaplain of the Christian Church (Disciples of Christ). Chaplain Norton is a native of Virginia and received his A.B. degree from Lynchburg College, Lynchburg, Virginia. His B.D., M.A., and Ph.D. degrees were earned at Vanderbilt University, Nashville, Tennessee, where he has taught since 1951. He served as a chaplain for two years in the Pacific during World War II, and has been active in the United States Army Reserve since 1947. He has attained the grade of Brigadier General in the Army Reserve.

> ORRIS E. KELLY
> Chaplain (Major General) US Army
> Chief of Chaplains

PREFACE

With few exceptions, articles and books about the United States Army and its historical development deal with battles, campaigns, organization, and certain leaders. Most of the writing tends to reinforce the stereotype of a large, nebulous, impersonal machine. Left largely unnoticed are the many activities, services and persons within the organization that make it a more significant institution than is generally realized.

In recent years some of the neglected aspects of Army life have received scholarly attention. Serious studies have been made, for example, of the historical development of the medical services; the same can be said regarding the social and cultural aspects of soldier life. There remain, however, several facets not yet thoroughly investigated and reported.

One such activity is the chaplaincy. Dedicated ministers, priests and rabbis rendered invaluable service for over 200 years from within the Army, yet there is no thorough study of the Army chaplaincy. This volume, like the others in the series, is primarily an attempt to rectify that situation; additionally, it is meant to show some Army dimensions that make it a significant institution.

The narrative spans the 75-year period from 1791 through 1865, a time of successive national struggles for survival. The chaplaincy is considered against the background of those struggles and their impact upon it, institutionally and otherwise. The primary emphasis, however, is on ministerial performance, the activities of typical chaplains. Restrictions on space preclude detailed accounts of many worthy accomplishments and contributions; hopefully, those included provide a representative cross section of the many who served. A genuine effort has been made to be objective, to render a balanced, impartial, accurate composition of good and bad, pleasant and unpleasant, achievements and failures.

The author acknowledges with gratitude the many who assisted with the production of this volume. Mrs. Mafie Capps and Mr. Alan Aimone of the United States Military Academy deserve special mention; so do those who shared their own research and insights with me, my colleagues in this series, Chaplains Earl F. Stover, Parker C. Thompson, and Roger R. Venzke. Chaplain Wayne C. King, museum curator; Mrs. Rita A. Harris, office secretary; and Chaplain William E. Paul, Jr., History Project Manager, all at the United States Army Chaplain Center and School, deserve special thanks for their valuable contributions.

Appreciation is due Vanderbilt University, especially Dean Walter Harrelson of the Divinity School, for a semester's leave of absence to accomplish detailed research and writing. I am indebted to my colleague, Richard C. Wolf, for editorial assistance and support. To my wife, Alma, foremost among several persons who aided in the preparation of the original manuscript, my profound thanks.

vi

TABLE OF CONTENTS

I

AN OLD ART IN A NEW COUNTRY

March 4, 1791, was a fairly pleasant and enjoyable day for most of the country. It was a momentous one for John Hurt. He would never forget it as long as he lived. Early in the morning official notification arrived informing him that he was awarded a chaplaincy commission in the United States Army, the first of its kind. The appointment was made by an old friend and colleague, President George Washington.

Only the day before Congress had authorized the position for an Army of two regiments, with 104 officers and 2,128 enlisted men.[1] Prior to that legislation, Army strength was the equivalent of a regiment; and most legislators, from the time the Constitution went into effect, consistently felt a regiment too small a unit to have a chaplain. When the constant threat of Indian warfare on the frontier prompted Congress, on 3 March 1791, to authorize the creation of a second regiment, the brigade-size structure that resulted appeared to warrant a chaplain. "To this toy army there was attached a major general, brigadier general, brigade major, quartermaster and chaplain."[2] The concern of Congress was a pragmatic one and the question of a religious establishment was not raised. Ironically, the chaplaincy was authorized at a time when religious interest in the United States was at an unusually low ebb and spiritual deadness characterized the American churches.

The position specified was essentially that of brigade chaplain. It carried no rank, and total compensation, including pay, rations, and forage, was $600 annually.[3] The stipend was slightly above that paid surgeons and from six to nine dollars more than the monthly pay of captains. Duties were not specified, but the chaplain was

———

(See notes at end of chapter)

expected to perform as brigade chaplains functioned during the Revolutionary War.

Hurt had both professional and military qualifications for the new position. As an Episcopal clergyman, after the American Revolution, he served some important parishes in Virginia, his native state. Theologically sensitive and homiletically alert, he was a good pastor and an able preacher. Several of his sermons were printed and circulated by some of his parishioners who were tremendously impressed by the content and structure of the discourses. Each manuscript contained the hallmark of an artisan.[4]

Hurt's military career dated back to the Revolutionary War; he was one of the very few chaplains on the Colonial side to serve throughout the conflict. On 1 October 1776, at the age of 24, he was appointed chaplain of the 6th Virginia Regiment. By the time of the New Jersey campaign of 1777, he was also serving as chaplain for the 4th and 5th Virginia Regiments. On 18 August 1778, after the three regiments were consolidated into a brigade, he was appointed brigade chaplain, holding that position until the end of the war.[5] Appointment to the chaplaincy in 1791 was, in effect, a reappointment.

The military career of Chaplain Hurt was not uneventful. In 1780, he was taken prisoner by the British while "endeavoring to gain intelligence for the Baron de Steuben" and suffered "the most ignominious treatment at different times on board different ships. . . ."[6] He encountered additional difficulty when he lost his horse, and his pay for 12 months was in arrears. When Hurt asked for Washington's assistance in securing another horse and getting paid, the Commanding General responded with the discouraging statement that he could not get a horse even for himself and that "want of pay is a common misfortune attending the army and which at present cannot be relieved by me. . . ."[7] A horse was soon secured, however, and eventually his financial compensation was received. On 13 January 1784, in recognition of his seven years' service in the Continental line, Virginia awarded him a tract of 7,000 acres in what is now Kentucky.[8]

The brigade chaplaincy position did not remain firm for long. After only a year, and in response to a Congressional act of 5 March 1792, the chaplain became a functioning member of the General Staff, composed of two generals, a surgeon, a quartermas-

---

(See notes at end of chapter)

ter, and an adjutant, in addition to the chaplain.[9] Hurt, the Army's only chaplain, served on the General Staff until he resigned on 30 April 1794. From the time of his resignation until his death in 1824, at Pamplin City, Virginia, the community of his birth, Hurt remained active in the ministry of the Episcopal Church.[10]

Although the Regular Army maintained a chaplain, none was authorized for the militia of the new states. One of Washington's cabinet members tried unsuccessfully to correct the situation. On 18 January 1790, Henry Knox, Secretary of War, submitted a plan to the President, who forwarded it to Congress; it called for the general arrangement of the militia into self-sufficient units called legions, each to consist of 153 officers and 2,880 men. A chaplain was proposed for the staff of each legion. Secretary Knox had deep feeling for the chaplaincy position:

> Every legion must have a chaplain, of respectable talents and character, who, besides his religious functions, should impress on the minds of the youth, at stated periods, in concise discourses, the eminent advantages of free governments to the happiness of society, and that such governments can only be supported by the knowledge, spirit, and virtuous conduct of the youth—to be illustrated by the most conspicuous examples in history.[11]

The plan was not adopted. In 1792, the first federal militia law was enacted, and the general and vague wording of the legislation opened up the possibility of appointment of chaplains to state militia units. It was about two decades, however, before any chaplains were appointed.

Meanwhile, the successor to Hurt, and the second Regular Army chaplain, was another veteran of the Revolutionary War, David Jones. A Baptist and native of Delaware, Jones served as chaplain with Pennsylvania troops throughout the entire engagement with England, the greater part of the time with a boyhood friend, General Anthony Wayne. Jones, who had an affection for military life, was appointed on 3 May 1794, only 13 days after the resignation of Hurt.[12] The commission was awarded at the insistence of General Wayne, who had been commissioned a Major General and put in command of the American Army. In his endeavor to construct a reliable military organization, he attempted

(See notes at end of chapter)

to secure the services of several former aides and staff; David Jones was one of those he sought.

Jones had hardly reported for duty when Wayne was involved in a series of skirmishes with Indians in the Northwest territory. The General lost in the first encounter, primarily because his plan was leaked to the Indians by a disloyal staff member. Chaplain Jones, during a visit to the stockade to converse with prisoners, discovered the source of the leak and promptly reported his find to the commander.[13] Tight security resulted. In the next encounter, on 10 August 1794, the Indians were defeated near what is now Toledo, Ohio; a year later the Indians surrendered, largely due to Wayne's skill at convincing them of the hopelessness of their cause. In the peace councils with the Indians, Wayne was almost invariably accompanied by three staff members and his trusted and intimate advisor, Chaplain David Jones. A painting of the chief participants in the final council portrayed Jones positioned very prominently near General Wayne.[14]

While on duty with Wayne in the campaign against the Indians Jones, continuing a practice started much earlier, kept a carefully written diary. It is filled with details about his activities and interesting insights into some aspects of army life. The entries indicate that Jones considered preaching to be his primary function. He preached whenever military conditions allowed, and the texts he used conveyed the kind of discourses the chaplain felt the soldiers should hear. A few selected texts from the later part of 1794 are illustrative.

On 3 August 1794 Jones reported: "I spoke to the soldiers from Luke 3:14 'and the soldiers likewise demanded of him, saying, and what shall we do?' and he said unto them, do no violence to any man, neither accuse any falsely; and be content with your wages!"[15]

Two weeks later he wrote that he preached "at 6 in the afternoon in the garrison from Exod. 20; 'Thou shalt not take the Name of the Lord Thy God in vain: for the Lord will not hold him guiltless, that taketh his Name in vain.' "[16]

On 19 October, the chaplain "preached to the Troops from Rom. 13:1, 'Let every soul be subject to the higher Powers.' "[17]

Following a service on 23 November, Jones wrote: "My text was John 18:36, 'Jesus answered, My Kingdom is not of this world; if

(See notes at end of chapter)

my kingdom were of this world, then would my servants fight, that I should not be delivered to the Jews: But now is my kingdom not from hence.'" Jones continued: "I made several preliminary observations, respecting the way in which this Text had been quoted, by such as refuse to bear arms and observed, that it was one of the most decisive Texts for bearing arms, in all of Scripture. . . ."[18]

Other duties which occupied the chaplain's time included visiting the sick, burying the dead, performing marriages, and preaching in civilian churches. Jones did not neglect scholarly pursuits and attempted to spend several hours each day reading. On 12 October 1790 he was "engaged in reading 'Plutarch's Lives,'" and reported that he had read "'Cato the Younger' and Mark Anthony's life. . . ."[19]

The chaplain enjoyed his work, but there were some unpleasant moments. In his diary Jones wrote: "Sergeant Kesting was to be executed by being shot, and Corporal Reading by being hanged by the neck. The dreadful hour came, the solemn process was performed . . . we came to the place. The day was rising. I spoke about 20 minutes and prayed."[20] But in that instance the unhappiness ended in joy; at the last moment, both were granted reprieves.

Late in 1796, Jones contemplated resigning his commission. He was deeply grieved by General Wayne's death on 15 December 1796, at the age of 52, from complications of gout and a severe stomach disorder. The two men had been almost inseparable on the battlefield, in camp, and in council. With the death of his intimate friend, the Army would not be the same. But his love for military life prevailed, and he decided to continue in service. He remained a chaplain in the Army until 15 June 1800, when he resigned.[21]

In the spring of 1798 it appeared that Jones would be joined by other chaplains. The United States seemed headed for war and an increase in the size of the Army was deemed necessary to safeguard the interests and welfare of the country. The prospective conflict was the culmination of a series of events that began almost at the time of Washington's inauguration as President.

Early in the closing decade of the 18th Century, England's highhandedness on the oceans, along with the efforts of Revolutionary France to enlist the cooperation of the United States in war against England, carried the United States swiftly toward a new conflict with the Mother Country. The new Republic, however, was

(See notes at end of chapter)

too feeble to risk such a prospect, and President Washington used the diplomatic energies of his administration to avert hostilities. John Jay, Washington's envoy to London, succeeded in doing so through a treaty, but with some sacrifice of America's concept of neutral maritime rights. While Jay's Treaty patched up relations with Great Britain, it did so at the expense of friendship with France, which saw the treaty as a secret agreement of partnership between England and her former colonies. The French became the most notorious violators of American commercial rights, and the two nations drifted into increasing hostility. By 1798 matters reached such serious proportions with France that the United States began preparations for war. A frenzy of legislation was passed: In April, the Army was authorized 4,000 additional troops, which more than doubled its size; in May, Congress made arrangements for the creation of a provisional Army; and in an act of 11 July 1798, which provided for over 14,000 more soldiers, provision was made for four chaplains to be attached to the General Staff. Each chaplain was to receive the pay and allowances of a major.[22]

War did not become a reality. Relations with France became less tense, and the troops were not mobilized. Congress immediately began the work of dismantling the greater part of the military structure it had envisioned. A Congressional act of 14 May 1800, which established Army strength at less than 5,000 officers and enlisted men, provided for the retention "of the general and other staff," including the chaplain. But in a subsequent act, on 16 March 1801, setting the size of the Army at less than 3,000, no specific mention of chaplains was made.[23]

Chaplains were a part of the military, however. Any chaplain in service in the early years of the 19th Century had support for his religious activities reinforced by an act of Congress. On 10 April 1806, Congress, in approving rules and articles for the regulation of the Army, "recommended to all officers and soldiers, diligently to attend divine worship service. . . ." To eliminate a possible competitive gathering place, the legislation declared that "no settler (would) be permitted . . . to keep . . . shops open . . . Sundays during divine services. . . ." To make sure the troops abided by sermonic directives given in worship services, the legislation prohibited profanity, gambling, and the drinking of intoxicants. Penalties were prescribed for offenders; for example, any soldier who used a

_____

(See notes at end of chapter)

profane oath incurred the penalty of seventeen cents for the first offense, and the same amount "and confinement for each offense thereafter." Commissioned officers had to forfeit pay in the amount of one dollar "for each and every offense."

To keep the chaplain at his task, the same act declared that "every chaplain commissioned in the army or armies of the United States, who shall absent himself from the duties assigned him . . . shall, on conviction thereof before a court-martial, be fined . . . or be discharged, as the said court-martial shall judge proper."[24]

Although war with France was avoided, an uneasiness continued to characterize American relations with European nations. The possibility of armed conflict with one or more European powers had to be faced; with an Army of regimental proportions, alternatives had to be considered. Attention again focused on the militia. With the Militia Act of 1791 in mind, Congress moved to regularize and strengthen the militia in each of the states; on 2 March 1803, it approved an act "more effectively to provide for the national defense by establishing a uniform militia throughout the United States." To achieve uniformity, each state would have the regiment as the basic military unit, with every citizen in the militia provided arms and ammunition and required to train with the nearest regiment. Officers were prescribed and each regiment was to have a chaplain. That legislation was significant; Congress for the first time provided for chaplains in the militia of the states.[25]

The legislation was appropriate, but the states did not move with dispatch to provide for its implementation. The act specified that each year the Adjutant General would report to the President on the condition of the militia in each state. In January 1804, when the first scattered reports came into Washington, only minimal conformity was achieved. Slight improvement was made during the next year, but Delaware, Maryland, and Tennessee did not bother to submit reports.[26] The militia remained the same ill-trained mass it had been before the passage of the act of 1803. The system seemed to defy all attempts to create better readiness; before another year passed, however, Congress was discussing a new organization for the militia.

Meanwhile, the relations of the United States with England and France deteriorated. Seizures of American vessels increased because of the policies of France and Britain. Americans were more anxious,

_____

(See notes at end of chapter)

however, about England's practice of "impressment"—taking seamen from American ships who, the British claimed, sometimes rightly, were deserters from the Royal Navy. Matters reached a climax on 22 June 1807; the British warship *Leopard* fired on the American warship *Chesapeake,* killing three men and wounding eighteen, and forced it to yield several alleged deserters. When the *Chesapeake* "hobbled back to Norfolk with its tale of woe, the response was immediate and loud . . . American opinion not only supported but demanded war."[27]

Instead of war, however, President Jefferson resorted to the Embargo Act of 1807, which withdrew American ships from the seas. Congress, meanwhile, discussed and planned for the eventuality of war. On 12 April 1808, it approved an act providing for an "addition to the present military establishment" of the equivalent of three brigades; a chaplain, with the pay and allowances of a major of infantry, would be assigned to each brigade.[28] The additional forces were not immediately mobilized.

About that time the militia seemed to take on new life, primarily in several New England states; however, it appeared to be more in opposition to the Federal Government than in support of it. Although all parts of the country were affected by the embargo, the New England shipping interests felt the impact most directly. Vociferous protests came from the area, meetings remonstrated with the government, and local courts refused to enforce federal laws. Policies designed to avoid a foreign war brought the country to the verge of civil war. Citizens rushed to staff and man militia units. Ministers competed for the militia chaplaincies. The increase in the militia strength was amazing, and a large number of clergymen became militia chaplains. By 1809, there were 64 chaplains in Massachusetts units, principally company size, and 42 chaplains served in Connecticut. The next year one chaplain was added to the Connecticut list, but the number in Massachusetts had increased to 81.[29] New England returned to relative calm when Jefferson, in one of his last acts, signed a bill repealing the embargo; the militia, nevertheless, maintained its strength.

Tensions in Europe did not abate. President Jefferson's successor, James Madison, attempted to secure peace and maintain the neutral rights of the United States by diplomatic negotiations and economic coercion. By this time, however, the British maritime

(See notes at end of chapter)

policy was deeply wounding both the pride and commerce of the United States; worse, England began to support the Indians in their warfare on the frontier. Relations with England deteriorated steadily, yet Congress did nothing to prepare for war. A bill to raise a military force of 50,000 volunteers was allowed to die even as pro-war sentiment swept the country.[30]

In the Congressional elections of November 1810, nearly half of the incumbents, denounced as ineffective and complacent, lost their seats. In the new Congress a young and aggressive group of legislators, sometimes called "war hawks," took the lead in advocating new and stronger measures regarding foreign adversaries. They forced the abandonment of peaceable coercion and laid the groundwork for a policy backed by force that ultimately led to war.

The "war hawks" were instrumental in securing legislation early in 1812 that increased the size of the Army, on paper at least, from 10,000 to 35,000. The legislators envisioned 13 regiments. The regiments were to be very large, numbering more than 2,000 infantry officers and enlisted men and nearly that many in the artillery; chaplains, however, were still provided only for brigades.[31] In less than a month another bill became law; it authorized the President to accept 50,000 volunteers to be officered by state authorities and called into service by the President when needed. Chaplains were again authorized for each brigade. Then, in April, Congress authorized each regiment in the militia to have a military minister, with the pay and allowances of a captain of infantry.[32] Within a short period of 30 days, Congress thus approved both brigade and regimental chaplaincies, the former for regular forces and the latter for nonregular. The implication seemed to be that volunteers needed more chaplains than regulars; that, or the action was simply a political expedient. Perhaps Congress didn't give much real thought to what it was doing. . . .

These measures. appeared woefully insufficient as genuine preparation for serious fighting; nevertheless, Great Britain's provocations took precedence, and on 18 June 1812 Congress declared war on England. The military force was little more adequate than it was in 1775. The Regular Army numbered slightly over 11,000 despite an authorized strength of 35,600, including eight chaplains.[33] The President did have authority to call up a sizeable contingent of volunteers and to mobilize the militia; however, that had to be tempered by the realization that some states, reflecting the general lack of patriotic fervor, would not raise the suggested quota of men. Several New England states, where the militia was best organized, showed hostility about the loss of maritime trade profits and announced they would not send any militia to "Mr. Madison's war," as they referred to it.[34] Although New England governors occasionally refused to furnish militia for federal service, individual New England men participated.

Before the war ran its course, more than 400,000 men were called into military service; yet at no time was there an effective force of more than 20,000 men. Fortunately for the United States, the British were preoccupied with war in Europe at the outset; furthermore, they had barely 7,000 soldiers in Canada, along with a small Canadian militia and the support of Indian allies.[35]

The battles throughout the war were, on the whole, minor skirmishes, with the rival armies averaging about 1,500 to 2,000 men. Most of the action occurred close to the Canadian border or along the Atlantic coast. During the first two years the fighting was mainly along the northern border, in accord with the United States' plan of operations that called for a three-pronged drive into Canada. The United States military force was made up largely of ill-trained and undependable militia. However inadequate in quality, they did turn out in quantity. Kentucky, New York, Ohio, and Pennsylvania furnished men generously; Maryland and Virginia had impressive contingents. In early 1813, the Army Paymaster estimated that over 30,000 militia were in service, compared to 18,945 regulars.[36]

The militia, generally in regiments, were accompanied in many instances by a chaplain; as a rule, he remained with a single regiment and provided ministerial services to that organization. There was no arrangement for transfer from one regiment to another. Approximately 20 chaplains were on duty with militia regiments in the early phase of the war and about half that number remained until the conflict ended. The states with the largest representation were Pennsylvania and New York, with five each.[37]

While chaplains for regiments was fairly standard practice in the militia, the Regulars continued to be authorized chaplains only for brigades. This position was reinforced when Congress, on 20 January 1813, reported that the Regular force would have chaplains

(See notes at end of chapter)

appointed to each brigade who were entitled to the pay and allowances of a major of infantry. By an act of the same Congress, militia chaplains, carrying out the same functions as brigade chaplains but for a smaller organization, received the pay and allowances of a captain of infantry.[38]

Obviously, the vast majority of chaplains in the militia did not enter federal service. The report of the Secretary of War on the status of the militia at the war's beginning indicated that 134 ministers had commissions as chaplains. Some were unable to secure significant active duty no matter how hard they tried. For example, immediately after the declaration of war, the governors of Massachusetts and Connecticut refused to furnish troops to the Federal Government. In these two states, where more than half of the militia chaplains were located, when restrictions were occasionally relaxed and a unit was federalized, it was for only a brief period, and a chaplain's tour of duty was quite short. For instance, in Connecticut, eight chaplains accompanied their units on active duty in June and July 1813; all were out of service within three months.[39]

Among the eight was a well known and somewhat eccentric clergyman, David Austin, who attempted to extend his period of duty because he was without a pastorate at the time. Austin was widely known because of his predictions and writings regarding the millennium and the return of the Jews to the Holy Land. Born to wealth in 1760, he became pastor of a Presbyterian Church in Elizabeth, New Jersey, in 1788. He was interested in prophecy and soon declared that the millennium was at hand; he even set a date, 15 May 1796, for the second Advent. His following was fabulous; whenever and wherever he spoke, the auditorium always filled to overflowing. When his prophecy failed to come true at the appointed time, his ingenuity found excuse for his mistake.

Austin's congregation, which at first respected and then simply tolerated him, eventually became agitated and church leaders asked the Presbytery to dissolve the pastoral relationship. Austin returned to New Haven, the place of his birth, and began to preach that the Jews of America were literally about to return to the Holy Land. He felt New Haven would be the place of embarkation, and spent his considerable fortune on houses and a wharf for their use. Unable to

(See notes at end of chapter)

pay incurred debts, he was imprisoned for a time. Upon his release, he served as a supply preacher in and around New Haven.

During this period Austin became chaplain for the militia unit commanded by his friend, Colonel Hezekiah Howe. His tour of federalized duty began 3 August 1813 and concluded on 17 September 1813, his attempt to extend it having failed. After the war he became pastor of the Congregational Church in Bozrah, Connecticut, and remained there, accepted and successful, until his death on 15 February 1831.[40]

A new theater of operations opened in the south in 1813. Andrew Jackson, commander of the Tennessee militia, sought to lead a force of 2,000 into Spanish territory in what is now southern Mississippi and northern Florida. Congress, after extended debate, approved a more limited expedition and sent Brigadier General James Wilkinson and his Regulars to do the job; the Tennesseans, who had journeyed south from Nashville, were left out entirely, encamped at Natchez, Mississippi Territory.

When Jackson organized his forces at Nashville for the abortive campaign into Spanish territory, he selected a chaplain to minister to his command. It was Learner Blackman, the most prominent Methodist minister in Middle Tennessee, chosen on 28 December 1812. Concluding that he "could be of some use to the Army especially that part of them that (were) Methodist," Blackman accepted the appointment. Compensation was $125 per month, far more than regimental chaplains in other states received, and twice the stipend for brigade chaplains.[41] Apparently half of the salary, or more, was supplemented by state funds.

Blackman was a good choice. A native of New Jersey, born in 1781, he was a Methodist missionary in Kentucky, Tennessee, and Mississippi territory from 1802 until 1808, the year he became Presiding Elder of the Holston District in East Tennessee. In 1810, he was transferred as Presiding Elder to the Cumberland District of Middle Tennessee; he held that position, except for his period of military service, until his death by drowning on 7 June 1815.

On 29 December 1812, Blackman preached his first sermon to the troops and made preparations to accompany them. He decided to keep a written record of his experiences; the voluminous journal which resulted affords insight into the activities of a militia chaplain.

(See notes at end of chapter)

Jackson and his force departed Nashville in boats on Saturday, 10 January 1813. In the evening most of the officers assembled on the commander's boat and Blackman conducted a worship service. An aide to Jackson reported: ". . . we had a very appropriate and sensible discourse delivered by the Revd. Mr. Blackman, Chaplain to the army. . . ."[42] In the course of the service, Blackman "read a part of the 10th Chapter of the Gospel by St. Mathew and preached some on fear. . . ." At the conclusion of the worship experience, he reflected: "I am in a critical place but that God that preserved Daniel among the Lions can preserve me among the wicked. . . . I feel now that the army is my charge while I am with them."[43]

Blackman kept busy visiting among the men and giving special attention to the sick and injured. The first Sunday out from Nashville he established a pattern that permitted him to conduct worship services where everyone had opportunity to attend. Since it was not practical to stop and assemble for a general service, Blackman held services on the individual boats. Each one carried a company numbering between 80 and 100 troops. Beginning at the headquarters vessel at 10 a.m., he moved in a canoe from boat to boat until services had been held on all. The last was reached about dusk. After the first Sunday, several of the company commanders lashed their boats together for the worship period to cut down the number of services Blackman had to conduct.

The apparent success of the Sunday services prompted Blackman to attempt them throughout the week. It was impractical to do this during the day, so he developed a routine of holding about two services after the boats had tied up at the bank for the night.

When the boats reached the confluence of the Cumberland and Ohio Rivers, the ice on the latter appeared to be too thick for navigation; the expedition camped at the mouth of the Cumberland for almost a week, waiting for the condition of the Ohio to improve. The chaplain used the opportunity to hold general worship services each day on the parade field after the troops had exercised. Here, as elsewhere, Blackman also used the delay as an opportunity to minister to the settlers residing in the vicinity.

When the flotilla reached Fort Massac, near Metropolis, Illinois, Blackman went ashore and preached to "the regulars" stationed there. The contact with the Regular Army left the militia chaplain somewhat despondent. He commented: "My sympathy was excited

(See notes at end of chapter)

when I considered the situation of soldiers. They are not better off than slaves. . . . I am awfully afraid our officers in the regular service are very wicked. We have much to fear when that is the case. . . . Profane swearing prevails among the soldiery and likewise among the officers. . ."[44]

About that stage of the trip General Jackson appeared less than satisfied with some aspects of Blackman's ministry, especially to the sick. The chaplain wrote: "The Gen. in presence of the Col. & Lieutenant Col. of the first Redgement examined me a little to know how I talked to the sick signified that it would be highly improper to tell a person he would die if Simtoms were unfavorable I let him know on that point that I should be independent and that I should do as I thought best." As an afterthought, he added: "I find the Gen. cannot bare much opposition. He is a good General but a very incorrect Divine."[45] Blackman felt less at ease visiting the sick than in any other phase of his ministerial activity. After the encounter with Jackson, he penned: "I feel my defficiency more when I attempt to visit the sick than in any other instances. . . ."[46]

By the time the expedition reached Natchez a sizeable number of men were sick and hospitalized. The chaplain increasingly spent more time visiting them. For those who died, military funerals were conducted which included a short address. But Blackman still had ample time to hold several worship services each day for both civilian and military congregations. He received some satisfaction from his preaching and felt success was evident in one area at least. "Preaching . . . had had great effect to prevent profane swearing. . . . I do not hear as much of it as I did when we first embarked."[47]

On the journey back to Tennessee from Natchez in late March and early April, after Jackson was ordered by Congress to abort the campaign, the troops traveled nearly 500 miles in about 12 days. There was hardly time for Blackman to do anything but keep pace with the movement.

On Sunday, 4 April, his last day as a militia chaplain, Blackman preached in Nashville to a "crowded congregation" and "road after (the) meeting to General Jackson's dwelling to see his family according to his request prayed with them at night."[48] About the time Blackman was mustered out of service, serious attempts were made to use the militia less and the regular forces more. Insistence by the militia on narrowly interpreted constitutional rights; the inability of militia and regular commanders to establish and remain

---

(See notes at end of chapter)

on good terms; and reorganization and new leadership for the regulars, all led the Federal Government to rely primarily on the regular forces.

The reorganization of the military establishment into nine military districts early in 1813 had important implications for the chaplaincy. Indeed, it ushered in a new concept. The plan for reorganization called for chaplain assignments to the headquarters of each district rather than to tactical units, although for purposes of pay they were considered brigade chaplains.[49] In each district, these staff chaplains provided or arranged for ministerial services to all regular forces in the area. When there were militia units located in the district, with or without chaplains, the staff chaplain of the district was responsible for co-ordinating their religious activities, most of the time without success—the militia refused to be assimilated into the program of the regulars. The plan could never function effectively, anyway, because six of the nine districts were without chaplains throughout the war.

The first chaplains to serve the regular forces came into service after the country was divided into military districts. Two chaplains, Peter Van Pelt and the venerable David Jones, were commissioned on 2 April 1813; on 20 May, Robert Elliott, Joseph Hughes, and James Wilmer were appointed. The quintet was joined by Aaron Googe, commissioned 16 June, and Stephen Lindsley, commissioned 2 July; Thomas Hersey reported on 20 August. Van Pelt became chaplain for the 3rd District, with headquarters in New York City. Lindsley, Hersey, and Wilmer served in the 8th District, headquartered in Detroit. Booge, Elliott, and Jones were in the 9th District, with headquarters at Buffalo. These were the only chaplains on duty until late in 1814 when Solomon Aiken, commissioned 16 September 1814, and John Brannon and Carter Tarrant, both commissioned 10 December 1814, began tours of duty.[50] These eleven Regular Army chaplains were all that ministered to regular combat forces during the war.[51] The War of 1812 was a very unpopular conflict with the American people, and lack of support for it, especially by the New England clergy, was an important factor in keeping the ranks of the chaplaincy very low. Most of the regular chaplains were capable ministers. Two of them, David Jones and James Wilmer, were particularly well known.

(See notes at end of chapter)

With over 12 years of experience as a military chaplain, this was the third tour of duty for Jones. Over the opposition of his family, Jones, on 15 February 1813, wrote from Pennsylvania to his intimate friend, General James Armstrong, the Secretary of War:

> Dear General . . . Lately I saw a number of newly enlisted Dragoons going to Carlisle, the place of rendezvous. They took my fancy. I wish to act with them. Should the President think it proper to appoint me their Chaplain, I hope he will not be dishonored by the appointment. I will serve anywhere he may make it my duty and if I get no appointment, I will go a volunteer chaplain, which will be a new phenomenon.[52]

On 20 May 1813, at the age of 77, he started out for duty with the troops.

On 13 June Jones preached his first sermon to the soldiers. The forces, some 2,000 in number, assembled on the parade field. As they stood, drummers in front gave a drum roll, and Jones began his sermon on the importance of courage. An hour later, the service ended with another roll of the drums.[53] The chaplain's diary records the texts and sermon topics he used over the months, and on every occasion the Scripture selections and the discourse were relevant and appropriate.

Highly respected and known personally to every general, Jones seemed to have unlimited freedom. He traveled at will throughout the Army and into civilian communities, holding services and giving patriotic addresses. When preaching in civilian pulpits, he loved to have some troops present. When asked to preach at First Baptist Church, Philadelphia, he allegedly "sent to the Navy Yard for Marines to sit for he fancied he could preach better if there were soldiers around."[54]

His effectiveness was hampered somewhat by long periods of illness; once he required an extended leave of absence. But when active, there was no abler patriot. Once when offering prayer before a sermon in Canada, he "prayed so full of patriotism, that when he closed, the soldiers took off their hats and gave three cheers for the chaplain!"[55]

James Wilmer, the chaplain who shared national publicity with Jones, was a native of Maryland and a very versatile Episcopal minister. Educated in England at the expense of an uncle, he spent a sizeable part of his younger years traveling between Maryland and

(See notes at end of chapter)

England as claimant to an elusive "fortune." The death of the rich uncle and Wilmer's mistaken belief that his share of the estate would make him wealthy prompted the journeying. Eventually he settled down, however, and between 1779 and 1789 was rector of four Maryland parishes in succession. It was he who first proposed the name Protestant Episcopal for the American branch of the Anglican Church.

In 1792 he published "Memoirs by James Wilmer," and in subsequent years he appeared in many roles: "As schoolmaster, pamphleteer, newspaper publisher and editor, versifier, litigant, advocate before Washington and the Congress for Swedenborgian-ism as a national religion, inmate of debtor's prison, and finally a reconvert to his old faith, again a clergyman of the church. . . ."[56] After his return as a clergyman of the Episcopal Church he held rectorates in Delaware, Maryland, and Virginia.

On 24 May 1809, Wilmer was elected Chaplain of the United States Senate. He held this position, along with his parish, until appointment as an Army chaplain on 20 May 1813. His service as a regular chaplain was to be for less than a year. On 14 April 1814 he died, the only chaplain casualty of the War of 1812. The cause of death was pneumonia, contracted from overexposure during a campaign in the Great Lakes area. A somewhat garbled account of the contributing events was published in *The Ohio Vehicle,* based on a news item from Detroit:

> On the 14th instant, the Rev James T. Wilmer, brigade chaplain in the North Western Army, died in this place after a lingering and painful illness. The loss of this good and venerable man will be severely felt by his relatives as well as his country. He was cast away in a small vessel which was run along the Chippeway in October last. This vessel was run ashore at an Indian settlement about 22 miles below Malden, but fortunately for the passengers and crew, the Indians had run off upon the appearance of the American Army. Mr. Wilmer was for 13 years chaplain to Congress. . . ."[57]

Except for Wilmer, all of the Regular Army chaplains served until the end of the war. Aiken, Booge, Brannon, Jones, Lindsley, Van Pelt, and Hersey were honorably discharged on 15 June 1815. Only Elliott and Tarrant remained on duty, a situation made possible by an act of 3 March 1815, which provided for a peacetime Army of 10,000 and authorized the retention of four chaplains.[58]

(See notes at end of chapter)

The act detailing the organization of the "peace time establishment" separated the country into two military divisions. In the military Division of the South, commanded by Major General Andrew Jackson, Robert Elliott was the chaplain; Carter Tarrant was the chaplain for the military Division of the North, commanded by Major General Jacob Brown. After these appointments, a chaplain vacancy still existed in each division. In a few months there was no chaplain in the Northern Division, for Tarrant died on 17 February 1816.[59]

The Army was again reorganized in response to a Congressional act of 24 April 1816. The four chaplain positions were retained, and in a very short time filled. On 29 April 1816, two new chaplains, Cave Jones and William McCalla, entered on active duty. Chaplain Aaron Booge, less than a year our of service, was reinstated on 3 May. Booge and Jones became the chaplains for the Northern Division. Joining Elliott, McCalla became the other chaplain for the Southern Division.[60]

With McCalla in his command, Jackson had a chaplain from the same mold as himself. Aggressive, pugnacious, controversial, McCalla was a strong supporter of the War of 1812. In an effort to serve as a chaplain, he had attempted, in 1813, to become licensed for the Presbyterian ministry. When the license was not issued, McCalla blamed the Reverend James Blythe, an opponent of the war and especially of ministerial participation in it. The firebrand got involved in a fist fight with Blythe over the issue, which was eventually settled through litigation. Soon afterward, McCalla moved from Kentucky to Ohio. On 31 March 1813, he married the daughter of General Samuel Finley; 29 days later he secured his commission as a chaplain.

Tall and of commanding presence, McCalla was an effective speaker. His preaching services were always well attended, and his deep commitment to the country and its military made him a very popular preacher with the soldiers. But his tenacity and pugnaciousness, his militancy, and his sharp tongue kept him in constant turmoil with many of the officers. He remained in the Army a little less than two years.

After his release from service, McCalla became pastor of the Presbyterian Church in Augusta, Kentucky, where he stayed until 1822. For the following 20 years his ministry in and around

(See notes at end of chapter)

Philadelphia made him one of the most conspicuous figures in his denomination. He wrote a number of books and achieved fame as a debater, primarily from an indecisive debate with Alexander Campbell, one of the leaders of what was to become the Christian Church (Disciples of Christ). The pugnacious preacher later sought to serve as a chaplain during the Mexican War.

Booge, Elliott, and Jones, along with McCalla, remained as chaplains until 14 April 1818, when all four were honorably discharged and given three months' pay and allowances. The discharges were the result of a Congressional act of 14 April 1818, which reduced the size of the Army and abolished the chaplain positions, along with those of surgeons and judge advocates.[61]

With this legislation no chaplain was authorized to regular soldiers. But chaplains continued to serve the military. Over 210 of them were with state militia units at the time and the number remained fairly stable for the next few decades.[62] Also a chaplain was on duty at the Military Academy to minister to the cadets.[63]

NOTES

[1] *The Public and General Statutes Passed By The Congress Of The United States of America* (Boston: Wells and Lilly, 1827), 1: 205 (hereafter cited as *Statutes*).

[2] William A. Ganoe, *History of the United States Army* (New York: Appleton and Company, 1924), 97.

[3] *Statutes*, 1: 205; Russell Weigley, *History of the United States Army* (New York: The Macmillan Co., 1967), 81–94, contains an authoritative account of the emergence of both the professional army and state militias.

[4] John Hurt, "An Address to the Virginia Brigade," *Virginia Magazine of History*, XVII, (2 April, 1909), 213–214.

[5] Francis B. Heitman, ed, *Historical Register and Directory of the United States Army*, 2 vols, (Washington: Government Printing Office 1903), 1: 559.

[6] Roy Honeywell, "John Hurt, First Regular Army Chaplain," *The Army and Navy Chaplain*, XVI, (July–August, 1954), 7.

[7] Stewart Robinson, "Washington—The Chaplain's Friend," *The Military Chaplain*, XXIII, 2 (October, 1952), 15.

[8] "American Army Chaplaincy," *The Army and Navy Chaplain*, XVI, (1 July–August 1954), 30.

[9] *Statutes*, 1: 222.

[10] Honeywell "John Hurt" 7.

[11] Henry Knox, "A Plan For the General Arrangement of the Militia of the United States," Proceedings of the Massachusetts Historical Society, Series 1, VI (1862–1863), 386.

[12] Heitman, *Historical Register and Directory* 1: 580.

[13] Harry Emerson Wilder, *Anthony Wayne* (New York: Harcourt, Brace and Company, 1941), 431–432.

[14] Richard Knoph, ed, *Anthony Wayne: A Name in Arms* (Pittsburgh: University of Pittsburgh Press, 1960), between pages 504, 505.

[15] Diary of David Jones, 18 June 1784 to 13 July 1796, Jones Papers, American Baptist Historical Society, Rochester, N.Y. Entry of 3 August 1794.

[16] *Ibid.*, Entry of 24 August 1794.

[57] *Ibid.*

[17] *Ibid.*, Entry of 19 October 1794.

[18] *Ibid.*, Entry of 23 November 1794.

[19] *Ibid.*, Entry of 12 October 1794.

[20] *Ibid.*, Entry of 30 November 1794.

[21] Heitman, *Historical Register and Directory,* 1, 580.

[22] *Statutes,* 1: 552.

[23] *Ibid.*, 794–795, 830–836.

[24] *Ibid.*, II: 992.

[25] *Ibid.*, II: 888.

[26] Walter Lowrie and Matthew Clark, eds., *American State Papers, Documents, Legislative and Executive, of the Congress of the United States, Military Affairs* (Washington: Gales and Seaton, 1832–1861), 1: 187 (hereafter cited as *American State Papers*).

[27] Harry L. Coles, *The War of 1812* (Chicago: University of Chicago Press, 1965), 7.

[28] *Statutes,* 11: 1090.

[29] *American State Papers,* I: 259, 298.

[30] Coles, *War of 1812,* 14.

[31] *Statutes,* II: 1210.

[32] *Ibid.*, II: 1285, 1425–1426.

[33] Maurice Matloff, ed., *American Military History* (Washington, DC: U.S. Government Printing Office, 1969), 124.

[34] Richard B. Morris, ed., *Encyclopedia of American History* (New York: Harper and Brothers, 1953), 141–143.

[35] Matloff, *American Military History,* 124.

[36] *Niles Weekly Register,* CI(1814), 94–95.

[37] John Linn and William Egle, eds., *Pennsylvania Archives* (Harrisburg: State Printers, 1852–1935), Second Series, XII, XIII; Mrs. Rutlege Smith, "Roster of Ancestors of Members of the United Daughters of the War of 1812," (Typed manuscript, Tennessee State Archives, Nashville, 1943), 1–62.

[38] *Statutes,* 11: 1285.

[39] Henry Johnson, ed., *Connecticut Military Records 1775–1848* (Hartford: The Case Lockwood and Brainard Company, 1889), 1–215.

[40] William B. Sprague, *Annals of the American Pulpit,* 9 vols. (New York: Robert Carter and Brothers, 1857–1865), 1:195–199.

[41] Dawson A. Phelps, ed., "The Diary of a Chaplain in Andrew Jackson's Army: The Journal of the Reverend Blackman–December 28, 1812–April 4, 1813," *Tennessee Historical Quarterly,* XII (1953), 268. The original manuscript is part of the Winans Collection, Mississippi Department of Archives and History, Jackson.

[42] John S. Bassett, ed., *Correspondence of Andrew Jackson* (Washington: Carnegie Institute: 1926–1935), 1: 257.

[43] Phelps, "Diary of a Chaplain," 268.

[44] *Ibid.*, 271.

[45] *Ibid.*, 272.

[46] *Ibid.*, 275.

[47] *Ibid.*, 276.

[48] *Ibid.*, 281.

[49] *American State Papers,* I: 432–433.

[50] Heitman, *Historical Register and Directory,* 1: 230, 241, 402, 526, 580, 634, 653, 945, 983.

[51] Confusing the militia with the regulars, some writers give a higher number.

[52] Horatio Gates Jones, "A Memoir of the Rev. David Jones A.M." (Typed manuscript, American Baptist Historical Society, Rochester, 1859), 33.

[53] *Ibid.*, 70.

[54] *Ibid.*, 70–71.

[55] *Ibid.*, 70.

[56] Allen Johnson, ed., *Dictionary of American Biography* (New York: Charles Scribner's Sons (1928–1936), XX: 313–314; J. Hall Pleasants, ed., "Memoirs of the Rev. James Jones Wilmer," *The Maryland Historical Magazine,* XIX (1924), 220–246.

[57] *Ibid.*.

[58] *Statutes,* 11: 1509–1510.

[59] Heitman, *Historical Register and Directory,* 1: 945.
[60] *Niles Weekly Register,* X(1816), 188–189.
[61] *Statutes,* 111: 1671.
[62] *American State Papers,* I: 770–771.
[63] *Ibid.,* 783.

II

WEST POINT

The impressively named United States Military Academy was struggling for its existence when Adam Empie was appointed chaplain on 9 August 1813. Founded in 1802, the fledgling Academy, located in semi-isolation on the high bluff of the west bank of the Hudson River, was on the verge of being closed; it offered small promise of becoming an outstanding educational institution, let alone ever bearing a marked influence upon the security and future of the nation.

The Academy in 1813 represented only a partial fulfillment of President Washington's dream—advanced in the closing decade of the eighteenth century—of providing unexcelled training for the Army's officers. He concluded that if the Army must be small, it must also be very good. Timothy Pickering, Secretary of War, suggested West Point as the place to institutionalize the leadership training aspect of Washington's concept. Threat of war with France prompted Congress to create the rank of cadet, in effect a junior officer designated to receive training at the Academy, and authorized teachers to instruct him. The number of cadets was quite small and the scope of instruction limited. After "the institution ran into disorder and the teachers into contempt"[1] Congress on 16 March 1802 officially established the Military Academy, identical with a corps of engineers.[2]

Even after the Act of 1802, the Academy showed little improvement. Only a few of the authorized cadets were appointed. The two instructors, frequently ordered away for such duty as erection of fortifications, made intermittent appearances in the classroom; they gave instruction in academic and military subjects that was elementary at best. A third instructor was dismissed after fighting with a cadet. The Superintendent, Major Jonathan Wil-

(See notes at end of chapter)

22

liams, a nephew of Benjamin Franklin, came to the position with a direct commission and had never won a military uniform.

There were no entrance examinations and no established age or physical qualifications for appointment to the Academy. The 10 enrolled cadets ran the gamut in age, ability, and stamina. The youngest was 12 years of age, the oldest 34; a few even had families. Some were college graduates, but most had very little formal education. Within the group was a former British officer. All cadets were quartered in the old "Long Barracks" of the Revolutionary period; they received instruction in a two-story "academics" building, which was also the dwelling of the Superintendent.[3] It was not surprising that during the first year Williams declared: ". . . the Military Academy as it now stands is a foundling, barely existing among the mountains and mustered at a distance out of sight, and almost unknown to its legitimate parents. . . ."[4]

Superintendent Williams, who tried to change what was essentially an engineering school into a genuine military academy, encountered one insurmountable hurdle after another. Despondent, he resigned in 1803, only to have President Jefferson persuade him to return for another frustrating tour of duty that ended in disgust and resignation in 1812.

The resignation of Major Williams alerted many national leaders, including some in Congress, to a basic fact: There was no National Military Academy on the plains above the picturesque Hudson. Over a 10-year period, only 71 men graduated from the school, with its irregular and elementary curriculum. At a time when the country faced war and the Army was being expanded, Congress felt compelled to act. On 29 April 1812, legislation was enacted that attempted both to meet the immediate problem and to set the foundation for the emergence of a real military school. The Act of 1812 set admission requirements; raised the number of authorized cadets to 250; augmented the faculty and staff; established regulations for discipline; and specified that cadets were to be recognized as a part of the United States Army.[5]

While not a part of the legislation, Congress envisioned a chaplain as one of the augmented staff. The debate prior to the passage of the Act stressed the necessity of a chaplain at the Academy. Congress was led to understand that one would be appointed.[6] Many felt that a chaplain would be able to do

(See notes at end of chapter)

something about overcoming the conditions described by one of the cadets. The youngest member of the first class wrote: "All order and regulation, either moral or religious, gave way to idleness, dissipation and irreligion. . . ."[7] The situation at West Point, however, only reflected the religious climate that prevailed at the time in academic communities. Yale "was in a most ungodly state . . . the college church was almost extinct . . . the students were skeptical, and rowdies were plenty." The college at Princeton, which but a generation before had been noted for its evengelical fervor, had less than 10 students who professed to be Christian.[8]

Captain Joseph R. Swift, the first graduate of the Academy, became Superintendent. But Swift, continually absent, delegated authority to Captain Alden Partridge, who attempted to reshape the school under the specifications of the Act of 1812. Partridge, an energetic officer, erected several stone buildings to replace the spartan structures left from the Revolutionary War. In these building projects he proved to be a competent construction chief. Partridge also worked hard to strengthen the academic program and bring in competent faculty and staff. When it came time to appoint the chaplain, Swift exerted his authority and selected a friend, Adam Empie, an Episcopalian. Apart from friendship, Captain Swift felt that an Episcopalian would make the best chaplain because "the service of that church was . . . the most appropriate to the discipline of a military academy."[9] Empie's military appointment was effective 9 August 1813. Although he was officially listed as Chaplain, he had additional duties as "acting Professor of Geography, History and Ethics."[10]

Empie, a native of North Carolina, came to West Point from the rectorship of St. James Episcopal Church in Wilmington. He was overawed by the setting and assuredly shared the inspiration and sentiment of a gifted writer's sentiments:

> It is, indeed, a spot formed by nature to be the nursery of heroes. As its name imports, it is a point of land on the Western shore, of the river Hudson; sixty miles from the city of New York and one hundred from Albany. Viewing it as you ascent the river, it appears to be nothing more than a rugged and almost inaccessible promontory; but having gained the summit of the bank, you are at once struck with surprise and admiration at finding yourself on a beautiful verdant plain, containing nearly eighty acres, and forming the area of an

(See notes at end of chapter)

amphitheatre; the one half of which is encircled by the river, and the other by the lofty mountain upon which stand the mouldering ruins of the old Fort Putnam.[11]

Empie, a handsome man of engaging personality, worked diligently at both of his assignments, but under the hardship of continuous bad health. He attempted to give the classroom, and the preparation for it, half of his waking time. The remainder he gave to his ministry. His religious program was quite simple but apparently successful; services consisted of a series of daily liturgical prayers and two Sunday worship periods.

The prayers were said in the morning at roll call and at the end of the day following a parade. The cadets participated in the parade "with an easy elegance and regularity of motion, unsurpassed by the best disciplined soldiers."[12] Before the cadets were dismissed, they were "drawn up in an open square," and the evening prayers were "delivered by the chaplain," who reverently knelt, sometimes in the snow.[13]

On Sundays, the church services were in the morning and afternoon. Although attendance was not mandatory, most students and staff attended. Services were first held in the "old wooden academy." Later they were "transferred to the Mess Hall," and subsequently, in 1815, to a room in the new stone building housing the Academy.[14] The chaplain's sermons, well prepared and organized, were generally favorably received. Frequently visitors were impressed by the religious discourse, and one who spent a Sunday at West Point wrote:

> The writer of this cannot refrain here from expressing the high gratification he derived from hearing two of this gentleman's sermons, during his stay at West Point. The classical purity of the language, the soundness of their religious doctrine, and the unaffected fervor of manner in which they were delivered, were alike calculated to interest and delight the hearer.[15]

Empie worked hand in hand with Captain Partridge and was one of his most ardent supporters. For over a year, at the urging of Partridge, he even served as Treasurer of the Academy. After two years, Partridge, with the assistance of his staff, allegedly had brought order, regularity, and discipline to every aspect of the institution.[16]

(See notes at end of chapter)

The chaplain supported Captain Partridge so diligently and consistently that when the Captain was replaced as Superintendent by Sylvanus Thayer, Empie felt compelled to resign. Apparently a sizeable number of cadets also wanted to leave; they protested the dismissal of Partridge, and refused to obey the instruction of his successor until an Army inquiry cooled the simmering affair.[17]

Following his resignation on 30 April 1817, Empie reassumed the rectorship of St. James in Wilmington. He remained there until 1829, when he left to become President of the College of William and Mary, Williamsburg, Virginia. In his later years, he became totally blind. Empie died 6 November 1860.

Thayer took over the superintendency determined to carry the school to the heights of Washington's dreams. Using European military schools as his models and standards of excellence, he began the process of transforming an engineering institution into a National Military Academy.[18] Wisely he built upon the foundation laid by his predecessors. He was convinced his own success depended largely upon getting Congressional support, securing a higher caliber of cadet, and attracting an eminent faculty. Congressional support and a student body of better quality came slowly. Faculty vacancies at the time he took command remained unfilled for a period, the result of a determination to appoint only the best qualified instructors.

The position left vacant by Empie was one of those not immediately filled. As a temporary expedient, Chaplain Cave Jones was transferred to West Point. He was one of four chaplains in the Regular Army at the time, and assigned to the staff of the Army's Northern Division. But Congress, on 14 April 1818, in an act to reorganize the Army and reduce its strength, abolished the four chaplain positions.[19] Jones, along with his three colleagues, was honorably discharged from the Army.

The Act of 14 April 1818, however, reaffirmed and strengthened the chaplaincy at West Point. It declared "that there shall be... one chaplain, stationed at the military academy at West Point, who shall also be professor of geography, history, and ethics, with the pay and emoluments allowed the professor of mathematics. . . ."[20] Although listed in the official Army Register as an officer, the chaplain did not have rank. As it developed, the chaplain at West Point was the only Regular Army chaplain officially on duty for the

(See notes at end of chapter)

next two decades. There were, of course, chaplains attached to the various state militia units during the period.

About the time of the passage of the Act of 14 April, Superintendent Thayer felt he had located the proper man for the Academy chaplaincy. It was Thomas Picton, a native of Wales who emigrated to New Jersey. Picton was appointed 23 July 1818.[21] He came to West Point from Westfield, New Jersey, where he had been pastor of the Presbyterian Church for 13 years. Prior to that he served two small Presbyterian churches in or near Woodbury, New Jersey; in addition, he was superintendent of an academy, essentially an elementary school for the children of his congregations.

Picton's duty at the Military Academy began on 15 September 1818. He liked the position and the place. A letter to relatives in Wales, written two years after he came to West Point, affords unusually sensitive insights into his roles of chaplain and professor, the routine of the cadets and soldiers, and the general atmosphere of the school:

> My present location is about 56 miles north of New York City, on the western side of the Hudson River. Here is a large school of young soldiers (military academy), which is maintained by the government. The number of students is around 250 from 14 years up to 22 or 23 years old. I am serving here in the dual capacity of *minister* and *teacher*. As a *minister,* my chief duty is to preach on Sundays; as *teacher,* I have this year 25 of the students (cadets) to teach two hours every day. . . . I am trying to teach them World Geography, World History, Morality and Law among Nations; that is, in the English language, Geography, History, Moral Philosophy, and the Law of Nations. In addition to the students and teachers and their families, there are about 100 soldiers, many of them with families too. This is my entire congregation. No others reside here other than tailors, shoemakers, laundry-women and two shopkeepers. I preach to the teachers and students in the morning and to the soldiers in the afternoon. Worship is carried on according to the usual order among the Presbyterians except that musicians join with singers in the praise. I have reason to commend the young men for their respectful behavior toward me and especially for their proper conduct in worship. I am residing at present in a *wild,* but *healthful* and very *comfortable* place. Near a large river and a steep pile of rock . . . about 200 feet above the water, is a wide plain of about 60 acres of land. On this plain we all live, and here the cadets learn to use their weapons, etc.

(See notes at end of chapter)

All around this plain are high mountains except where the river breaks through. . . .[22]

Chaplain Picton's pleasant life on the banks of the Hudson lasted just over 6 years. His discharge came about in a most interesting manner. A Board of Visitors was created in 1815, which functioned annually after 1819; composed of distinguished officers, educators, and government leaders from around the country, its purpose was to help the Academy escape parochialism and achieve some focus of outside interest. The Board made on-campus visits and submitted its report, with recommendations, to the Academy and to Congress. When the Board visited West Point in June 1824, about a third of its members signed a privately written recommendation to the Superintendent that Picton be discharged; the minority document was not included in the published report for that or the following year.[23] The recommendation was based on Picton's role as a preacher. Apparently far better on the lecture platform than in the pulpit, he did not possess the eloquence some of the Board of Visitors desired. They wanted him discharged and replaced with a great pulpit orator.[24]

The Superintendent accepted the minority report and made plans to have Picton discharged. The latter was informed of his dismissal in a message from the Secretary of War. This aroused a sizeable segment of the faculty which, in addition to supporting Picton, a highly esteemed and respected colleague, saw its own security threatened. At issue was the matter of the rights of an Army officer. Both Army Regulations and those of the Academy provided for a Court of Inquiry to determine the validity of any allegations. Jared Mansfield, Professor of Philosophy, in a communication to a United States Senator, set the issue in perspective: ". . . the discharge of Professor Picton . . . without any alllegation of fault . . . any investigation or Court of Inquiry which the rules and regulations promise . . . if it be made a precedent . . . will annihilate all the prospects of those, who have raised the academy to its present state of excellence. . . ."[25]

A related factor in Picton's dismissal was student criticism and hostility, which began over an unwelcome innovation at his first service. His initial sermon coincided with the inauguration of compulsory chapel attendance, a practice Superintendent Thayer began in Order 21, issued 21 September 1818. The chapel service

(See notes at end of chapter)

was Protestant. No provision was made for either Catholic or Jewish services. Mandatory attendance and lack of worship opportunity for those who were not Protestants fueled controversy, and the chaplain became the object of cadet discontent.

Picton's forced resignation was effective 1 January 1825.[26] Before the month was out the "eloquent pulpiteer," who the Superintendent and Board of Visitors felt should be the chaplain at West Point, was appointed. It was Charles McIlvaine, an Episcopalian native of New Jersey, and a graduate of both Princeton University and Princeton Theological Seminary.

Apparently the right man was selected. McIlvaine, only 26 years of age, was already famous as a preacher. Because of his superior ability in the pulpit, he was destined to become the only chaplain at West Point selected for inclusion in a history of American preaching.[27] At the time of his appointment, he was Rector of Christ Church, Georgetown, and Chaplain of the United States Senate, where his father was one of the Senators from New Jersey. He attracted some of the most influential people in America to his services, and they, in turn, spread abroad their very favorable comments about his discourse. Among those who heard several of his sermons were some members of the Board of Visitors, as well as the Secretary of War, John C. Calhoun. When Picton was criticized for his lack of preaching ability, McIlvaine logically came to mind among those who had heard him and were charged with giving advice and direction to the Academy. When the offer of appointment came, a number of Army officers, aware of the lack of religious sympathy at West Point, urged McIlvaine to decline. His intimate friend John C. Calhoun, however, persuaded him to accept.

McIlvaine arrived on campus in the spring. In his very first service, the tall, stately man of arresting personality made known the emphasis he placed on the position of chaplain. McIlvaine informed the congregation that he would try to do his duty both as a professor and minister, but he wanted it understood that he regarded the chaplaincy "much the more important" and desired to be thought of primarily as a minister.[28] During his three years at West Point, McIlvaine did not alter that stance.

McIlvaine's first year at the Academy was something of a disappointment to him. Facilities for worship were less than

---

(See notes at end of chapter)

desirable and opportunities for visits with cadets were exceedingly limited. The place for worship at that time, a room in the basement of the library, could accommodate only the "corps of cadets, the officers, and the families of the latter . . . and these with so much crowding, that the cadets sat on benches without backs or rails and these so near to one another. . . ."[29] The Board of Visitors recommended a new chapel in its report for 1825.[30] It wanted a facility to match the new preacher. McIlvaine continued to preach to his military audience in spartan surroundings, however, without the slightest indication of any effect or response, although his eloquent and decisive manner was long remembered.

By the rules of the Academy, occasion for conversation with the cadets was virtually nonexistent. Even when opportunity existed, their own shyness and the fear of being thought religious prevented them from calling on the chaplain. After leaving West Point, McIlvaine wrote:

> Only on Saturday afternoon was any cadet allowed to visit an officer, or anybody else out of the barracks, without special permission from the Superintendent: and such was the feeling and prevalant sentiment about coming to see me, lest it should indicate something towards religion, that for a whole year I cannot remember that a single cadet ever visited me, or sought acquaintance, or that I had any knowledge of one of them, other than that formed by seeing them in the chapel, or meeting such as came under my professorship in the class-room.[31]

McIlvaine began a Sunday School in the chapel on Sunday afternoons. Ladies assisted in it, but few cadets attended. A worship service followed the Sunday School session; it was primarily for soldiers stationed at West Point, families, and any others who had not been able to crowd into the morning service.

McIlvaine's second year was quite different, a year of leading the forces of evangelical Christianity against the citadel, to take it. Before he finished, the chaplain, able to combine preaching ability with missionary zeal, was accused of trying to transform a military academy into a seminary.

What eventually became a massive religious revival began with a deeply serious conversation between McIlvaine and one of the cadets. Leonidas Polk, a "young man of fine form and graceful bearing," one of the leaders of the Class of 1827, came across a tract

(See notes at end of chapter)

and a book that treated of doctrine and the duties involved in being a Christian. Polk read the material with an attention he had not previously given to the claim of Christianity. A week after reading the material, deeply troubled, he appeared at McIlvaine's house, too choked with emotion for coherent speech; after a considerable struggle he poured out the story of an inner conversion, against which he had struggled in vain. After the long confession, McIlvaine resolved many of the difficulties troubling the young cadet, and "let him talk out what he feared most—the ridicule of his comrades."[32] Polk asked the chaplain what he should do. McIlvaine urged him to step out immediately and take a stand. Polk left the chaplain's study a confessed Christian.

The next day was Sunday. The cadets trooped into chapel, among them Robert E. Lee, Albert Sidney Johnston, Joseph E. Johnson, Jefferson Davis, and Robert Anderson. Also present was Cadet Martin Parks, who would return to West Point as Chaplain 14 years later. McIlvaine preached for the better part of an hour, then went to the altar to conclude the service. As he did, Polk, to the astonishment of the cadets, went gently, deliberately to the front end and knelt in a symbolic dramatization of his Christian commitment.

Later, in a letter to his brother, Polk described his feeling:

> This step was my most trying one; to bring myself to renounce all of my former habits and associations, to step forth singly from the whole corps acknowledging my convictions of the truth of the holy religion which I had before derided and was not anxious to embrace, and to be put up, as it were, a mark for the observation of others; were trials which unaided by the consolations of the Bible, humble and fervent prayer, and above all the strong hand of Him who is all powerful to shield and protect all such as do earnestly desire to make their peace with Him, I should have sunk under.[33]

Polk, who eventually became a bishop in the Episcopal Church and a Lieutenant General in the Confederacy, more than held his own in the heated religious discussions that erupted in the barracks. Several other cadets soon asked for conferences with Chaplain McIlvaine, who began holding regular prayer meetings in his home. Attendance increased so rapidly it became necessary to shift the services to the chapel.[34] Forty days after their first conference McIlvaine baptized Cadet Polk, together with another cadet, William B. Magruder, later a general. The baptism service took place in the

_____
(See notes at end of chapter)

presence of the entire corps of cadets, and its impressiveness was
not lost on them.

Polk's conversion and subsequent baptism became the signal for
a dramatic revival of religion that swept the entire institution.
McIlvaine's bold and uncompromising preaching, which had not
previously produced the slightest observable effect, finally forced
into view an influence that existed below the surface. When the
"dashing and handsome cadet, a leader among his fellows, had
dared to declare for Christ, others, who had, perhaps, been too
timid to speak out before, no longer lacked the courage to come
forward, and conversion followed conversion, until it seemed that
the entire corps had been touched."[35] Feeling ran so high that on
one occasion McIlvaine felt obliged to stop in the middle of his
sermon, lest the emotions of his hearers might get out of control.[36]
Nightly meetings for the purpose of worship became routine. All of
the renewed religious interest was confined to West Point; there was
no widespread religious revival in the country at the time.

The religious excitement at West Point attracted attention.
McIlvaine's preaching and evangelistic activity led at least one college
and several churches to decide that he was the answer to their
needs. Early in 1827 he was offered the rectorship of St. Ann's
Episcopal Church, Brooklyn. In July the vestry of St. Paul's Church,
Rochester, extended him an unanimous invitation to become its
rector. In August he was offered the Presidency of William and
Mary College.[37]

McIlvaine did not want to leave West Point; at the same time,
he was anxious to devote full time to religious activities. Reluctantly,
on the last day of 1827, after nearly three years at the Academy, he
resigned to accept the rectorship of St. Ann's in Brooklyn.[38] An era
had ended.

The administrators of the Academy were aware of the offers
that came to McIlvaine; they undertook a diligent search for a
successor, should one be needed. When McIlvaine's resignation
became effective on 31 December 1827, Thomas Warner was
appointed his successor on 1 January 1828.

Warner, a native of New York and an Episcopalian, studied law
before preparing for the ministry. Striking in appearance, he so
strongly resembled Andrew Jackson that he was sometimes mistaken
for the General. Equipped with mental gifts approaching genius,

---

(See notes at end of chapter)

and a practicing Christian of high moral standards, he was quite at home in the classroom but somewhat out of his element in the pulpit.

In the lecture hall he was probably without peer. Students in his classes declared that they "learned more from Professor Warner . . . than from any other teacher."[39] His well-structured lectures were given in highly polished language; his rich tenor voice was ideal for communicating his thoughts and keeping the students awake. The Board of Visitors was aware of his superiority as a teacher and singled him out for commendation in 1829 and again in 1831.[40]

In the pulpit, however, Warner was little more than acceptable. One observer felt that he was superior in reading the Episcopal service, but he was virtually alone in that judgment.[41] A student, provoked by having to attend services, reflected the sentiments of many fellow cadets when he wrote: "I have just got back from church, after hearing rather a dry sermon. . . . When I go to church here, I am obliged to sit for two long hours on a bench without a back, squeezed up among a parcel of cadets."[42]

The Board of Visitors felt that not only was Warner less a chaplain than they desired but also that the religious program, confined to a single Sunday service, was weak. Aware of his superiority in the classroom, the Board took a daring step and in 1836 unanimously recommended that the "Secretary of War . . . separate the chaplaincy from the professorship. . . ."[43] Perhaps the completion of a "neat chapel" during the school year helped focus attention on the inadequacy of the chaplain's program and kindled the desire for a better orator.

Chaplain Warner also had two serious personal failings that tended to nullify his best endeavors; he possessed an excitable temper that quickened at the slightest provocation, and an impetuosity that he never learned to curb. Together they kept him in difficulty and eventually forced his resignation.

A former cadet reported witnessing the anger of Chaplain Warner on many occasions. He wrote of one incident:

> One Sunday morning he came to the chapel following the cadets. It was evident from the expression of his face and the nervous movements of his hands that he was out of humor, and when he observed that one cadet did not rise with all others, as prescribed by the ritual, he leaned over his desk,

---

(See notes at end of chapter)

pointed sharply at the seated youngster, and exclaimed: "I'll thank you to rise!" The color left his face, and his voice and eyes displayed the extreme of anger. After holding the young cadet under his wild gaze a whole minute, he resumed his erect position, and proceeded with the service. His anger continued, and in his sermon he evidently strayed from his notes to attack sin and the indifference of sinners, with unusual vehemence. [44]

Another episode jeopardized his relationship with the staff and made continuation as chaplain and professor very tenuous. The incident occurred after a cadet had been fatally wounded in a fencing match with an intimate friend. Hearing of the accident, Warner hastened to the hospital to console the dying youth; however, he went without first seeking the permission of the Superintendent, as required. At the hospital he took the surgeons to task for what he considered their casual manner of attending to the cadet. Almost immediately the chaplain was placed under arrest for his disregard of regulations and was confined for approximately three weeks. The Board of Visitors made its annual inspection during the same period and in its report noted "The chaplain had been under arrest. . . ." It urged an inquiry into the case. [45]

The Court of Inquiry learned that Warner, disregarding command structure, confronted General Winfield Scott, verbally attacked the Superintendent, then upbraided the surgeon for incompetency. One who was present said. "I . . . can never forget how fiercely the fire of resentment can burn . . . as . . . the torrent of vengeful eloquence . . . poured out. . . ." [46] The chaplain's attitude toward military orders and regulations, coupled with his temper tantrums, made his retention at West Point all but impossible. He was forced to resign.

The experience with Warner and some of his predecessors as they tried to function in a dual role prompted the Board of Visitors to prod Congress and the War Department into separation of the chaplaincy from the professorship. On 24 January 1838 a bill introduced in the Senate to increase the size of the Army contained a section providing for the separation; in subsequent debate, however, it was deleted, and the old practice continued. [47]

As the academic year began in 1838, there was a new chaplain at the Academy, an Episcopal clergyman named Jasper Adams. He brought impressive credentials: Professor of Mathematics at Brown

University, President of Charleston College in South Carolina, President of Geneva College in New York. On the basis of his reputation as a scholar and administrator he was appointed by the Board of Visitors in 1837.[48]

The arrival of Adams coincided with that of a new superintendent, Major Richard Delafield. The appointments of both the Superintendent and the chaplain were effective 1 September 1838. Adams, aware of the inexperience of the Superintendent, appeared determined to run not only the religious program but the Academy as well. Like McIlvaine, he considered himself a chaplain first and then a professor; as chaplain, he moved aggressively to replace the "Military Academy with a Holy Commonwealth."

About the time Adams completed gathering evidence to justify a "moral cleansing of the Academy," Superintendent Delafield was totally in control of affairs. The two men were soon in conflict over Adams' understanding of his own role and his view of moral conditions at West Point. Adams felt that as chaplain he should have free run of the Academy; Delafield was determined that he abide by the rules and regulations. Adams believed that moral conditions were deplorable; the Superintendent felt they were no worse than those on other campuses.

Adams made up his mind to get the issues, as he saw them, into the open. In an accusatory letter of 18 pages to the Superintendent, Adams charged that excessive drinking of intoxicants, affairs with lewd women, and widespread use of profanity were all common practices among the cadets. Regarding consumption of alcohol, he specifically charged that "from twenty to fifty cadets (were) drunk every Saturday night; that there (was) some drunkenness on other nights;" and "that there is plenty of liquor among the cadets and . . . it is constantly kept in many of the rooms."[49]

Moving beyond the matter of the moral climate, Adams charged that the Superintendent burdened him with professorial duties to the extent that he had no "time to prepare for chaplaincy duties." "The most that a chaplain can do, under the circumstances," he wrote, "is to keep things from becoming worse."[50]

In an effort to improve conditions, the chaplain urged the Superintendent to enforce a stricter observance of Sunday "by all connected with the Academy"; to reinstate "daily and morning

(See notes at end of chapter)

prayers"; to provide for more religious instruction; to separate the chaplaincy from the professorship; and to allow total freedom in counseling and visiting cadets.[51]

The Superintendent took the charges seriously, especially that of excessive drinking, the one most documented. He asked for witnesses. Adams made a lengthy reply and recommended more than a dozen; he also suggested a technique to be used in questioning them. Publicity about the episode spread beyond the Academy, and it was now necessary to have an investigation of "the moral conditions and discipline" at the Military Academy. A court of inquiry was appointed, which consisted of four Army officers, presided over by Major General Winfield Scott.[52]

Adams apparently believed the court was nothing more than a face-saving technique for the military. He was present for the opening session and those that followed. He participated in questioning the witnesses, most of whom were suggested by him. The court, however, took its task seriously and probed deeply into all aspects of the affair.

After the proceedings were completed, the court's lengthy written opinion found that Adams' charges were based almost totally on rumor, were exaggerated, and in a few instances were falsified. It felt that although things were not ideal, only a few drank, and no more than a dozen used profanity or associated with lewd women. Also the court was of the not totally unbiased but "unanimous opinion that the moral discipline of the Military Academy (was) excellent, and that its moral condition (was) also, very generally, sound and improving."[53]

The most serious and damaging statement of the court related not to the moral conditions but to Adams himself. It concluded that he was an inefficient chaplain and totally neglected pastoral duties to the extent of not visiting a single sick cadet during his tour of duty. The hospital surgeon testified "that he never knew . . . Adams to visit a sick cadet in the Hospital."[54] The negative atmosphere he helped to create offered the chaplain no alternative but to leave the Academy.[55] He resigned, effective 15 November 1840, but for all practical purposes the school had been without a chaplain for over six months; some felt there had been none for over two years.

The departure of Jasper Adams impressed upon the Secretary of War, the administration of the Academy, and the Board of

(See notes at end of chapter)

Visitors the fact that every Academy chaplain except Charles McIlvaine had been forced to resign. It was not an impressive record; success did not seem to attend the efforts of ministers chosen to serve as chaplains. It was not a matter of incompetence; all were unusually well qualified academically, and two approached eminence. The main difficulty appeared to be an inability to adjust to the rules and regulations of military life. Sentiments arose for the appointment of a minister who appreciated the military and, ideally, had served in the Army. Standards were not to be lowered to secure such a person. Martin Parks, a graduate of the Academy, came to mind almost immediately.

Parks, a member of the Class of 1826, was a convert to Christianity in the religious revival during McIlvaine's chaplaincy. A North Carolina native, he resigned from the Army in 1828 to study for the ministry. Parks served successfully as rector of several Episcopal congregations and was well known throughout both his denomination and the Army. His return to the Academy on 5 December 1840 marks the only time that a graduate came to serve as chaplain.

The appointment proved to be a good one. His ministry was effective as he functioned smoothly within the framework of the institution. For six years he worked diligently without arousing controversy or attracting unfavorable publicity. He resigned on 31 December 1846 to return to a civilian pastorate.[56]

The successor to Parks represented a break with tradition and also with the desire for a minister with military experience. A Presbyterian, William Sprole, minister of the First Presbyterian Church, Washington, D.C., where President James K. Polk was a parishioner, became the eighth chaplain of the United States Military Academy.[57] President Polk, impressed with Sprole's preaching ability, apparently urged the appointment. Sprole was not a good selection; upon his arrival, the Academy chaplaincy was again surrounded by controversy.

Academically, Sprole was not of the same caliber as the seven men who previously held the position. He was acceptable as a preacher, but sermons that inspired many in his Washington congregation did not motivate the young cadets. Almost from the start, Sprole labored in an atmosphere of suspicion, distrust, and unfriendliness. Lack of academic credentials made him unacceptable

(See notes at end of chapter)

to many of the faculty; the very fact that he was a chaplain made him unwelcome to many of the cadets.

Reports of successive Boards of Visitors expressed dissatisfaction with Sprole's performance as a professor and said very little that was complimentary about his chaplaincy.[58] One member of the Board declared Sprole did not have the competency "to discharge, properly, the duties of the professorship" and that evidence of this was visible everywhere.[59] The report of the Board of Visitors in 1856 "was quite explicit," and it was evident "that a change should be made."[60] Ironically, the two members of the Board who were the strongest advocates for his removal were fellow Presbyterian ministers.[61] Sprole was not completely surprised when he received a letter, dated 21 August 1856, from Jefferson Davis, Secretary of War, informing him that "he had been superseded" as chaplain by the Reverend John W. French, recommended to the President by Secretary Davis on 14 August 1856.[62]

French, a native of Connecticut, was rector of the Church of the Epiphany in the nation's Capital at the time the appointment was offered him. He did not seek the position and knew nothing of his name "being considered" until after Secretary Davis was authorized to offer him the post. He hesitated a week before he agreed to accept.

French, who in addition to his ministerial experiences was once a professor at Bristol College in Pennsylvania, moved to West Point in late August and began his duties in early September. After a few months it appeared he might be dislodged. Sprole, who did not want to leave the Academy in the first place, attempted to remove the new incumbent and sought reinstatement into his old position.

A new President, James Buchanan, was elected in November, and some friends of Sprole were selected for important positions in the new administration. Soon after the inauguration, efforts were made to induce the new President to remove French and restore his predecessor. Buchanan appeared willing to accept the proposal. The former Secretary of War, Jefferson Davis, himself a graduate of the Academy, was concerned for its welfare; in an effort to protect French's position, he wrote Buchanan "a statement of the causes which led to the removal of Mr. Sprole and the appointment of Mr. French."[63] The letter was prompted by a communication from some of the faculty who declared there were "strong probabilities that Mr.

_____

(See notes at end of chapter)

French is to be taken from us and Mr. Sprole returned in place." They wanted to know "what can be done to turn this calamity from us?" The letter of Davis seemed to steer Buchanan away from intervention.[64]

The episode brought French a degree of faculty support not enjoyed by most of his predecessors. The support was not without justification; he was an able scholar and effective teacher, as well as a good preacher. At last it appeared that the Academy had secured a person capable of being both professor and chaplain.

One student, however, did not appear to hold a high estimate of French and thought he was out of place at West Point. Yet, begrudingly and in an offhanded fashion, he complimented him for his abilities as teacher and preacher. Cadet Tully McCrea, Class of 1862, in a letter to his cousin in Dayton, wrote:

> . . . I have just returned from church, where I heard a sermon from the text "Thou Shalt Not Kill," and I thought it was a singular one for a minister to select to preach to officers and cadets, but he twisted it around to suit all cases. Our minister is Professor French. He has the double office of chaplain and prof . . . and he is no more qualified to fill the place than the man in the moon. He is a very good preacher and a smart man and would make a very good professor in some Theological college but he is out of his sphere at the Military Academy. He is always introducing something into the course, that is of no practical use. Last year he introduced a work of his own, "Practical Ethics," which is merely a collection of verses from the bible, and the year after our class had finished studying . . . Grammar he had us begin on another Grammer . . . it is a very good work, and might have been very interesting to those that had studied the ancient language, but we had finished our work on grammer, and to think we are studying the mean stuff to the exclusion of History and studies of far more practical use is not very pleasant; it is needless to say that the Prof is very unpopular with the cadets.[65]

French was at West Point during the trying times of the Civil War. One episode brought him national attention. A friendship with Jefferson Davis, president of the Confederacy, resulted in regular correspondence between the two, including a short period after the war began; French's loyalty to the Union was therefore questioned by some students and alumni. The chaplain was highly incensed and in a letter to the Secretary of War declared that of "all men in the

(See notes at end of chapter)

land" he was the "last on whom such suspicion should rest."[66] About the same time, practically every general in the Union Army who was an alumnus of the Academy came to the support of the chaplain. The issue soon simmered down and was not raised again; while French nursed the hurt caused by the accusation, it did not hamper his chaplaincy. He remained at West Point longer than any other chaplain, and was there when he died on 9 July 1871. In a published document, the Superintendent announced the chaplain's death to the cadets and wrote that it would awake "recollections of the triple relationship he sustained toward them, as a Father, Teacher, and Friend."[67] The statement was a good summary of his ministry. Funeral services were held in the chapel, and in tribute a "badge of mourning" was worn by all officers, professors, and cadets for thirty days. It was an appropriate honor for a chaplain who served long and well.

NOTES

[1] William A. Ganoe, *History of the United States Army* (New York: Appleton and Company, 1924), 109.

[2] *Statutes*, II: 830–836; Stephen Ambrose, *Duty, Honor, Country, A History of West Point* (Baltimore: John Hopkins Press, 1966), 22.

[3] Ganoe, *History of United States Army*, 109.

[4] E. D. Waugh, *West Point* (New York: The Macmillan Company, 1944), 46.

[5] *Statutes*, II: 1241–1242.

[6] *American State Papers*, V: 350.

[7] Waugh, *West Point*, 48.

[8] William W. Sweet, *The Story of Religion in America* (New York: Harper and Brothers, 1950), 223, 224.

[9] Harrison Ellery, *The Memoirs of General Joseph Gardner Swift* (Privately Printed, 1890), 123, 138, 219. At this time the right of appointment rested with the superintendent.

[10] George W. Cullum, *Biographical Register of the Officers and Graduates of the U.S. Military Academy* (New York: James Miller, 1879), 83.

[11] *Niles Weekly Register*, IX (1815–16), 17.

[12] *Ibid.*, 18

[13] *Ibid.*

[14] Mrs. Charles Davis, *Reminiscences of West Point* (East Saginaw: Evening News Printing and Binding House, 1886), 27.

[15] *Niles Weekly Register*, IX (1815–1816), 18.

[16] *Ibid.*

[17] *Ibid.*, XIII (1817–1818), 31.

[18] West Point was modeled most after the Military Institute of France. Because of this the French influence was strong. Many of the textbooks were in French and French was one of the two courses required in the first year. It was natural that French fashions in theology should prevail there, even after they began to lose popularity elsewhere.

[19] *Statutes*, III: 1617–1672.

[20] *Ibid.* Total pay amounted to $1,180 annually.

[21] Francis B. Heitman, ed., *Historical Register and Directory of the United States Army* (Washington: Government Printing Office, 1903), I: 559.

[22] Thomas Picton Papers, 1 May 1799 to 11 October 1834, Manuscript Collection, United States Military Academy.

[23] *Niles Weekly Register,* XXV (1823–24), 366–368; *American State Papers,* XVIII: 144–149.

[24] Thomas Picton Papers, Letter by Jared Mansfield, dated 21 January

[25] *Ibid.,* Picton at the time was listed as an officer without rank in the official *Army Register.*

[26] Heitman, *Historical Register and Directory.* 791.

[27] Frederick Webber, *A History of Preaching in Britain and America* (Milwaukee: Northwestern Publishing House, 1957), III: 266–273.

[28] William Carus, *Memorials of the Right Reverend Charles Pettit McIlvaine* (New York: Thomas Whittaker, 1882), 22.

[29] *Ibid.*

[30] *American State Papers,* III: 148.

[31] Carus, *Memorials,* 25.

[32] Thomas Fleming, *West Point, The Men and Times of the United States Military Academy* (New York: William Morrow and Company, 1969), 60.

[33] *Ibid.,* 60–61.

[34] *Ibid.*

[35] William Manross, "Leonidas Polk: Early Life and Presbyteriate," *Historical Magazine of the Protestant Episcopal Church,* XVII, 4 (1938), 332.

[36] *Ibid.*

[37] Carus, *Memorials,* 30.

[38] In 1832, McIlvaine began a long and distingusihed career as bishop of the Diocese of Ohio. Under his influence both Kenyon College and the Episcopal Seminary in Ohio became centers of evangelical life. He died in 1873.

[39] E. D. Keyes, *Fifty Years Observation of Men and Events* (New York: Charles Scribner's Sons, 1884), 77.

[40] *American State Papers,* IV: 177, 736.

[41] Keyes, *Fifty Years Observation,* 77.

[42] Sidney Forman, *Cadet Life Before the Mexican War* (West Point: United States Military Academy Printing Office, 1945), 15.

[43] *American State Papers,* XXI: 907.

[44] Keyes, *Fifty Years Observation,* 78.

[45] *American State Papers,* V: 706.

[46] Keyes, *Fifty Years Observation,* 79.

[47] *Congressional Globe,* LXXVI (1838), 134, 477.

[48] Callum, *Biographical Register,* 84.

[49] Jasper Adams Papers, 1 September 1838 to 15 November 1840, Manuscript Collection, United States Military Academy, Letter dated 3 February 1840.

[50] *Bid.*

[51] *Ibid.*

[52] Jasper Adams Papers, Opinion of the Court of Inquiry, dated 6 July 1840.

[53] *Ibid.*

[54] *Ibid.*

[55] Adams departed an embittered man. In less than a year he was dead, at the age of 48, at Charleston, South Carolina.

[56] Heitman, I: 771; George McIver, "North Carolinians at West Point Before the Civil War," *North Carolina Historical Review,* VII, L (January 1930), 17. Parks had a son who also graduated from the Academy; he preceded his father in death by one year. Chaplain Parks died in 1853.

[57] Earl West, "Religion in the Life of James K. Polk," *Tennessee Historical Quarterly,* XXVI, 4 (Winter, 1967), 368; Milo Quaife, ed., *The Diary of James K. Polk* (Chicago: A. C. McClurg Company, 1910), I: 20, 32, 37, 44, 73, 108, 128, 148, 177, 206, 270.

[58] Dunbar Rowland, *Jefferson Davis, Constitutionalist, His Letters, Papers and Speeches* (Jackson: Mississippi Department of Archives and History, 1923), 117.

[59] *Ibid.,* 114.

[60] *Ibid.,* 117.

[61] *Ibid.*

[62] Manuscript Collection, West Point Military Academy, Jefferson Davis letters dated 21 August 1856 and 14 August 1856.

[63] Rowland, *Jefferson Davis,* 117.

[64] *Ibid.,* 113, 114.

[65] Manuscript Collection, United States Military Academy.

[66] John French Papers, 19 August 1856 to 1 July 1871, Manuscript Collection, United States Military Academy, letter dated 17 July 1861. The correspondence between Davis and French is found, in part, in this collection.

[67] *Ibid.,* General Orders Number 75.

III

POSTS WEST

Richard J. Cadle, an Episcopalian, was appointed chaplain at Fort Crawford, Wisconsin, on 10 September 1838.[1] With that appointment, the Army officially recognized an arrangement that existed for approximately two decades.

Military outposts established on the frontier after the War of 1812, mainly along the Mississippi and its tributaries, were visible signs of American power and authority. Detachments of troops, often no larger than a company, entered the wilderness to construct forts at strategic spots on waterways and key terrain. Small, isolated, and insignificant in terms of fortification, the garrisons were erected to overawe the Indians and prevent outbreaks of hostility while guarding the frontier. In the event of Indian warfare, they offered refuge and security. When settlers moved into the area, it was usually around these tiny citadels in the vast wilderness that they congregated.

Quite naturally the clergymen sent out by various denominations to minister to the westward-moving population found initial accommodation at such outposts. Often the first religious service in the region was at an army post, for a congregation made up of soldiers and settlers. When the settlers moved out and established their crude shops, stores, taverns, and residences, creating a satellite community that eventually became a town, the military commander ordinarily made arrangements to continue a ministry to the troops on a part time basis. Gradually, in a number of instances, some ministers were employed full time as chaplains by post commanders; it was strictly a local arrangement, neither authorized nor prohibited by the War Department.

In all probability, the first post to have unofficial chaplains was Fort Smith, on the Arkansas River. Epaphras Chapman and Job Vinall, missionaries from New York, began holding services for the rifle company there in 1819.[2] A few years later Eleazer Williams, an

(See notes at end of chapter)

Episcopal missionary who afterwards became famous as the pretended Dauphin of France, conducted services at Fort Howard in Wisconsin territory. He even had an enlisted assistant to copy "from old manuscript sermons, a set for his use, to preach to the garrison at Fort Howard."[3] Using old sermons and new ones, Williams was effective and the assembly hall was always filled to capacity to hear him.

Before 1830, civilian clergy also functioned as post chaplains at Fort Brady and Fort Mackinac in Michigan territory; Fort Crawford and Fort Winnebago, Wisconsin territory; Fort Leavenworth, Kansas territory; and Fort Snelling, Minnesota territory, the farthest outposts on the Northwest frontier. The same practice existed at several posts in the East. Mark L. Chevers, Episcopal rector at Hampton, for example, began work as chaplain at Fort Monroe in 1827 and resided on the post.[4] Although not provided for by law, most of the military posts had the services of an unofficial part-time chaplain.

The civilian clergy were generally welcomed by the military community. For instance, William Ferry, who organized the Presbyterian Church and established a mission for Indians on Mackinac Island, held services on Sunday and conducted prayer meetings on weekday evenings at the garrison; most of the enlisted men and officers attended.[5] An added inducement to be present seems to have been Mrs. Ferry's beautiful singing voice.[6] Reports of excellent attendance also came from other posts.

At Fort Snelling, as the result of an act by the commander, only the most seriously ill were likely to be absent. One Sunday following an inspection, while the soldiers were in formation and about to be dismissed, the Snelling commander, with the expectation of getting most of the troops to attend religious services, asked all who planned to attend to step forward. Only six men moved. These went on to services, and the colonel had the Articles of War read to those who remained in the ranks. "This reading continued long after the benediction had been pronounced. On the following Sabbath the same option was allowed them, when about half of the command stepped to the front to attend church. On the next Sabbath the same routine was gone through . . . every one (moved) to the front. . . ."[7] There was virtually complete attendance as long as that commander was stationed at the post.

_____

(See notes at end of chapter)

One of the ministers who served with unusual effectiveness as an occasional post chaplain was Abel Barber, a Presbyterian. Barber was cordially received by Lieutenant Colonel Enos Cutler and other officers at Fort Winnebago. In addition to regular Sunday services, he started a series of weekly prayer groups, a Bible study class, and a temperance society. Unfortunately, an impasse occurred when a number of officers objected to worshipping in common with the enlisted men. Barber would not hear of separate services and relinquished his chaplaincy.[8]

By 1830 clergy serving both civilian and military communities discovered that an increasing amount of time was expended at the posts. That was especially true after the establishment of schools there to furnish instruction for the children of officers, soldiers, and prominent citizens living in the vicinity of the forts. Almost without exception the clergy were asked to take charge of the educational enterprises.[9] At the urging of post commanders they began to relinquish the civilian phase of their ministry and devoted full time to the military, with responsibility for all the religious and education activities. While the functions were those of minister and school administrator, the term applied to the position was chaplain. Financial compensation, generally $40 a month, was from voluntary contributions and post funds, not from War Department appropriations.

Among the first clergy employed as post chaplains were Jeremiah Porter and Richard Cadle. Porter's first ministry, just after leaving Princeton Theological Seminary, was to troops at Fort Brady, where he became chaplain in 1831.[10] One of his first acts was to assist in the baptism of two soldiers and an Indian woman. Porter recorded in his journal that on Sunday morning, 27 November, he and the Reverend Mr. Boutwell, a Baptist, broke ice in the St. Mary's River to perform the ceremony. Porter indicated that while the occasion was very impressive, it would have been more solemn and meaningful had the converts been completely immersed.[11]

During his ministry at Fort Brady, Porter witnessed many conversions and baptisms, among them that of the commanding officer. Something of the era's intense anti-Catholic sentiment was seen in Porter's elation at observing the conversion of several Catholic soldiers who "renounced papacy cordially and entirely as a

(See notes at end of chapter)

system of priest-craft and ridiculous mummery."[12] Porter assisted in the establishment of a temperance society at the post and encouraged the men to establish savings funds with money ordinarily used for liquor.

Two events touched Porter deeply during his tour at Fort Brady, both indications of the import of his ministry. After considerable personal effort, Porter found that the wife of one lieutenant was ready to make a decision to join his denomination. The woman's background astonished the chaplain. She had been reared in a Catholic school but came from a home where her father practiced orthodox Judaism and her mother followed the precepts of the Society of Friends.

The second event involved Sergeant and Mrs. Cooper, who appeared before Porter with their two children to request that he perform the marriage ceremony. After a few awkward moments, Porter found that the couple had been united in a civil ceremony some ten years before; their goal now was to have the marriage sanctified in a Christian rite.[13]

Cadle became unoffical post chaplain at Fort Howard in 1832. Founder of the first Protestant church in Green Bay, Christ Episcopal, he had conducted services at the fort since 1827.[14] As full time resident chaplain, Cadle was able to have a room in the barracks set apart for public worship, start a small Sunday School, and secure a sizeable number of people for the secular school. His successful chaplaincy attracted the attention of the commanders at both Fort Crawford and Fort Winnebago.[15] Each attempted to get him to transfer. Cadle moved to Fort Crawford in 1836.

Success attended his efforts at Fort Crawford. The post commander urged Cadle to organize a school for Indian children. By December 1837 an Indian school with 41 pupils, 15 boys and 26 girls, was in operation. The girls were taught to sew and the boys to farm. In two years enrollment reached 79. To assist with the teaching in the two schools, Cadle employed his wife and Bradford and Patsey Porter, husband and wife from Kentucky. For their services in attempting to bring the white man's learning to the children of red men, the teachers were paid $300 annually. The chaplain received $500.[16] Payments were from post funds.

The employment of unofficial chaplains by the post commanders at Forts Brady, Howard, and Crawford, and at several other

_____
(See notes at end of chapter)

posts, reflected their recognition of the need for religious exercises and spiritual guidance at those installations. Eventually Washington officialdom began to see the merit in providing posts with chaplains. Among the first to see the advantage in regularizing the military ministry was Secretary of War Lewis Cass. He expressed his concern in his annual report for 1831:

> The American soldier is well paid, fed, and clothed . . . but . . . there is no arrangement in our service for his . . . religious improvement. And there is perhaps no similar service in which such a measure is more necessary . . . I am satisfied that the appointment of chaplains and their employment at . . . our garrisons . . . would be productive of great advantage to the service; and to the soldiers individually the measure would be equally beneficial.[17]

The cabinet official thus planted the seed of a wholesome proposal; others would cause it to germinate. A number of religious journals and several military periodicals soon carried articles endorsing a chaplain for troops stationed at army posts. Interest in the project mounted among the more thoughtful officers on the frontier. In a lengthy letter to one military publication, the writer declared that the vast majority of Army officers desired the appointment of chaplains.[18]

From Fort Brady, Lieutenant Joseph Gallagher wrote several letters to Benjamin Swift, the United States Senator from Vermont, to urge passage of a bill authorizing chaplaincy appointments. In contrast to the Army's plight, he pointed out that the Navy had spent over $10,000 a year for fleet chaplains, and that Congress had appointed chaplains for its own use and for the Military Academy. Gallagher further cited the case of a clergyman employed as an unofficial chaplain at Fort Brady whose good guidance sharply reduced the number of stockade inmates. Lieutenant Gallagher estimated that willing and competent clergy could be appointed at an annual salary of $200 to $400 each and that 50 "such chaplains at. . . . military posts (would) be equivalent to increasing the army by more than a thousand men."[19] That was a persuasive argument to an economy-minded senator who wanted to increase the efficiency of an army with a total strength of 6,238, but with only 4,282 present for duty.[20]

(See notes at end of chapter)

A similar appeal was written to Senator John Davis of Massachusetts by Lieutenant Colonel Josiah Voss, Commander of the 3rd Infantry, stationed at Fort Towson, a frontier post:

> I now take the liberty to request that you will use your influence for the passage of a law authorizing the appointments of chaplains for the army.... I have been in the army for nearly twenty-four years, and I am now convinced from past experience, that nothing will add so much to the respectability and efficiency of our army as the appointment of chaplains and the regular public worship of God at our military posts on the Sabbath.
>
> It is found that when the Sabbath is properly observed, and public worship held, that there are fewer desertions, less intoxication, and a more healthy and efficient command....
>
> Let there be chaplains appointed for every military post, and let officers, as well as men, be required to attend public worship on the Sabbath, and we shall see, very soon, an astonishing change in the moral character of our army: Provided, however, that the chaplains are the right kind of men.[21]

Suggesting an income higher than that of lieutenant, Lieutenant Colonel Voss concluded his communication by declaring that clergymen of "undoubted piety...would cheerfully enter the service for a compensation of $800 to $1,000 per year." And since the government had an "overflowing treasury," Voss felt an expenditure of $50,000 or $60,000 a year for the benefit of soldiers would hardly be a burden.[22]

Senator Davis moved with haste; shortly after receiving the letter from Voss, he was able to get the Senate on 3 March 1836 to instruct the Committee on Military Affairs to "inquire into the expediency of providing for the appointment of chaplains for the Army of the United States."[23] Before the year was out, Benjamin F. Butler, the New York statesman temporarily holding the two cabinet posts of Attorney General and Secretary of War, made specific proposals in the annual report of the Secretary of War. He recommended that Congress pass legislation authorizing the post "councils of administration to select and employ chaplains and give the persons employed the pay and emoluments of such grade as congress may prescribe."[24] The council of administration, provided for in the Army Regulations of 1835, was essentially a committee of the three senior officers at a post; Secretary Butler believed that

(See notes at end of chapter)

such councils would be better qualified to select chaplains more satisfactory to the local garrisons than might be chosen by national authorities.

It was over two years before Congress finally passed a bill enacting Secretary Butler's proposals into law, and that bill greatly modified the original suggestions. On 5 July 1838, Congress approved the act that made it "lawful for the officers composing the council of administration at any post . . . to employ such person as they may think proper to officiate as chaplain, who shall also perform the duties of schoolmaster at such posts." Final approval of appointments, however, rested with the Secretary of War. The chaplain's compensation was set at $40 per month with an allowance for four rations a day and an allotment of fuel and quarters comparable to that of a captain.[25] Had the act been implemented, as many as 70 chaplains could have been appointed.

Two days after the authorization of post chaplaincies, however, the number of posts at which chaplains could be employed was limited by Congress to the twenty "approved by the secretary of war" and "most destitute of instruction."[26] The employment of chaplains at all 70 existing posts was considered too expensive. While modification of the Act of 5 July was an effort to keep expenditures within boundaries, it did inaugurate a program that could eventually be expanded.

The number of posts allowed chaplains was reduced even further by the War Department; on 18 August 1838 it released a list of posts where chaplains were authorized to be employed. Only 15 installations were specified: Hancock Barracks, Jefferson Barracks, and Forts Brady, Crawford, Gibson, Gratiot, Jessup, Leavenworth, Monroe, Morgan, Pickens, Pike, Snelling, Towson, and Winnebago.[27]

Thus on 10 September 1838 Richard Cadle was appointed chaplain at Fort Crawford; however, the invitation by the post council of administration and the actual appointment by the Secretary of War were simply a formalizing of an existing relationship. Cadle had been the unofficial chaplain at the fort since 1836. The clergymen appointed later in the year at Forts Brady (Abel Bingham), Gratiot (Charles Reighly), Leavenworth (Henry Gregory), Monroe (Mark L. Chevers), Snelling (Ezekiel Gear), and Hancock Barracks (Charles Beaman), also represented switches from unoffi-

(See notes at end of chapter)

cial to official chaplains.[28] In 1839 more chaplains were engaged, including John J. Ungerrer and Charles Hedges, successively, at Jefferson Barracks; Stephen P. Keyes at Fort Winnebago; Henry J. Lamb at Fort Jessup; and David E. Griffith, who received an appointment to replace Gregory at Fort Leavenworth. William Scull became chaplain at Fort Gibson in 1840.[29]

Other posts that had chaplains within the next few years included: Fort Washington and Fort Arbuckle, Indian Territory; Fort Atkinson, Iowa Territory; San Antonio, Fort McKavett and El Paso, Texas; Fort Laramie, Nebraska territory; Fort Scott, Kansas territory; Fort Washita, Arkansas territory; Fort Moultrie, South Carolina; Newport Barracks, Kentucky; and Fort Monterey on the west coast. Later as Washington territory opened, chaplaincies were established at various posts in the region.

The individual posts authorized chaplains changed periodically, but the number of chaplains remained static. Only 20 were allowed until 1849, when an Act of 2 March provided for 10 additional appointments.[30] That act was primarily to provide for the appointment of chaplains to some of the new posts established in the territory acquired from Mexico. Interestingly, of the 15 posts originally authorized chaplains, only Forts Gibson, Leavenworth, Monroe, Snelling, and Towson remained on the approved list issued by the War Department in 1849.[31] A few of the posts listed in 1838 ceased to exist and others were no longer "destitute" enough to qualify for the services of a chaplain. The criteria for establishing chaplains at posts were still based on the size of the garrisons and the degree of isolation from local churches and mission stations.

Because a few commanders did not place much emphasis on the role of the chaplain, and some councils of administration did not function effectively, a few men who were not clergymen received chaplaincy appointments. Occasionally "a superannuated sergeant or sometimes even a retired cook, would be appointed to undertake the religious ministrations. . ."[32] To prevent future occurrences of that sort, the Adjutant General, implementing the Act of 2 March, specified that after the "Council of Administration" had selected "a person to officiate as chaplain," the submission of the nomination to the War Department had to be accompanied by "the recommendations of the highest ecclesiastical authority of the communion to which the applicant" belonged.[33] The vast majority of post

(See notes at end of chapter)

chaplains were conscientious clergymen who possessed the traits and characteristics one looked for in a minister. Yet there were never enough to fill all of the positions. For instance, on the eve of the Civil War there were 16 posts in the Department of the West, 10 of which were authorized chaplains, with only five on duty.

Army Regulations made explicit the duties of the chaplain. The primary one was to conduct "appropriate religious services" at least once each Sunday.[34] Facilities for services were conveniently located and were generally adequate. In most cases it was the largest room on post, designed to serve as a chapel on Sunday and a classroom during the week; equipped with benches, platform, and lectern, it was usually on the first floor of a two storied barracks. Soldiers occupied the upper level. The building was one of four long, rectangular barracks strategically located to enclose a square parade and drill field of more than an acre. A second barracks housed the commissioned officers, including the chaplain, and their families. In the third, noncommissioned officers and their families lived on the upper floor and the lower level housed the hospital. Soldiers occupied the second level of the fourth building and the first floor was divided into offices and public rooms. A flag pole was located at the end of the parade field. A building for the storage of weapons occupied one corner of the enclosure. At another corner was the powder house, and at a third was the quartermaster's storehouse and a sutler's store (the equivalent of a modern post exchange). The guardhouse was positioned in the final corner. A picket fence of squared logs, approximately twenty feet high, enclosed all of the buildings.[35] On posts where houses were available, the chaplain was normally provided with residence. When permanent buildings were scheduled the chapel was ordinarily the first structure erected.[36] In most places chapels were built with funds raised through private subscription. At some posts special funds were provided by the council of administration. A few officers felt the expense should be borne by the Quartermaster Department; however, appropriated funds were not used for chapel construction.

The form of the religious service was not prescribed; each chaplain was free to devise his own mode of worship. A few years after the chaplaincy was recognized, Army Regulations did specify that as part of the service the chaplain deliver "a short practical sermon, suited to the habits and understanding of soldiers."[37] From

---

(See notes at end of chapter)

the very beginning, attendance at Sunday worship was compulsory; in addition, the soldiers were required to march, in formation, "to and from church or place where divine services (were) performed."[38] Further, the Second Article of War provided, as it had during all of the nineteenth century, that any officer found guilty of indecent or irreverent behavior at church could be court-martialed. Any noncommissioned officer found similarly guilty could be fined one-sixth of a dollar for his first offense, and for subsequent offenses be fined the same amount and confined to quarters.[39] The regulations also recommended that wives and families be encouraged to cooperate by attending church, but without the element of compulsion. Although most posts never had a population exceeding 300, when the bugler sounded church call, the provisions of compulsory and recommended attendance provided a capacity congregation at each service.

At least one commander, Colonel Stephen Kearny, openly questioned the undemocratic nature of compulsory church attendance in the light of the traditional concept of religious freedom. The Adjutant General, in response to Kearny's concern, made it clear that all commanding officers had a right to require troops under their command to attend church on Sunday. Wrote Colonel Roger Jones, the Adjutant General: "It may be made a part of the military duty, and they could be paraded and marched to the place of worship." In the same communication, Jones conveyed a view expressed by Lewis Cass, who championed the movement to provide chaplains at posts, that as Secretary of War he would feel particularly grieved if he should hear that any portion of the troops should object to attending public worship.[40] The comments, however, did not answer the question that bothered Colonel Kearny.

At Fort Monroe, where Mark Chevers was chaplain, Lieutenant John O'Brien, a staunch Catholic, dramatized his opposition to compulsory attendance. On a Sunday in January 1843 he marched a battalion to a Protestant chapel service, and, to protest the requirement, remained outside alone during the worship period. At the conclusion of the service the troops filed out and O'Brien marched them back to the barracks area. Immediately, the post commander, Colonel J. deBarth Walbash, himself a Catholic with a brother in the priesthood, had O'Brien arrested and requested higher authorities to order a court-martial. The matter was not

(See notes at end of chapter)

resolved until April, when it reached President John Tyler, a man with impressive military credentials; he declined to convene a court-martial and declared that no man's right of conscience should be infringed.[41] Neither the case nor the decision was publicized; compulsory attendance at worship services remained the practice.

Sunday services at the posts became focal points of organized religion, especially on the frontier. Soldiers have generally not been noted for deep piety or exemplary religious lives. To many observers they have been symbols of dissipation and debauchery, and there is no question that regular soldiers of the early nineteenth century justified such a concept. Many were certainly low characters, enslaved by habits of intemperance and immorality that no amount of discipline could eradicate. But as a result of church attendance, however mandatory, there appeared on every post where a chaplain served the nucleus of a church organization that usually matured into a permanent parish. At every post a number of dedicated religious workers emerged who assisted in teaching Sunday School, led prayer meetings, sang in the choir, and even formed small orchestras to add a more refined touch to the worship.

One group of soldiers that received special attention from the more thoughtful chaplains was the Catholic. A sizeable segment of the troops at any post was Catholic, largely immigrants from western European countries. Exact figures are not available, but at most posts the majority of troops were Catholic. Although all chaplains were Protestant until shortly before the Civil War, and the compulsory services were Protestant, arrangements were frequently made to have priests visit the post and celebrate Mass. The first priests were from among missionaries laboring in the area; later, they were resident clergy. The priests were treated respectfully, and in the main the soliders appreciated the attention they received from them. At Fort Riley, Father Maurice Gailland had such enthusiatic response to his activities from Catholics that he soon spent more time on the post than in his civilian parish.

On some posts there was an undercurrent of anti-Catholic feeling, reflecting the spirit of the times. This developed into an unpleasant situation on one post. A young officer stationed at Fort Gibson in 1847 complained to the Adjutant General that the post commander refused to allow a priest to preach at the post. The Adjutant General, Colonel Roger Jones, sent a blistering letter to the

(See notes at end of chapter)

commander admonishing him severely for his open anti-Catholic views. In a second letter Jones reemphasized the necessity of respecting all religious bodies and creeds.[42]

In addition to providing for garrison services, chaplains, with the endorsement of the commanders, generally held services in the civilian settlements that grew up around every post, and in neighboring communities. Many of the churches in these places were organized through the influence of post chaplains; but many were too small to support the services of a resident minister, and the visits of missionaries were infrequent. Ezekiel Gear, chaplain at Fort Snelling for 20 years and the first resident Christian minister in Minnesota, ministered to the settlers outside the fort, conducted services in St. Paul, and was active in the establishment of Episcopal congregations throughout Minnesota.[43] Richard Cadle, chaplain at Fort Crawford for five years, organized Episcopal congregations in several Wisconsin communities.[44] Solon W. Manney, the Fort Ripley chaplain for over 10 years, frequently preached in the small settlements that dotted the upper valley of the Missouri and was instrumental in organizing a few congregations. One writer declared that Fort Ripley "should be remembered as the place . . . under which for nearly forty years the Episcopal Church did its work in Minnesota."[45] More than any other religious leaders it was the post chaplains who kindled a definite religious spirit in the civilian communities.[46]

The lack of opportunity for Christian worship among the Indians also attracted the attention of chaplains. While obstacles were many and almost insurmountable, efforts were constantly made, most times successfully, to establish congregations in the Indian communities. In a few instances the Indians themselves took the initiative and invited chaplains to conduct worship in their midst.[47] The fruits of those endeavors more than repaid the effort expended and attempts of the two groups to live together in peaceful relationship became more dependable. For their part the Indians were constantly giving chaplains timely notices of proposed raids which prevented the garrisons from being surprised; because of this general massacres were averted.

Sunday services at the post were supplemented by weekly prayer meetings and ethical lectures. At some places there were prayer meetings every evening. A number of chaplains maintained

(See notes at end of chapter)

both weekday Bible classes and Sunday Schools as means of giving instruction in scripture to the entire post population.

The prevailing sins became the objects of the chaplains' pugnaciousness as they attempted to uplift the social level along with the cultural and religious. During the course of a year a soldier was likely to be assigned to a variety of tasks: farming, gardening, cooking, making bricks, burning lime, cutting wood, hunting game, shooting wolves, building a house, milking cows, clearing the grounds, and going on trips for supplies.[48] Garrison duties, however, did not exhaust the energies of the soldiers and many were continually engaging in shady amusements that sometimes led to courts-martial, but nearly always elicited the chaplains' wrath. Gambling, profanity and excessive drinking of intoxicants were vices the army ministers attempted to suppress. Efforts to curb drunkenness received priority and "temperance societies," organized under chaplain asupices, appeared everywhere in the isolated environment that encouraged habits of intemperance.

Despite all this activity there was time for chaplains to officiate at weddings, baptisms, and funerals, and to make visits to the sick in the hospitals, prisoners in the guardhouses, and soldiers in the barracks. Unfortunately the monthly reports of chaplains to the commanders were very terse; they merely reported the number of deaths, marriages, baptisms, and visits, without comment about events related to them.

Although the religious duties were enough to command the time and energies of the chaplain, he was also legally responsible for operating the post school system. As schoolmaster all secular educational enterprises came within his purview; therefore an applicant had to have the ability to teach in order to secure a chaplaincy appointment. The work in the schools was not without its side rewards; for instance, the classrooms became excellent places for the chaplains to extend their influence.

At first instruction was limited to children of officers serving at the post, and the number hardly ever exceeded a dozen.[49] Soon the schools were available to all of the children at a post. Later there developed a policy of having not merely a post school but a free public school at the post for all persons of school age on and adjacent to the garrison. After the War with Mexico this trend received an impetus through the desire to educate the Mexican

(See notes at end of chapter)

population that was acquired. Assistants were allowed in the enlarged programs, but chaplains continued to retain full responsibility.

The troops were not overlooked when opportunities for learning were provided. Many soldiers had not gone through even the most basic courses in elementary education. Not surprisingly, a sizeable number were unable to read and write.[50] To assist in overcoming these deficiencies schools were established. Mathematics, spelling, geography, reading, and writing were the areas of instruction. In the beginning the remedial courses were held at night, after duty hours. Shortly before the Civil War, recruits entering service were examined to determine their educational attainments; those found deficient were detailed to attend school as part of normal military duty. Many were enrolled, but few attended. Teachers were detailed from among the educated enlisted men for the school term, which ran from November to May.

Initially, classes were usually held in the same room used by the chaplain for worship service. The hard benches on which the parishioners sat for religious instruction on Sunday accommodated those who received secular instruction during the week. As the programs expanded so did the facilities; it was not long before a building was set aside on most posts for use as a school.

Closely related to the duties of schoolmaster were those of post librarian. On practically every post there was a library housed in one of the public rooms, and the chaplain was usually the librarian. The library, which tended to relieve the sense of isolation, was maintained from post funds and fines paid for failure to observe the rules regulating the use of books.

An unusually good collection of books and magazines could be found in the libraries. The volumes the chaplain selected for purchase were meant to elevate the mind and morals of the reader; in addition, a number of religious works were sent free of charge by denominational publishing houses. Concerned persons in the neighborhood of a post donated books they thought soldiers would be interested in reading. Most of the volumes dealt with history, biography, geography, and mathematics. The librarian generally subscribed to the leading periodicals; the reading rooms contained copies of the *National Intelligencer*, *National Gazette*, *Niles Weekly*

(See notes at end of chapter)

Register, *North American Review*, *Gentlemen's Magazine*, *American Repository*, and an agricultural review.[51]

At some posts there were chaplains who engaged in activities that went beyond those connected with being a chaplain and schoolmaster. Chaplain William Scull was assigned the duty of post gardener at Fort Washita.[52] At Fort Ripley, Chaplain Solon Manney voluntarily became post gardener. He not only raised fresh vegetables for the garrison, but also gave instruction to others on techniques of planting, cultivating, and harvesting vegetables and fruit. That was important because at some posts the chief activity appeared to be gardening, or farming. At times Manney was also called up to be either a defense lawyer or a prosecuting attorney at military trials.[53] Cases in which he participated involved sleeping on duty, shooting cows and hogs, shooting a wife, whipping a laundress, beating a corporal, breaking windows, selling government clothing and guns, stealing preserves, and failing to wash dishes and dump ashes in the right place. Chaplain David Clarkson spent much time as a male nurse in the hospital at Fort Riley. During a cholera epidemic he, along with his wife, worked full time at the hospital; he also helped prepare for burial the bodies of those who succumbed to the disease.[54]

Chaplains were expected to confine their military ministry to the garrison and did not normally take part in operations beyond the post. There were chaplains, however, who sometimes accompanied soldiers on such movements. At the insistence of the commander, the Fort Leavenworth chaplain went on practically every operation that set out to quell disturbances, especially the police and punitive expeditions against the Indians. The chaplain, Leander Kerr, "seemed to possess the whole secret of winning the good graces of the Indians" and had the uncanny ability, because of specialized training in ritual and languages, to comprehend the dialects and communicate with them.[55] Several times Kerr was credited with averting bloodshed because of the special relationship he had with the Indians.

The post chaplain in the performance of duty helped many a soldier solve personal problems; meanwhile, many of his own problems seemed insoluble. Money was a major difficulty. Even after long years of service and despite academic preparation or personal satisfaction, meager remuneration permitted the military

(See notes at end of chapter)

minister and his family no more than the basic necessities of life. After chaplain salaries were raised to $60 a month in 1857, in addition to rations, fuel and quarters, their total compensation was still less than that of infantry captains. But the relative security, especially in terms of monthly salary and a stable congregation, induced some civilian clergy to embrace the chaplaincy. As the ink was drying on the Act of 1838, the Reverend Charles S. Hedges wrote to his bishop for help in finding a chaplaincy position. He bemoaned the fact that the stipend from his civilian parish was not large enough to maintain himself, much less his family.

Episcopal Bishop Jackson Kemper aided Hedges in acquiring the position of chaplain at Jefferson Barracks, Missouri, where he served until the troops were withdrawn in 1844.[56] The Reverend Ezekiel Gear also indicated in a letter to Bishop Kemper that he accepted the position at Fort Snelling because it provided greater security than a civilian parish. Bishop Kemper was instrumental in getting several Episcopalians into positions as chaplains. In 1856 there were five Episcopal post chaplains in his diocese alone.[57]

Chaplains were plagued by awareness that there was no opportunity for promotion, no matter how long and how well they served. Other officers could anticipate subsequent promotions that carried an increase in salary, allowances, and prestige, but not so the chaplains. The situation was addressed many times by chaplains and commanders, but no solution was forthcoming.

The military minister also faced the difficulty of confronting the whims and fancies of his isolated congregation, whose attitude predictably ranged from enthusiasm to indifference to hostility. Apathy and indifference were problems, but the existence of hostility made chaplains most uneasy. There was pronounced opposition from those antagonized by efforts to suppress vice and upgrade entertainment and recreational pursuits. A number of practices fixed in Army tradition were considered unwholesome by several chaplains; efforts to curb, eliminate, or change these annoyed some of the military and aroused their opposition. West Point graduates who recalled four years of forced chapel attendance frequently had no taste for religion and simply opposed its representatives.

The tenuousness of chaplaincy positions vis-à-vis the post councils of administration led to much anxiety. The normal term of

(See notes at end of chapter)

office was only three years. At the end of that time a chaplain had to have the support and good will of the post council of administration for reappointment, or his services were abruptly terminated.

The reality of the problem was well illustrated in the case of William Scull, chaplain at Fort Washita from September 1844 to October 1847. When Scull applied to the post council of administration for renewal of his appointment in 1847 he found the council and the commanding officer, Major George Andrews, opposed to his remaining at the garrison. That opposition was mainly because of the chaplain's innocent involvement in a military-political feud between Colonel William Harney, who commanded Fort Washita from 1834 to 1847, and his successor, Major Andrews.

In 1844 Harney personally selected Scull to be chaplain at Fort Washita without consulting other officers at the post, including the council of administration. When Scull and his family arrived at the Fort, they were welcomed by Harney and snubbed by the members of the council of administration, who refused to recognize the validity of the appointment. Major Andrews, chairman of the council, made life almost unbearable for the chaplain. Scull was furnished the most meager facilities and compulsory church attendance was not enforced.

When reappointment was denied, charges and countercharges were vehemently exchanged. Scull charged that Andrews, in manifesting clear and definite opposition to him from the beginning, considered all sermons too bothersome and would like to see all chaplains removed from frontier posts. Andrews rebutted with the contention that Scull's service was of no benefit to the command, because he had not taken steps to make himself acceptable to the command or to the cause of religion; besides, declared Andrews, Scull's sermons were much too formal for his personal taste. Andrews recommended that the office of chaplain be abolished at Fort Washita and that missionaries be invited to hold any services that might be needed from time to time.[58]

Irritated when Scull made several attempts to reinforce his appeal for reappointment, the obstinate Andrews hastened his departure with a piece of evidence about Scull's previous chaplain position. A few years before, Scull had run from a similar disagreeable situation at Fort Gibson. Asked by the post adjutant to

(See notes at end of chapter)

return or resign his position at Fort Gibson, where his contract had not expired, Scull chose to resign.[59]

Having dispensed with Scull's services in 1841, the Fort Gibson council of administration did not consider appointing another chaplain until four years later, and then they approached the matter with considerable caution. When the Reverend Daniel McManus applied to the council for appointment to the vacancy, he was appointed "to officiate as Chaplain for the period of one year (and) to be reemployed at the expiration of that time, should the Council of Administration think it proper to do so. . . ."[60] McManus apparently proved to be a satisfactory choice, for he was reappointed and continued to serve at Fort Gibson until June 1857.

The post council's power was similarly illustrated in 1860 when Colonel Edwin Sumner requested the Secretary of War to remove the Reverend James De Dui from his post at Fort Kearney. The Adjutant General, Colonel Samuel Cooper, replied for the War Department; he explained that according to Army Regulations only the post council of administration could appoint or remove a chaplain from his post, and that no other means was legal.[61]

A number of denominations were represented among the clergymen who served as post chaplains; Episcopalians, however, predominated. From 1838 to the eve of the Civil War, over half of the post chaplains appointed were from that church. During most of the period there were Episcopal chaplains at West Point (Chaplains Adams, Parks and French) who exerted some influence on the cadets to whom they ministered as well as on the War Department itself. Graduates of the Academy from about 1842 to about 1850 who became post commanders seemed to prefer Episcopalian chaplains. Since chaplains also functioned as schoolmasters at Army posts, the educational requirements for Episcopal ordination made its clergy eminently qualified for the work.[62] Many Episcopal missionaries were early arrivals near military posts, and visited and conducted worship services for the garrisons; when the position of post chaplain became official, they often were appointed first. Some bishops of the church worked aggressively to place their men in the post chaplain positions.

Presbyterians were the second largest representation among post Chaplains. They were followed, in order, by Baptists and Methodists. There was one Catholic, Samuel Milley, post chaplain at

(See notes at end of chapter)

Monterey, California, from September 1849 to February 1850. Another Catholic, Ignacio Ramirez, replaced him.[63]

Down to the Civil War, the post chaplains did notable work in fostering opportunities for religious activities and secular education. For a time during the early 1850s there was some opposition to chaplains as a group. The ". . . irresponsible conflict. . .," as Senator Seward's melancholy phrase put it, gathered momentum; actual civil war broke out briefly in Kansas in 1856. Religious leaders and church bodies became increasingly involved, which led to growing turmoil in Congress. Some of that spilled over into relationships with Army chaplains and there was a period of criticism and opposition. But all that was soon submerged in a flurry of activity in Congress that helped pave the way for the tragic war that divided the nation and provided chaplains with opportunities for service previously unequaled.

NOTES

[1] Francis B. Heitman, ed., *Historical Register and Directory of the United States Army* (Washington: Government Printing Office, 1903), I: 272.

[2] Ed Bearss and Arrell Gibson, *Fort Smith; Little Gilbralter on the Arkansas* (Norman: University of Oklahoma Press, 1969), 32.

[3] Albert G. Ellis, "Fifty-four Years Recollections of Men and Events in Wisconsin," *Collections of the State Historical Society of Wisconsin*." VII(1873–1876), 226.

[4] Parish Records, St. John's Church, Hampton, Virginia.

[5] Charles Anderson, ed., "Frontier Mackinac Island, 1823–1834, Letters of William Montague and Amanda White Ferry," *Journal of the Presbyterian Historical Society*, XXV(December, 1947), 199.

[6] *Ibid.*, XXVI (June, 1948), 123f.

[7] Richard Johnson, "Fort Snelling From Its Foundation to the Present Time," *Collections of the Minnesota Historical Society*, VIII (1898), 439–440. The first church established and the first marriage performed in what is now Minnesota were at Fort Snelling. See Edward Neill, "Fort Snelling Echoes," *Magazine of Western History*, X (1889), 610.

[8] Richard Gamble, "Army Chaplains at Frontier Posts, 1830–1860," *Historical Magazine of the Protestant Episcopal Church*, XXVII (December, 1958), 291.

[9] W. C. Whitford, "Early Education in Wisconsin," *Collections of the State Historical Society of Wisconsin*," V, Part 3 (1869), 330.

[10] *Army and Naval Journal*, 1 March 1884.

[11] Jeremiah Porter, "Journal of Incidents, 1831, 1833," microfilm copy of manuscript in Phillips Collection, University of Oklahoma, entry of 27 November 1831.

[12] *Ibid.*, entry of 14 April 1832.

[13] *Ibid.*, entries of 28 January 1832, 13 February 1832, 20 February 1832; Gamble, "Army Chaplains at Frontier Posts," 291.

[14] Howard Greene, *The Reverend Richard Fish Cadle* (Waukesha: Privately printed, 1936), 42.

[15] *Ibid.*, 101.

[16] Bruce Mahan, *Old Fort Crawford and the Frontier* (Iowa City: University of Iowa Press, 1926), 214–216.

[17] *American State Papers*, IV: 709.

[18] *Military and Naval Magazine of the United States*, III (May, 1834), 187–189.

[19] *American State Papers*, VI: 119–120.

(See notes at end of chapter)

[20] *Ibid.*, 806.

[21] *Ibid.*, 148.

[22] *Ibid.*

[23] *Ibid.*, 147.

[24] *Ibid.*, 812.

[25] Richard Peters, ed., *The Public Statutes at Large of the United States of America*, 1789–1845 (Boston: Charles C. Little and James Brown, 1848), V: 259.

[26] *Ibid.*, 308.

[27] *Niles Weekly Register*, LIV (1838), 404.

[28] Heitman, *Historical Register and Directory*, I: 218, 223, 298, 450, 477.

[29] *Ibid.*

[30] Richard Peters, ed., *The Statutes at Large and Treaties of the United States of America, December 1, 1845 to March 3, 1851* (Boston: Little Brown and Company, 1862), IX: 351.

[31] *Niles Weekly Register*, LXXV (1849), 227.

[32] Aidan H. Germain, *Catholic Military and Naval Chaplains*, 1776–1917 (Washington: Catholic University of America, 1929), 36.

[33] *Niles Weekly Register*, LXXV (1849), 227.

[34] War Department General Order No. 29, 18 August 1838, Records of United States Army Commands, Department of the West, Letters Received.

[35] Mahan, *Old Fort Crawford*, 223–224. Graphic accounts of the construction of several posts can be found in Grant Foreman, *Advancing The Frontier 1830–1860* (Norman: University of Oklahoma Press, 1933.)

[36] George Tanner, "History of Fort Ripley, 1849–1859, Based on the Diary of Rev. Solon W. Manney, D. D., Chaplain of the Post from 1851 to 1859," *Collections of the Minnesota Historical Society*, X, Part 1 (1905), 183; Henry Shindler, *Public Worship at Fort Leavenworth, Kansas, 1827–1907* (Fort Leavenworth, 1907), 14.

[37] *General Regulations of the Army of the United States, 1841.* (Washington: Government Printing Office, 1841), 34.

[38] *Ibid.*

[39] Alfred Mordecai, ed., *A Digest of Laws Relating to the Military Establishment of the United States* (Washington: 1833), 44 quoted in Gamble, *Army Chaplains at Frontier Posts*, 295.

[40] Colonel Roger Jones to Colonel Stephen W. Kearney, 3 May 1839, Records of United States Army Commands, Department of the West, Letters Received, Army Section, War Records Division, National Archives. Quoted in Gamble, "Army Chaplains at Frontier Posts," 295.

[41] Isabel O'Reilly, "One of Philadelphia's Soldiers in the Mexican War," *American Catholic Historical Society Records*, XIII (1902), 273–284.

[42] Gamble, "Army Chaplains at Frontier Posts," 304.

[43] Samuel Edsall, "Rev. Ezekiel Gilbert Gear, D. D., Chaplain At Fort Snelling, 1838–1858." *Collections of the Minnesota Historical Society*, XII (1908), 691–695.

[44] Greene, *The Reverend Richard Fish Cadle*, 90, 100, 105–110; James Lockwood, "Early Times and Events in Wisconsin," *Collections of the State Historical Society of Wisconsin*, II (1856), 147.

[45] Tanner, *History of Fort Ripley*, 196.

[46] Francis Paul Prucha, *Broadax and Bayonet. The Role of the United States Army in the Development of the Northwest, 1815–1860* (The State Historical Society of Wisconsin, 1953), 211.

[47] George Tanner, "Early Episcopal Churches and Missions in Minnesota," *Collections of the Minnesota Historical Society*, X, Part I (1905), 206; Tanner, "History of Fort Ripley," 211.

[48] Edgar B. Wesley, "Life at a Frontier Post," *American Military Institute Journal*, III (Winter, 1939), 207.

[49] Gamble, "Army Chaplains at Frontier Posts," 301.

[50] Ernest S. Stapleton, "The History of Baptist Missions in New Mexico, 1849–1866," unpublished M. S. thesis, University of New Mexico, 1954, 130. This thesis contains information about John M. Shaw, chaplain at Fort Defiance, 1852–1856.

[51] Wesley, "Life at a Frontier Post," 208.

[52] Gamble, "Army Chaplains at Frontier Posts," 300.

[53] Tanner, "History of Fort Ripley," 197–200.

[54] Woodbury F. Pride, *The History of Fort Riley* (Fort Riley, Kansas, Cavalry School, 1926), 68–73.

[55] J. Henry Carleton, *The Prairie Logbook: Dragoon Campaigns to the Pawnee Villages in 1844, and to the Rocky Mountains in 1845* (Chicago: The Claxton Club, 1943), 100.

[56] Gamble, "Army Chaplains at Frontier Posts," 297.

[57] *Ibid.* In addition to Gear, they were Joshua Sweet, Fort Ridgely; Richard Vaux, Fort Laramie; James Du Pui, Fort Kearney; Solon Manney, Fort Ripley.

[58] Gamble, "Army Chaplains at Frontier Posts," 297–300.

[59] *Ibid.*, 300.

[60] *Ibid.*

[61] *Ibid.*, 301.

[62] *Ibid.*, 306.

[63] Heitman, *Historical Register and Directory*, 712, 844.

IV

SOUTH OF THE BORDER

1 January 1846 ushered in a new year in the United States; it also brought an increase of tensions in the simmering feud with Mexico. There seemed to be no stopping the force of American conviction of "manifest destiny" regarding expansion south and west. As they regained confidence after the hard times of the Van Buren administration, the people savored the prospect of acquiring Texas, and more.

War had been brewing since the mid-1830s, when American settlers rebelled against Mexico and established the Republic of Texas. Mexico refused to recognize their independence and protested strongly when Texas formally accepted annexation to the United States in July 1845. President James K. Polk ordered an American force to move from the Louisiana border into Texas to combat any invasion from Mexico. After some months at the mouth of the Mieces River, near Corpus Christi, General Zachery Taylor was ordered in February 1846 to advance to the Rio Grande River, where he built a strong fort opposite Matamoros. Not long after that the Mexicans were reinforced, and the day following they opened hostilities. The battles of Palo Alto and Resaca de la Palma followed on close succession. On 11 May, Polk delivered a fiery message to Congress, stating that Mexico had "invaded our territory and shed American blood upon the American soil." On 13 May Congress passed a declaration: "By Act of the Republic of Mexico, a state of war exists between that Government and the United States!"[2] The legislative body at the same time increased the size of the Army to more than 15,000 and authorized the raising and supplying of 50,000 short term Volunteers.[3]

The force that invaded Mexico under General Taylor consisted almost entirely of soldiers and officers from the Regular Army. The ranks gradually swelled with Volunteers. Although the war was seen by many as a crusade by Protestant America to subdue Catholic

(See notes at end of chapter)

64

Mexico, ironically the troops went into battle unaccompanied by chaplains. This was true not only of Taylor's command but also of Colonel Stephen Kearney's forces, which marched westward to take possession of all northwestern Mexico to the shore of the Pacific.[4]

The failure to provide chaplains for tactical units was not because they were unavailable. There were 13 chaplains in the Army when hostilities began, 12 at as many posts and one at West Point.[5] Most of the troops had been at posts where there were chaplains, but the chaplains were obliged to remain behind when the soldiers departed. Also, an estimated 85 chaplains were serving state militia units when the longsmoldering embers were fanned into flame.[6]

Nor did lack of support from the denominations prevent chaplaincy assignments to combat forces. Except for denominations traditionally opposed to war, along with the Congregationalists and Unitarians who reflected the regional antiwar sentiments of their New England constituents, religious bodies, with varying degrees of enthusiasm, supported the conflict.[7] Some communions even saw the conflict as a blessing in disguise, an opening of Catholic Mexico to Protestant proselytism. In general, however, American Protestantism did not go to the extreme of correlating the defeat of Mexico with the elimination of Catholicism.[8]

Chaplains did not go with troops into the early engagements because of two factors: First, existing legislation did not authorize their assignment to tactical units such as regiments and brigades; chaplains were permitted by law only at the Military Academy and at 20 posts. Second, the bad experience with most militia units in the War of 1812 prompted President Polk to call on the states for Volunteers but not for militia units as such. To prevent repetition of militia organizations refusing to cross national boundaries, as some had done in the War of 1812, the summons went to militiamen to volunteer on an individual basis. Because units were not mobilized, militia staffs, on which the chaplains served, did not enter on active duty. Many men from militia organizations responded to the call, and chaplains who volunteered went either as officers or soldiers.

The Americans were early bombarded with Mexican propaganda designed to exploit religious sensitivities and hamper the effectiveness of the Army. Both the Mexican secular and religious presses circulated articles extensively that represented the conflict as

(See notes at end of chapter)

being, on the part of the United States, a war of rape and plunder, a war of "impiety" conducted by "vandals and heretics" determined to confiscate church property and destroy Catholicism.[9] The propaganda had a twofold purpose: First, to incite Mexicans to resist the American military as a matter of religious duty; and second, to disturb and upset Catholic soldiers in the American Army, even to the point of considering desertion.

The propaganda had some appeal for Catholics who, at the time, made up about one-fourth of the Regulars. Many knew firsthand the extreme expressions of the native American movement, when anti-Catholic sentiment resulted in some riots and the burning of several Catholic churches.[10] Liberty of conscience was infringed upon as they were forced to attend Protestant worship services at various posts before marching into Mexico. On the other hand, there was the need to demonstrate patriotism, since the suspicion was passed by word of mouth that Catholic soldiers would not be loyal fighting a government ostensibly of their own faith.[11] Thus, for many reasons, Catholic soldiers were in something of a quandry and susceptible to propaganda.

Since the propagandists also found the desired response among many Mexicans, President Polk and his advisers realized that some action must be taken to counteract the religious fears aroused. The President was convinced of the necessity to reduce the anxieties of Catholic soldiers fighting in a predominantly Protestant army; he knew it was equally important to assure at least Mexican priests that their churches and religion would be secure. James Buchanan, Secretary of State, suggested that assignment of Catholic chaplains to the Army be considered as a means of dealing with the situation. He argued that the large number of Catholics in General Taylor's army justified such assignments; further, that Catholic chaplains could not only serve the military but could also show that the government possessed no anti-Catholic bias and had no intention of destroying churches and warring on religion in Mexico. The President wisely surmised that the presence of priests with the Army should also remove from the campaign the fears and suspicions that disturbed American Catholics both in and out of the Army.[12] To make sure that the war reflected no aspect of a Protestant crusade, Polk and his advisors made no effort to provide for Protestant chaplains.

(See notes at end of chapter)

Meanwhile, bishops of the Catholic church were at a gathering of the hierarchy in Baltimore. At the invitation of Secretary Buchanan, Bishops John Hughes of New York, Peter Henrich of St. Louis, and Michael Portier of Mobile, traveled to Washington to discuss with the President the advisability of appointing priests as chaplains. The response of the bishops was enthusiastically positive. Polk asked them to reommend two priests suitable for appointment to Taylor's army; they in turn took the request to the Jesuit Fathers of Georgetown College, and together with them selected John McElroy, Pastor of Holy Trinity Church, Washington, and Anthony Rey, Professor of Philosophy at Georgetown College. The "three bishops dined at the College and returned to the President with the names of the two Fathers; all was concluded in one half hour."[13]

It appears that the bishops and fathers chose well. Although neither of the priests was native born, both possessed the training, experience, zeal, and stamina that the American Army positions required. McElroy, the older of the two, was born in Ireland in 1782 and immigrated into New York in 1803. After studies at Georgetown, he was ordained a priest in 1817. "As a preacher he was renowned for his eloquence, and as a theologian respected for his erudition."[14] Rey, a native of France, was 33 years of age when he arrived in the United States in 1840 to begin a successful career as educator, pastor, and administrator. He filled the Army position with ease.

There was no Congressional provision authorizing the appointment of chaplains to the Army; the President, however, in a discretionary move, appointed the two priests and issued them commissions, which delegated them to function as Army chaplains.[15] The Secretary of War, William Marcy, in a communication to General Taylor, stated that the priests would "attend to the army under his command and . . . officiate as chaplains."[16] Marcy's communication also stipulated that the priests were permitted to minister to soldiers of the Catholic faith—"to administer to their religious instruction, to perform divine services for such as may wish to attend . . . and to have free access to the sick and wounded in hospitals or elsewhere."[17] Each was to be provided with facilities, accommodations, and a salary of $1,200 annually.

Polk expected the appointments to arouse protests, especially from nativists and religious newspapers. The response was surprisingly mild. In general, Catholic publications applauded the action,

(See notes at end of chapter)

and Protestant periodicals simply reported the event as news, without comment. This was not surprising; newspapers often copied articles from contemporary papers, rather than prepare editorials, and simply echoed the information and sentiments written. Even the *American Protestant Magazine* did nothing more than declare the appointments the work of the Jesuits.[18] The editor of a Methodist publication based in Cincinnati expressed the hope that the two chaplains were not Jesuits. Immediately a Philadelphia Catholic publication responded: ". . . in the spirit of boldness but of late assumed by the Roman Catholics in this country, we are glad to assure him *that they are, and experienced ones*, moreover."[19]

Adamant and bitter opposition came from a former Regular Army chaplain, William McCalla, chaplain on the staff of Andrew Jackson from 1816 to 1818, who applied to Polk for appointment as chaplain. When Polk refused, the disgruntled Presbyterian personally confronted the President and, after violently attacking the priests, censured the administration for employing them. McCalla threatened to drive Polk from office over the matter. Fortunately the Chief Executive chose to ignore him and refused to enter into a newspaper controversy with him. Later, Polk wrote in his diary: "I have met with no man during my administration, among the numerous office-seekers who have beset me, for whom I have so profound a contempt."[20] But McCalla would not let the matter rest. As late as July 1847 he was still trying, adhering to the twisted logic that belittling the Catholic chaplains would strengthen his case. He announced publicly that the President told him, during a visit to his office, that the priests were sent to Mexico "nominally as chaplains, but really as spies."[21] The President, obviously too cautious to make a confidant of such an erratic cleric, was distrubed by the public attention the statement received, but chose not to dignify it with an answer. Several newspapers, however, took up the gauntlet and attempted to show that the charge was a fabrication. A New York paper referred to McCalla as a "bigoted knight-errant" and a Rochester paper labelled him a "Noodle of the first water."[22] A third paper came to the heart of the matter and declared McCalla's "hatred of the Catholics and his chagrin" in failing to secure a chaplaincy "had deprived him of his wits."[23] For Polk the matter was settled by a diary entry. On 29 July 1847, he penned: "I cannot adequately express the horrors I feel for a man who can . . . veil his

(See notes at end of chapter)

hypocrisy under the cloak of religion, and state the base falsehood he has done. If I were a private citizen I should have no hesitation in exposing him to the world."[24]

Meanwhile, on 6 July 1846 the two chaplains, without knowledge or experience of military life, reported to General Taylor at his headquarters near Matamoras. They were warmly welcomed, and the Army commander promised them full support in their endeavors. Their arrival coincided with the army's westward movement to attack and seize the Mexican fortified town of Monterrey. It was agreed that Rey should go with the combat troops and McElroy remain at Matamoras to minister to the sick and wounded in the base hospital.

Before settling down to his task, McElroy searched for a place to live. He found it in a boarding house operated by an American, who did not let his right hand of business be outdone by his left hand of patriotism. Compelled to pay $10 a week for a small room containing little besides an old cot with no mattress, McElroy learned that the cruelties of war had not been exaggerated.

When McElroy began his hospital chaplaincy, there were about 100 patients, but the number quickly increased to about 800, chiefly inexperienced Volunteers. Five buildings in the city made up the hospital complex, and the chaplain spent most of "each day visiting each ward and each bed."[25]

Despite a heavy regular schedule of visiting the sick and wounded, McElroy found time to organize a school for the children in the area. Four hours a day, beginning at six in the morning, he taught them reading, writing, spelling, arithmetc, and geography.

On Sundays McElroy offered Mass for the soldiers and the Mexicans. At least those Mexicans could not believe the charge that Americans were fighting them because of their Catholic faith. A number of Protestants also attended the Catholic services. One officer, Henry Lane, formerly an active layman in a methodist church in Indiana, became a regular participant in the services conducted by McElroy. After one service he wrote: "I went to church and heard a fine sermon from Father McElroy. In this land of the stranger it is sweet to hear the strains of Gospel Peace and grace."[26] Quite early the Methodist layman became especially fond of the Catholic chaplain, and in his journal he recorded: "He is I think the best informed man whom I have met in Mexico. He visits

---

(See notes at end of chapter)

the sick & afflicted & I think will do much good in his present position. If all Catholic priests were like him there would be not half as much prejudice against Catholicism."[27]

One task that the two chaplains attended to with great care was letter writing. McElroy constantly wrote letters for the sick and injured who were unable to write themselves. When death occurred, he always communicated with the bereaved. Nearly all of the letters were routine, but one which received much attention brought him unwelcomed notoriety.

At the request of a mortally wounded officer, Lieutenant John May, an Alabama Volunteer, McElroy wrote a letter of consolation to the youth's Catholic parents. In the letter the chaplain told of being with the youth in his final hour and baptizing him shortly before he died. Deeply moved by the letter, the bereaved family published it to convey to the public the value they placed on the military chaplainacy. The *American Protestant Magazine* published an extract from the letter and, by accident or design, said it was addressed to a Presbyterian minister in Pennsylvania, the Reverend James Woods, and pertained to his son. The editor lamented that a descendant of the "venerable Witherspoon, should have been in the hands of a Jesuit in his dying moments."[28] Several Catholic and Protestant weeklies copied the story as it appeared in the *American Protestant Magazine* and further spread the error. Tragically, the Reverend Woods believed his son was dead, and that he became a Catholic before dying. In his momentary grief he delivered a long discourse and took the President to task for appointing Catholic chaplains to the army of a Protestant country.[29] The minister learned soon after that his son was alive and active. As the heat of controversy grew, McElroy declined to make any allusion to it, and the affair soon faded from public view.

While McElroy carried on his chaplain activities in the hospital, Rey worked diligently with the troops, sharing in their dangers, privations, and trials as they advanced on Monterrey. During the bloody siege of the city in late September 1846, the chaplain distinguished himself in caring for the wounded on the battlefield. Letters from soldiers, testifying to his courage, found their way to the public press. It was related that during the fiercest stage of the siege this dauntless priest walked coolly, bravely, and unarmed through the streets of Monterrey, among the bursting shells,

(See notes at end of chapter)

holding aloft a miniature cross and shouting words of encouragement.[30]

From the time Taylor's army occupied Monterrey until January 1847, Rey served not only the soldiers there but also those stationed at Saltillo. In mid-January many of the troops went to Tampico to join the forces under General Winfield Scott that were forming for the seizure of Mexico City. The chaplain decided to visit his colleague in Matamoras. With a companion he set out. Near the village of Marina, on the road between Monterrey and Camargo, the travelers were waylaid by a band of Mexican guerillas. Rey's companion was killed immediately. The clerical dress caused the renegades to hesitate, but at the command of the leader the chaplain was also shot.[31] News of the assassination reached Marina and excited great indignation; virtually the entire population went out to recover the bodies and inter them in the village cemetery.[32] Ironically, some of the people who feared the American attack upon the Catholic Church killed the priest who came to their country as a messenger of good will.

McElroy was unaware that Rey had been murdered but became deeply concerned about his safety when, after two months, he failed to receive the customary monthly letters. Inquiries, even to General Taylor, provided no information except that Rey was not with the troops during the fighting at Buena Vista in February. McElroy was not told of the fate of his fellow chaplain until some time later.[33] In April, with military activity in northern Mexico at an end, McElroy, in bad health, was summoned back to Georgetown.

In late 1846, while Rey was still with General Taylor and McElroy was at the Matamoras hospital, both the foreign and domestic press circulated stories meant to show that the American Army had its share of problem soldiers. Some of the revelations were not surprising. From the beginning of the invasion many of the troops left a dismal trail of excesses and disorders. Reports of soldiers abusing civilians, insulting women, and brawling among themselves were commonplace. Pillage marked the route taken by the troops. Then, with almost all of northwestern Mexico in American hands, the soldiers stationed at Matamoras, Monterrey, Saltillo, Tampico, and Camargo were allowed more time off duty, and the situation became especially serious. Desertions mounted. Serious crimes such as rape and murder increased. In Matamoras

---

(See notes at end of chapter)

drunken officers and men committed numerous outrages on the inhabitants, and around Camargo depredations of all sorts were reported. In Monterrey one observer complained: "Nine tenths of the Americans here think it is a meritorious act to kill or rob a Mexican."[34] One officer noted in his diary that disgraceful brawls, quarrels, and drunken frolics became the order of the day.[35] To make matters worse, hostility between Regulars and Volunteers kept them at one another's throats. One of the really important problems of the war was keeping Americans fighting Mexicans rather than each other.

The shameful and unwelcome adverse publicity had a positive dimension. As it focused the attention of Congress and the administration on the baser side of soldier behavior, it also led to consideration of ways to moderate it. The initial debate in the Senate appeared to indicate that the best way of providing a positive force to overcome the rampant evils was to appoint chaplains to the tactical units. Senator Edward Hannegan of Indiana expressed the sentiments of other senators when he declared that had chaplains been provided for those who went into Mexico, "the crime and disorder, of which so much had been heard, would have been as 1 to 100."[36] He felt the Congress was under obligation to provide chaplains for the troops; he conveyed to his colleagues the belief that no power on earth was as well calculated to maintain order, propriety, and decency as the presence of chaplains.[37] The Senate at the time was debating a bill that would add 10 regiments to the Army's strength; Hannegan proposed an amendment that would authorize the appointment of a chaplain to each regiment. The Senate, apparently convinced of the need for chaplains, gave serious consideration to the amendment; debate on it took up most of one afternoon and nearly all of the following day.[38]

Most of the debate centered on the size of units to be allowed chaplains, the amount of compensation, and the method of appointment. A number of senators favored reinstitution of the brigade chaplaincy. Florida Senator James Westcott argued against appointment of regimental or brigade chaplains; instead, he favored appointment to the Army, for use when and where the occasion might designate.[39] In discussing compensation, Senator Hannegan proposed that it be the same as that of a major of dragoons, roughly $2,000 annually. Senator Ambrose Sevier of Arkansas

(See notes at end of chapter)

declared that sum to be excessive and informed the legislative body that the ministers he knew, all of them Methodists, preached every Sunday and prayed night and day for $100 a year, $200 if they were married. With tongue in cheek, he said he would be glad to supply the whole Army with chaplains from his state at the rate of $200 annually. Because the supply of men available for appointment was abundant, he saw no need for extravagant pay. Senator Sevier felt that compensation should amount to no more than $500 annually. He also expressed himself on the method of selection and urged that chaplains be elected by the regiments. He would not consent to having "a chaplain brought from Rhode Island to preach to Arkansas troops, or a chaplain from Vermont to preach to Kentucky troops."[40] Most senators held the opinion that chaplains for the Regular Army should be appointed by the President; they tended to agree with the senator from Arkansas, however, that chaplains for the Volunteers should be elected by the regiments.

During the debate, Senator Henry Johnson of Louisiana reminded his colleagues of the impressive reports and letters sent by officers and soldiers commending the valuable service rendered by the "2 chaplains that had been sent out." This prompted the senator from Florida, James Westcott, to declare that he would oppose the appointment of any Protestant chaplains because the Mexicans would become excited and seize upon the appointment as proof that the war was indeed a Protestant crusade against the Catholic Church.[41]

The House of Representatives, meanwhile, had approved a less ambitious proposal. Chaplains were authorized for brigades, and were to be compensated at the rate of $500 annually. The Senate and the House finally worked out a compromise, which became law on 11 February 1847 and contained two important features. First, chaplains were authorized for each brigade, with compensation set at $750 annually, plus rations and forage; selection would be by councils of administration.[42] In a brigade made up of three regiments, that involved nine officers, since each regimental council of administration consisted of three senior officers. Second, a new dimension was added by a provision that post chaplains could serve tactical units in the field. The legislation decreed that when more than one half of the soldiers at a post left to join the Army in Mexico, the Secretary of War, at his discretion, could order the post

(See notes at end of chapter)

chaplain to accompany them; if he failed to comply with such an order, his compensation would stop and his position would be declared vacant.[43] The House felt that all post chaplains should go to the field, but the Senate stressed the remoteness of some posts and the importance of the chaplain's work as schoolmaster. It was finally agreed to leave this matter to the discretion of the Secretary. Interestingly enough, the compensation for the post chaplain ordered to accompany troops was $270 less than that paid a chaplain directly assigned to a brigade, since the Act of 11 February did not alter the $480 annual salary for post chaplains.

The Act of 11 February, fully implemented, could have resulted in the appointment of as many as 14 chaplains. Less than half that number were awarded commissions, however, and no post chaplains accompanied troops to Mexico. John McVickar, post chaplain at Fort Columbus in New York harbor from 1844 to 1862, probably developed a closer relationship with soldiers headed south of the Mexican-American border than any other post chaplain. He "sent regiments to the Mexican war with individual Bibles and the Church's blessing."[44]

The clergymen, all Protestants, who were appointed chaplains with Volunteers came primarily from the states closest to the fighting. The majority—W. H. Crenshaw, John Powell, Levi Pressly—reported from Louisiana;[45] in the Mississippi Valley the war was popular among the clergy. In the older states there was little enthusiasm for it and much opposition. While Texas and the states bordering on the Mississippi eventually furnished over 48,000 Volunteers, the original colonies sent only 13,000.[46] Yet the clergyman with the most impressive record was a native of New York and a former Navy chaplain.

John McCarty, an Episcopalian born in New York in 1798, began his chaplaincy duties on 25 April 1847 with a brigade of Volunteers that contained many soldiers from New York and adjoining states. He was qualified both by experience and temperament for the position. Commissioned in the United States Navy in July 1824, be became chaplain on the *USS Constitution* in March 1825, and remained in the Navy until he resigned in April 1826. Until his Army appointment he served Episcopal congregations in New York and New Jersey.

(See notes at end of chapter)

McCarty began duty as General Winfield Scott advanced to seize Mexico City. Among those present for one of the chaplain's first services was Captain Edmund Kirby Smith, a member of the council of administration that selected McCarty for appointment. Shortly after the worship period, Captain Smith wrote his wife: "I attended divine services this morning. . . . The men were paraded in masses in the courtyard, the officers standing near the chaplain. After reading the service he preached a good sound, though unornamental sermon on the necessity of religion. . . . This is the first Protestant service I have heard since I left Syracuse in August, 1846"[47]

That is not to say that worship was completely neglected in the absence of official chaplains. Services were conducted occasionally in some units by officers and soldiers who were ministers before the war.[48] Clergymen from the United States, Texas and Arkansas in particular, visited units periodically to lead Protestant worship.[49]

By early May, Scott's army reached Puebla, about 75 miles east of Mexico City, where it spent 10 dismal weeks waiting for badly needed reinforcements. McCarty began serving as chaplain for all of the troops in General William Worth's division, of which his own regiment was a part. During late August, in one of the most decisive battles of the war, the rout at Contrerras, McCarty distinguished himself. Captain Edmund Kirby Smith, in a letter to his wife, reported: "All unite in the opinion that our chaplain, McCarty, deserves a wreath. He was under fire during the battle, pressing forward among the combatants, encouraging and exhorting all to deeds of gallantry, and it has been proposed that he be made a Brevet Bishop."[50]

The example of McCarty prompted another former Navy chaplain to seek duty with the Army. Jared Elliott, who served in the Navy as a chaplain from 13 July 1838 to 18 October 1842, was assigned as post chaplain at Fort Atkinson on 3 September 1845. He remained there until 29 January 1849. While at Atkinson he attempted unsuccessfully to secure duty with tactical forces in Mexico.

General Scott entered Mexico City on 14 September 1847. Peace terms were negotiated in February 1848, and the troops that remained in Mexico began to learn the tribulations of occupation duty. As enlistments and obligations expired, a steady stream of

(See notes at end of chapter)

Volunteers returned home, including their chaplains. McCarty was the only chaplain on duty with tactical troops when he resigned his commission on 6 July 1848. But he liked the military, and in a little over two months he reentered the Army as post chaplain at Jefferson Barracks. He left Jefferson Barracks the last day of 1852 and served successively as post chaplain at Columbia Barracks, Fort Steilacoon, and Fort Vancouver. He retired on 16 September 1867.[51]

No sooner was the war with Mexico concluded than Congress, as it had after previous armed conflicts, began to dismantle the Army. The Volunteers were discharged immediately, as were most of the new Regular regiments. When the reorganization was completed, approximately 10,000 officers and soldiers remained to guard the old and newly acquired frontiers, and the Army reverted to the system of post chaplains. In the process of dismantlement, the chaplains, along with the medical department, fared better than other groups. In a bill introduced on 16 January 1849 by newly elected Arkansas Senator Solon Borland, the medical staff was increased by 10 assistant surgeons; 10 additional chaplains were authorized for military posts, bringing the total number of chaplaincy positions to 30.[52] The bill passed the Senate and the House without serious opposition and became law on 2 March 1849.[53]

Not long after the reorganization of the Army, as the country enjoyed the blessings of peace, there developed a growing criticism of the military chaplaincy, though not of chaplains personally. The employment of chaplains for the Senate and House also came under attack. In early 1850 opposition reached a climax in the submission to Congress of a number of memorials signed by citizens from several states, but mainly from North Carolina and Tennessee. The petitions asked that the office of "chaplain in the Army, Navy, at West Point, at Indian stations," and in both houses of Congress be abolished.[54]

The basic claim was that employment of chaplains by the Federal Government was unconstitutional and portended a union of church and state. The petitions denounced compulsory military attendance at religious services and cited the case of a soldier alleged to have been fined and imprisoned for his failure to attend. They argued that the office was frequently dishonored by the appointment of unworthy men, and complained that with the "immense

(See notes at end of chapter)

increase" in the number of chaplains—30 in the Army, 24 in the Navy, and 2 for Congress—the cost, more than a quarter of a million dollars annually, was too great.[55]

The memorials were referred to the House Judiciary Committee. After long deliberation, the Committee reported on 13 March 1850. The report answered the objections and then defended, in a finely worked argument, the right of soldiers and sailors to Divine services:

> The spirit of Christianity has ever had a tendency to mitigate the rigors of war, if as yet it has not been entirely able to prevent it; to lead to acts of charity and kindness; and to humanize the heart. It was true philanthropy . . . to introduce this mitigating influence when, of all plans, its fruits were to be beneficially realized, namely into the Army and Navy, and to abolish it, in this Christian age of the world, would seem like retrograding rather than advancing civilization. While much good and no perceptible evil has resulted from the practice; while no constitutional prohibition exists in relation to it, and no tendency to a "religious establishment" is discernible under it; while diversity of faith is tolerated as freely as the constitutional requirement, in the minister, as well as in those for whom he officiates; and while the expense is so small as not to be felt by any one,—your committee do not think it necessary to interfere with the office of chaplain, as it exists at present in the army and navy.[56]

That did not silence the critics. On 19 January 1853 the House Judiciary Committee made a similar response to another set of memorials from citizens who wanted the chaplaincy abolished.[57] A third report of nine pages was issued by the Committee on 27 March 1854 in response to additional memorials; in it the Committee emphatically declared "that it was not able to come to the conclusion desired by the memorialists" and was convinced that "neither . . . the army nor the navy should be deprived of the services of chaplains."[58] But the debate continued; in February 1856 memorials came from some citizens of Missouri, and in April from 149 Tennesseans. In each case the Judiciary Committee reported it could not come to the conclusions arrived at by the memorialists.[59]

The persistency of the critics prompted a number of people to come to the defense of the chaplaincy and urge its continuance. Probably the most prominent was Lorenzo Dow Johnson, an Episcopalian layman residing in the nation's capital. In addition to many speeches delivered, he wrote two pamphlets on the subject. The first, *Chaplains of the General Government, with Objections to their Employment Considered*, appeared in 1856. The following year he published *An Address to Pastors and Peoples of these United States on the Chaplaincy of the General Government*.[60] His pamphlets constituted the first attempt to give a short and fairly accurate account of the chaplaincy.

Johnson stated that the leading spirits in the movement to abolish the chaplaincy were "those who avowed their disbelief in all revealed religions." Johnson may have been correct, but a more likely explanation was that the memorialists represented the continuing activity of those who opposed war, and especially "Mr. Polk and his war." Immediately after Polk assumed office and war with Mexico was almost an accomplished fact, opponents of war naturally became opponents of the President. Before the Mexican war their objections centered on the Military Academy, which they worked diligently to abolish; after the war, opposition centered on individuals they considered most responsible for it. Politics was also involved. For instance, the strongest-worded memorials came from Tennessee, where the Whigs were vehement in their efforts to discredit the former President and his political party. Tennesseans were reminded quite frequently that Polk appointed two Catholics as chaplains—and no Protestants—in the first year of war. In an almost totally Protestant state it was easy to get support for any proposal designed to prevent a reoccurrence of that, and at the same time to denigrate the person responsible.

With indisputable facts and sound logic, Johnson attempted to answer, point by point, the objections raised. He candidly pointed out certain glaring weaknesses that existed in the chaplaincy and followed that with constructive suggestions. Johnson specified reforms that were years ahead of their time. In one of his most prophetic proposals, he advocated:

> A Board of commission for government chaplains, composed of some eight, ten or twelve clergymen, chosen by as many denominations; then . . . let all candidates for the chaplaincy pass an examination of this Board, for which a certificate of approval should be made necessary to constitute the applicant eligible to an appointment . . . also let it be the duty of all government chaplains to make an annual report to the Board, containing statistical facts and general results of their work,

(See notes at end of chapter)

whether it be at a fort, on a campaign . . . or on a cruise at sea.[61]

Support for Johnson's activities came from across the nation. Financial contributions poured in to aid in the printing and distribution of his pamphlets. The efforts of the memorialists and petitioners to persuade Congress to abolish chaplains gradually subsided, due in part, at least, to the aggressiveness of the Washington layman.

In the midst of the negative criticism directed at chaplaincies, active and former chaplains received some good news. Two pieces of legislation, enacted into law on 3 March 1855, singled them out for financial reward. One stated that they would share in the extra pay authorized by a law of 28 September 1850 for officers and soldiers who served in California before 1 March 1852; for officers, that bonus was at the rate of two dollars for each day of service.[62] The other specifically included them in a grant of 160 acres of land to every officer or soldier who had served honorably in any war since 1790.[63] Chaplains were not mentioned in the original bill but were included as the result of an amendment sponsored by Senator James Shields of Illinois. In support of his motion he declared: "I can testify from my own knowledge that some of these chaplains hazarded their lives as much as any soldier in the army. . . . They are as meritorious as any class to whom the benefits of the bill are to be extended."[64] So many confusing alterations were made in the bill that the Senate swept them all away by adopting a concise substitute, but the indomitable Shields insisted that his provisions for chaplains be reinstated. In a restatement of his argument he said they should share in the bounty despite the fact they they were noncombatants and took no part in the fighting. Immediately his Illinois colleague, Stephen Douglas, jumped to his feet and declared that Shields was mistaken in thinking that chaplains took no part in combat. Douglas added: "I know some who did as much fighting as praying. Some of them were the most efficient men in the army—particularly in the western wars. I do think they ought to be placed on equality with the soldiers."[65] With that support, Shields' amendment was enacted into law.

Post chaplains received an additional benefit two years later. The pay of officers was increased $240 annually, and the Secretary of War was authorized to allow this additional compensation to

(See notes at end of chapter)

chaplains upon recommendation of the councils of administration. At the same time, the commutation value of the rations was raised from 20 to 30 cents.[66] That gave a post chaplain compensation valued at $1,159 annually, in addition to quarters and fuel.

The financial rewards were simply one of several expressions of appreciation for the overall military ministry performed for over half a century. The 23 post chaplains on duty when the law became effective, out of the 30 authorized, were grateful.[67]

NOTES

[1] *Congressional Globe*, 29th Congress, 1st Session, 783; This was a moot point, however, because Mexico, with at least equal legality held that the fighting had taken place on its soil.

[2] *Ibid*. 791; *Statutes*, IX: 9.

[3] *Statutes*, IX: 9.

[4] Dwight Clark and George Ruhlen, "The Final Roster of the Army of the West, 1846–1847," *California Historical Society Quarterly*, XL(1964), 37–43.

[5] *Congressional Globe*, 29th Congress, 2nd Session, 346.

[6] 30th Congress, 1st Session, Executive Documents, "Report of Secretary of War, W. L. Marcy, on Status of the Militia."

[7] Clayton Ellsworth, "American Churches and the Mexican War," *American Historical Review*, XLV(1940), 301–306, revealed the wartime stance of the major Protestant denominations to be as follows: Episcopalians, Lutherans, Dutch and German Reformed, neutral; Southern Methodists and Baptists, favorable; Presbyterians, Northern Methodists and Baptists, varying from lukewarm to favorable; Congregationalists and Unitarians, strongly opposed. Ellsworth surveyed the four major Catholic diocesan papers, which discussed both political and religious aspects of the war, and found them unanimously pro-war and patriotc.

[8] Thomas Hinckley, "American Anti-Catholicism during the Mexican War," *Pacific Historical Review*, XXXIC(1962), 125.

[9] Blanche McEniry, *American Catholics in the War with Mexico*, (Washington; Privately Printed, 1937), 47.

[10] *Ibid.*, 4.

[11] Benjamin Blied, *Catholics and the Civil War* (Milwaukee: Privately Printed, 1945), 12.

[12] John Smith, "The Military Ordinariate of the United States of America," (Unpublished J. C. D. thesis, The Catholic University of America, 1966), 64; McEniry, *American Catholics*, 155.

[13] John McElroy, "Chaplains For the Mexican War—1846," *Woodstock Letters*, XV(1886), 198.

[14] McEniry, *American Catholics*, 55.

[15] *Ibid.*, 199.

[16] *Ibid.*, 201.

[17] Ibid.

[18] *American Protestant Magazine*, 11 (1846), 221.

[19] *Western Christian Advocate*, 17 July 1846.

[20] Milo Quaife, ed., *The Diary of James K. Polk* (Chicago: A. C. McClurg Company, 1910), II: 187–190.

[21] *Ibid.*, 111: 104–105.

[22] McEniry, *American Catholics*, 68, 70.

[23] *Ibid.*, 70.

[24] Quaife, *Diary of James K. Polk*, III: 105.

[25] McElroy, "Chaplains For the Mexican War," XVI(1887), 38.

[26] Graham Barringer, "The Mexican War Journal of Henry S. Lane," *Indiana Magazine of History*, LIII(1957), 413.

[27] *Ibid.*, 415.

(See notes at end of chapter)

[28] *American Protestant Magazine*, 11(1846), 271.

[29] McEniry, *American Catholics*, 61.

[30] *Ibid.*, 67.

[31] *Niles Weekly Register*, LXII(1847), 160.

[32] McElroy, "Chaplains For the Mexican War," XVI(1887), 227.

[33] Shortly before McElroy left Mexico, he received unverified reports surrounding the death of Father Rey. The factual and detailed account was not available until he was back in the United States.

[34] Otis A. Singletary. *The Mexican War* (Chicago: University of Chicago Press, 1960), 145.

[35] Darwin Payne, "Camp Life in the Army of Occupation," *Southwestern Historical Quarterly*, LXXXIII(1969–70), 338.

[36] *Congressional Globe*, 29th Congress, 2nd Session, 216.

[37] *Ibid.*

[38] *Ibid.*

[39] *Ibid.*

[40] *Ibid.*, 220.

[41] *Ibid.*, 222.

[42] *Ibid.*, 347.

[43] *Statutes*, IV: 124.

[44] *Dictionary of American Biography*, XII: 172; Colonel Brooke Nihart, "A New Regiment in California, 1846–1848," *Military Collector and Historian*, Spring 1965. On page 5 is a picture of McVickar distributing Bibles to soldiers.

[45] Francis B. Heitman, ed., *Historical Register and Directory of the United States Army* (Washington: Government Printing Office, 1903), II: 48, 65.

[46] Samuel Elliot Morrison, *The Oxford History of the American People*, (New York: Oxford University Press, 1965), 561.

[47] Emma Blackwood, *To Mexico with Scott; Letters of Captain E. Kirby Smith to his Wife* (Cambridge: Harvard University Press, 1917), 145.

[48] Barringer, "Mexican War Journal," 391.

[49] George Furber, *The Twelve Months Volunteer or, The Journal of a Private in the Tennessee Regiment of Cavalry* (Cincinnati: A.J. and U.P. James, 1850), 88; Barringer, "Mexican War Journal," 394.

[50] Blackwood, *To Mexico with Scott*, 214.

[51] Heitman, *Historical Register and Directory*, II: 654.

[52] *Congressional Globe*, 30th Congress, 2nd Session, 263.

[53] *Ibid.*, 456, 520, 615; *Statutes*, IX: 351.

[54] 31st Congress, 1st Session, House of Representatives, *Report No. 171*.

[55] *Ibid.*

[56] *Ibid.*

[57] 32nd Congress, 2nd Session, House of Representatives, *Report No. 376*.

[58] 33rd Congress, 1st Session, House of Representatives, *Report No. 124*.

[59] 34th Congress, 1st Session, House of Representatives, *Report Nos. 2 and 63*.

[60] The latter was privately printed in Washington and the former in New York by Sheldon, Blakeman and Company.

[61] Johnson, *An Address*, 18.

[62] *Statutes*, IX: 504, X, 639.

[63] *Statutes*, X: 701.

[64] *Congressional Globe*, 33rd Congress, 2nd Session, 313.

[65] *Ibid.*, 361, 364.

[66] *Statutes*, XI: 163.

[67] Johnson, *Government Chaplains*, 70.

V

SERVING MR. LINCOLN'S REGIMENTS

Edmund Ruffin, a gray-haired Virginian, requested the "honor" of firing the first shot. Brigadier General P. G. T. Beauregard, a Louisiana Creole, commander of the military forces of the newly organized Confederate States of America, obliged. The target was Fort Sumter, a graceless hulk of masonry on a small island in Charleston harbor, occupied by a tiny Army garrison under the command of Major Robert Anderson. On that twelfth day of April 1861, at 4 A.M., Ruffin's aim was poor, but his shot triggered a bombardment that continued for almost two days. More importantly, it ignited a lengthy and bloody conflict that tore the nation asunder. Although the fires of rebellion burned in several different places, the decisive blaze flamed at Fort Sumter. The onus of the first shot fired and the stigma of rebellion were on the South.

The well-publicized incident at Sumter came as no surprise. It was the tragic culmination of a crisis that had smoldered for as long as most people could remember. For four decades the nation was agitated by the slavery controversy. Solutions were sought and compromises proposed, but to no avail. The shooting at Sumter declared that all attempts to reach a peaceful settlement were ended. The country was obliged to settle by force its great sectional quarrel.

The attack precipitated a widespread outburst of indignation in the North. Abraham Lincoln, President for just over a month, promptly issued a call for 75,000 militiamen. There appeared to be no alternative. Seven southern states declared their independence of the Union, set up a central government of their own, and defied with armed force any attempt to restrain them. (Four more states joined the Confederacy after the call for militiamen.) To put down the rebellion, Lincoln concluded that Union forces must invade the South, overthrow its government, and occupy its territory.

82

The call for militiamen came because the United States Army did not possess enough effective military power. Its approximately 16,000 officers and men were widely scattered, primarily on the western frontier; no sizeable unified effective striking force existed. Lincoln therefore turned to the militia—an unorganized, untrained crowd of some 3 million men—for his 75,000-man army, which was to be in service for 90 days.[1] Scarcely two weeks later, on 3 May, with Confederate forces in nearby Virginia a threat to the capital, the President called for an additional 42,000 volunteers and an increase in Regular Army strength of 22,714.

The process of raising the new Volunteer Army was turned over to the states; the Federal Government had but little voice in its composition and necessarily accepted any and all sorts of military organizations. Some units that came into service in response to the second call enlisted for three years, others for as little as nine months. Whatever the procedure, the growth of the Volunteer Army was fantastic; by the end of 1861 almost 650 regiments of infantry and cavalry were mobilized.[2]

When the militia units came on duty, many brought their chaplains. State and not federal authority, however, was responsible for unit structures and staff composition. 30 chaplain positions were authorized by federal law to provide a religious ministry to the Regular Army; 26 were occupied, however, by chaplains located mainly on scattered military posts. When Lincoln called on 3 May for additional Volunteers and for enlistments to augment the Regular Army, it was clear that state authorities and existing federal statutes could not provide enough chaplains.

For moral as well as political reasons, Lincoln wanted chaplaincy services available to the forces. When the War Department issued General Orders 15 and 16 on 4 May—the former for the organization of Volunteer regiments, the latter making similar provisions for new units of the Regular Army—both orders authorized a regimental commander to appoint a chaplain on the vote of field officers and company commanders.[3] The man thus chosen by Volunteer regiments had to be an ordained minister of a Christian denomination and approved by the state governor. All who met those conditions were officially commissioned chaplains by the War Department. While on duty they were to receive the pay and allowances of a captain of cavalry, approximately $1,700 annually. Some paymasters believed the two orders were issued without clear legislative authority and refused to pay chaplains with regiments in service for 90 days. Compensation was received, however, when the Secretary of War ordered payment of the same rate other chaplains received.[4]

All doubt about legislative authority was removed when the provisions of General Order 15 were incorporated in a 22 July act of Congress.[5] But the act did not become law without opposition. The issue was mainly financial. Opponents, while recognizing the need for chaplains, thought the salary too high and wanted it lowered. Senator Henry Wilson of Massachusetts, Chairman of the Committee on Military Affairs, was convinced that Congress had to honor the intent of General Order 15. He argued: "In the call made by the President for volunteers, it was provided that each regiment should have a chaplain, and that the compensation should be the pay of a captain of cavalry. These regiments have chosen their chaplains; they are in the service. . .under these circumstances, I think we had better adhere to the pledge we gave the country.[6]

During the debate over salaries, Representative Clement Vallandigham of Ohio discerned the future more accurately than he was ever able to do again.[7] He moved to amend the professional qualifications so that Jewish rabbis could become chaplains and serve the increasing number of Jews entering the Army.[8] His colleagues did not share his vision and voted down his amendment without discussion.

Congress did not deal with the appointment of chaplains to Regular Army regiments until late summer. An act of 3 August authorized a chaplain for each regiment, selected and approved as the President directed, and specified the same qualifications for appointment as those contained in General Order 16.[9]

Although General Order 15 and the act of 22 July seemed specific enough, the manner of appointment of chaplains for the Volunteers was not uniform. Most authorities followed the prescribed procedure, i.e., that chaplains be mustered into service by a Regular Army officer to whom a copy of the appointment proceedings was given, which he then forwarded to Washington.[10] The governors of many states, however, not the War Department, commissioned Volunteer unit chaplains. Regimental chaplains from Indiana and Maryland served without either state or federal

(See notes at end of chapter)

commissions. Wisconsin and Rhode Island gave commissions only when requested to do so. New Hampshire gave a certificate that specified that each of its chaplains held office at the pleasure of the regimental commander involved.[11]

Such diversity of Volunteer commissioning procedures carried with it important financial consequences for chaplains and their families. For instance, a properly commissioned chaplain who was disabled while in service received a pension of $20 a month; if he was killed or died in service, his heirs received the same amount. If not properly commissioned, the pension amount was that paid a soldier in the grade of private.[12] As chaplains became aware of the facts they made every effort to secure valid commissions.

Neither the War Department General Orders nor the Congressional acts established minimum educational qualifications or specified any age limit. The educational background of chaplains ran the gamut from no formal training to advanced university degrees. In the early months a few chaplains could neither read nor write. There was also tremendous variance in age. The youngest chaplain appeared to be in his late teens, and the oldest had passed the biblical allotment of three score and ten.[13] For the approximately 300 chaplains who entered service in 1861, the average age was 44.

Without educational qualifications or age requirements, and with neither close denominational nor government scrutiny, a sizeable number of undersirables filled chaplaincy positions in the early months. A veteran of the Army of the Potomac registered the opinion that at least 75 per cent of the chaplains commissioned during the first year were practically unfit for their work.[14] A Boston journalist concerned with that assessment, after a visit among Army units in late 1861, declared that a good chaplain was a rarity.[15] Because of the very early need for chaplains, numbers of ministers mistaken about their calling, and unable to find or keep churches at home, jumped at the chance to better their futures. Said one observer, "Many chaplains are men who could never command in civic life the position they now hold."[16] Many drifters, misfits, and ne'er-do-wells among the clergy wormed their way into the chaplaincy. Also, "men who were never clergy of any denomination" became chaplains, and in a few instances the position was "given to an irreligious layman, as a . . . favor to a friend."[17]

(See notes at end of chapter)

Political connections allowed some unqualified men to become chaplains. In one case Secretary of War Stanton was determined to keep an undesirable out in spite of pressure from the President. The procedure can be traced through a series of endorsements attached to the application:

> " 'Dear Stanton: Appoint this man to be chaplain in the army.—A. Lincoln.' 'Dear Mr. Lincoln: He is not a preacher.—E. M. Stanton.' Three or four months elapse, evidently, and then we have: 'Dear Stanton: He is now.—A. Lincoln.' 'Dear Mr. Lincoln: But there is no vacancy.—E. M. Stanton.' 'Dear Stanton: Appoint him a chaplain at large.—A. Lincoln.' 'Dear Mr. Lincoln: There is no warrant of law for that.—E. M. Stanton.' 'Dear Stanton: Appoint him anyhow.—A. Lincoln.' 'Dear Mr. Lincoln: I will not.—E. M. Stanton.' And he didn't."[18]

Stanton's will prevailed in another unusual case. Mrs. Ella Hobart, member of the Religio-Philosophical Society of Saint Charles, Illinois, was unanimously elected chaplain of the First Wisconsin Regiment of Heavy Artillery; after she served for nine months, a recommendation for a commission was forwarded to President Lincoln. Lincoln wrote: "The President has not legally anything to do with such a question, but has no objection to her appointment." Mrs. Hobart had to leave the Army, however, when Secretary Stanton refused to recognize her eligibility for a commission because of her sex and his desire not to establish a precedent.[19]

The unworthy stood out like sore thumbs because of their activities and the distinctive uniform worn by chaplains—a plain black frock coat with standing collar and one row of nine black buttons; plain black pantaloons; and black felt hat, or Army forage cap, without ornament. Those who disgraced the calling became objects of ridicule and derogatory comment. One writer declared that some chaplains were cowards, others were knaves, and a sprinkling were sots.[20] A surgeon accused one chaplain of selling supplies sent by benevolent organizations for free distribution, and a sergeant reported a chaplain stole a horse.[21] Soldier correspondents complained of the failure of chaplains to observe high moral standards and of their neglect of spiritual duties in favor of lighter activities, especially those that entailed absences from camp. One of Lincoln's private secretaries, W. O. Stoddard, charged that chaplains

(See notes at end of chapter)

were, for the most part, "broken down reverends," long since out of the ministry for incompetency or other causes; even the President, in anger, is reported to have said, "that army chaplains . . . as a class, are the worst men we have in the service."[22] A federal paymaster claimed that many chaplains were dishonest and complained that they did not "hesitate to draw pay for three horses, when it is known they keep but one."[23] A Yankee private, probably summarizing the sentiments of many, was quite to the point in a letter to his parents: "Our minister is no account."[24]

Chaplains themselves recorded stories of colleagues who were intemperate, unethical, unprepared, self-seeking, and lazy. Chaplain William Eastman reported that "many men who undertook the service fell short. . . ."[25] One ill-trained eccentric who came in for harsh denunciation was chaplain to a New York regiment. His every act and word appeared to elicit criticism. Typical was the complaint about the severance of his liquor ration, "from which he drew the inspiration for his Sunday labors, and for the articles which he published under the name of Q. K. Philander Doesticks, P. B. He said the college which had conferred his degree, registered him in full, as Queer Kritter Philander Doestick, Perfect Brick."[26]

Almost from the beginning unfavorable comments about inferior chaplains trickled into Washington. Since some were political appointees, nothing was done. In mid-summer, the Army committee of the Y.M.C.A. petitioned the Secretary of War to remove unsuitable chaplains and to require that applicants furnish evidence of good standing in some Christian denomination.[27] The Secretary gave an equivocating reply. In September, Y.M.C.A. workers were still irritated by the low quality of some chaplains. By October the complaints became numerous enough to prompt the Adjutant General's office, dissatisfied with the general laxity of standards, to order the discharge of chaplains who failed to meet the prescribed requirements. Only a few chaplains were dismissed, however, and in the waning days of 1861 criticism reached flood proportions.

In early December a group of clergymen representing three denominations was authorized to call on the President and report that notoriously bad examples were discrediting chaplains as a group. To correct the situation, they asked the President to change the system of appointing regimental chaplains in order to keep out

(See notes at end of chapter)

those deficient in education, ministerial standing, personal and religious qualities, and devotion to their task. Lincoln responded that little could be done, since chaplains were chosen by the regiments they served.[28]

At approximately the same time Benjamin Larned, Paymaster-General, reported to Senator Henry Wilson, Chairman of the Committee on Military Affairs, that many chaplains were utterly unworthy of their positions. To support his contention he cited, without vouching for its truth, the report that a regiment maintained a French cook by mustering him as their chaplain. Not desiring to deprive regiments of the services of competent chaplains, he urged that clergymen be appointed only with the recommendation of the highest ecclesiastical authority.[29]

Many members of Congress meanwhile felt that the criticism was overdone. Senator Wilson argued that the vast majority of chaplains were men of "capacity and character" who comprehended their duties and faithfully performed them. Only a minority were "unworthy, worthless, and a disgrace, and they had received their punishment—the scorn, derision, and contempt of officers and soldiers."[30] Senator David Clark of New Hampshire declared that no men were "doing more good than chaplains." He added that while "they do not fight, they do a great deal toward keeping the regiments ready to fight."[31] But several lawmakers were acutely aware that substandard appointees were disgracing the Army chaplaincy. Their earliest efforts to eliminate them, however, did not center on tightening the qualifications and standards of appointments, as most critics had suggested, but on reducing the amount of compensation. They seemed convinced that lower compensation would drive out the self-seeking while conscientious chaplains would remain regardless of the amount paid. Bills to reduce pay were introduced. One in particular received wide publicity. On hearing of the proposals, chaplains in the Washington area gathered on 15 January 1862 and drafted a petition to the Senate. In it they reasoned that a reduction as drastic as the one suggested—$900 annually, or approximately half the current stipend—would drive out the competent as well as the incompetent.[32] The bill was never brought to a vote.

As Congress debated the matter of pay, the Secretary of War attempted to focus attention on the real issue. In a communication

_____

(See notes at end of chapter)

to the House of Representatives he declared that the "radical vice of the system is the mode of appointment" and argued "until that is changed all legislation on the subject will be thrown away."[33]

In the spring and summer of 1862, Congress attempted to solve the chaplaincy problem by dealing with the issues of both pay and appointment. Attention centered first on the stipend. The consensus was that chaplains were overpaid, yet no member of Congress seemed to know just how much regimental chaplains received annually. The salary was approximately $1,700, but estimates ranged from $720 to $2,700. When debate concluded, both houses argued that each regiment should have a spiritual advisor who would receive a base pay of $1,200 annually, plus allowances valued at $200.[34] The net result of this legislation was reduction of compensation by $300. By some strange reasoning, the lawmakers felt the reduction would help drive out the mercenary-minded, yet adequately compensate worthy chaplains. In that action Congress fixed the pay of chaplains for the remainder of the war.

The problem of ministerial standards next demanded Congressional action. It was obvious that existing screening devices, even when observed, were virtually useless. How could the Army get rid of presently enrolled misfits and prevent future acceptance of incompetent ministers? On 17 July 1862, after prolonged debate, Congress approved legislation it hoped would provide the solution. The act stated that no individual was to be commissioned a chaplain "who is not a regularly ordained minister of some religious denomination and who does not present testimonials of his present good standing, with recommendations for his appointment as an army chaplain from some authorized ecclesiastical body or from not less than five accredited ministers belonging to said religious denomination."[35] The legislators were convinced that the requirement for testimonial letters from ecclesiastical authorities assured the military of obtaining qualified chaplains of good character; it also gave the denominations some control over who served as chaplains.

Agreement on legislation to raise the standards was difficult mainly because significant disparities divided groups of denominations. The older urban Eastern-based churches—Congregationalists, Episcopalians, Presbyterians—emphasized a highly educated ministry. The Methodists and other churches especially active in rural areas relied more on ministers who demonstrated practical ability,

(See notes at end of chapter)

although ordination normally followed a period of apprenticeship and a doctrinal examination. Other groups, such as some Baptists, traditionally felt that God's call to preach was the overriding criterion for ordination, and they tended to accept anyone into the ministry who had experienced the call. Any Congressional set of ministerial qualifications that limited acceptance to some ministers and not others could be expected to produce a public reaction both immediate and caustic, for it would give one type of denominational preparation an advantage over other types.[36]

As for getting rid of undesirable chaplains, the legislation—spelled out in General Order Number 91—instructed commanders to evaluate, within 30 days, "the fitness, efficiency and qualifications of the chaplains ... and to muster out of service such chaplains as were not appointed in conformity with the requirements of this Act, and who have not faithfully discharged the duties of chaplains during the time they have been engaged as such."[37] Unfortunately, the concluding clause of the act gave commanders such broad discretion that the legislation and General Order were widely disregarded. As late as October, another General Order called the attention of commanders to the Act of 17 July and General Order Number 91 and directed that they be complied with at once.[38] Gradually, most of the substandard chaplains were either weeded out by the implementation of the law or forced out by the pressure of ridicule and criticism.

Even if the legislation did not achieve the desired results, it was largely responsible for a much higher caliber chaplaincy during the last years of the war. Although the most accomplished and experienced ministers did not leave the security and congeniality of their parishes, the vast majority of the chaplain positions were filled by good men impelled by lofty motives and thoroughly devoted to the cause of righteousness. Both military and clerical authorities compelled new applicants to adhere rather rigidly to the qualifications and requirements spelled out in the Act of 17 July 1862. One unwholesome practice developed as a result of the stringent enforcement of the law; a few ministers who desired commissions but could not get the desired endorsements within their own denominations switched to others where they could be obtained. On the other hand, some of the unordained elected chaplains who had served effectively now secured ordination.[39] Although the com-

(See notes at end of chapter)

ments, letters, diary and journal entries of officers and soldiers did not do an about-face, references to chaplains began to show a marked positiveness.[40] Unfortunately, even when the requirements were totally met, a few unwholesome characters filtered through the screening process. In most instances they were soon discharged or eventually engaged in activities that forced their removal from office.[41]

In the Congressional actions that reformed and strengthened the Army chaplaincy, a precedent-setting feature emerged: The way was opened for the appointment of chaplains from the Jewish faith. Clearance for the appointment of Jewish chaplains occurred when the Act of 17 July 1862 dropped the provision that required chaplains to be ministers of the Christian faith. But the change did not come without intensive, persuasive, and unique prodding.

When the bill that authorized chaplains for Volunteer regiments was pending in the House of Representatives early in July 1861, Congressman Clement Vallandigham proposed an amendment to alter professional qualifications by changing the clause requiring chaplains to be members of a "Christian denomination" to read "religious society." His object was to allow Jewish rabbis to become military ministers. He called attention to the large number of Jews in the Army and stressed the piety and learning of the rabbis, but his colleagues did not share his views and rejected his proposal without discussion.[42]

In the meantime the officers of the 5th Pennsylvania Cavalry, unaware of or deliberately ignoring the provisions of the Act of 22 July 1861, elected Michael Allen, a pleasant, well balanced, unordained Jew, to be regimental chaplain. Allen was a Philadelphia Hebrew teacher who once intended to study for the rabbinate, changed his mind, and became a liquor dealer. Though not a rabbi, he was well educated and widely experienced in synagogue activities.

Allen's election was natural enough. The regimental commander, Colonel Max Freedman, and many of the officers and men of the unit were Jewish. In all likelihood they searched their membership for a qualified chaplain, found no ordained rabbi available, and requested Allen to serve them. Since governors usually commissioned nominees whose names were presented to them, confirmation was automatic.[43] Allen handled his assignment in an exemplary manner. His sermons, excellent in tone and

---

(See notes at end of chapter)

content, were obviously intended for a mixed audience of Christians and Jews.[44] Demonstrating remarkable ability in serving such a large contingent of men, he was enjoying his assignment when, in September, a Y.M.C.A. worker visited the regiment—camped at the time just outside of Washington—and discovered that its chaplain was neither a Christian nor an ordained clergyman. The Y.M.C.A. worker saw this as a flagrant and dramatic example of the general laxity of standards in awarding chaplaincy commissions and, without attacking Allen personally, he addressed an indignant letter to the religious newspapers. The resulting furor caused such a reaction that Allen was forced to resign.

Allen's supporters wanted to argue the issue as a test case for having Jewish chaplains legalized, but the chagrined Allen declined. Colonel Freedman and his fellow officers, however, in order to call attention to what they considered unjust discrimination, decided to press the issue. In an attempt to force Congress to permit Jewish chaplains, the regiment deliberately nominated Rabbi Arnold Fischel, a validly ordained clergyman and an experienced lobbyist. The Secretary of War was compelled by law to disapprove the nomination. Rabbi Fischel immediately began an intensive lobbying campaign "which lasted for almost a year and involved political pressures and techniques of every known variety."[45]

Fischel's lobbying paid dividends. When the Act of 17 July 1862 included the words "religious denomination" in place of "Christian denomination," legal discrimination against Jews ended. The maneuvering in the Senate that led to the change in words was revealing. Though most senators were willing to admit Jewish chaplains into the Army, a bill introduced to repeal the words "Christian denomination" did not pass, because passage would have made it appear that a majority was on record as favoring the repeal of Christianity. A stratagem was then devised whereby the words "Christian denomination" remained the law. An additional sentence was enacted which contained this semantic jewel: "That so much of section nine of the aforesaid act . . . as defines the qualifications of chaplains . . . shall hereafter be construed to read as follows: That no person shall be appointed a chaplain in the United States Army who is not a regularly ordained minister of some religious denomination. . . ." This was horrible lexigraphy, but it was good politics and excellent justice.[46] Strangely, the 5th Pennsylvania

Cavalry did not take advantage of the new law to secure a Jewish chaplain.

It was not until September that the first rabbi was commissioned as chaplain. In August the Board of Ministers of the Hebrew Congregation of Philadelphia petitioned Lincoln to appoint a Jewish chaplain for the military hospitals located in the City of Brotherly Love. Lincoln agreed to make the appointment if the board would select the rabbi it desired to have commissioned. A highly popular cantor, the Reverend Jacob Frankel, 54 years old at the time, was designated. Frankel received his commission on 18 September 1862, and thus became the first American Jewish functionary to receive a commission as a military chaplain.[47]

Ferdinand Leopold Sarner, a native of Germany, became the first rabbi to be commissioned a regimental chaplain. He was elected chaplain of the 54th New York Volunteer Regiment, made up primarily of German-speaking soldiers, on 10 April 1863. Quite likely he was chosen because of his fluency in German rather than because he was a rabbi. Sarner was severely wounded in the battle of Gettysburg and subsequently hospitalized. He left the hospital before being formally discharged and was reported absent without leave. Thus the first Jewish chaplain to be wounded also became the first Jewish chaplain to go AWOL.[48]

Two other minority groups, one religious and the other racial, received recognition at this time. Some Catholic priests officially received commissions as chaplains, and the Civil War became the first in which black clergymen served as chaplains.

Although two priests provided religious services in the Mexican War under special presidential appointment, and three others were employed as post chaplains, it was not until the Civil War that priests actually received Army commissions as chaplains and served in any sizeable numbers. The concern for the appointment of priests was expressed when the Volunteer bill was under consideration in July 1861. The day was past, Congress explained, when soldiers of the Catholic faith—approximately one-sixth of the Army's strength—could be attended by one or two itinerant chaplains. Many members of Congress felt that Catholics in the military should have the benefit of religious services provided by clergy of their faith; in most units, however, Catholics were a minority and Protestant chaplains were usually selected. An Illinois colonel who served in the Mexican War suggested a possible solution to Illinois Congressman John McClernand: appoint a Catholic chaplain to each brigade, "if no Catholic chaplain is in any regiment comprising it." The Congressman made the proposal on the floor of the House, but it was rejected.[49] A few days later the Secretary of War called upon Senator Henry Wilson and urged him to support the proposal, slightly altered, in the Senate; the Secretary suggested that a priest serve two brigades rather than one. Wilson urged this in the Senate next day, but it was rejected in the interest of economy. Some general officers, among them Rosecrans and Stanley, accomplished the purpose of the proposal by simply attaching Catholic chaplains to their headquarters.

During the course of the war, Volunteer regiments where Catholics were a majority generally elected priests as chaplains. In all, 40 Catholic chaplains saw service with regiments.[50] But no more than about half that number were in service at any given time. On 21 March 1862, for example, there were 22 Catholics among the 472 chaplains on duty.[51]

In addition to chaplains, many civilian priests rendered invaluable service to the men in blue. It was but natural that priests located near the lines should offer their services. In addition, local parish priests were frequently called upon to attend to the spiritual needs of Catholics in passing regiments. A few priests even followed regiments and did the work of chaplains; one of them, Father Paul Gillen of Notre Dame Univeristy, pitched his chapel tent wherever he found Catholic soldiers until stopped by an order of General Grant. But Gillen was undaunted; he promptly became chaplain to the 170th New York Infantry and served with it until the end of the war.[52]

Black chaplains did not enter the Army until after the war had reached mid-point, and then they served only black troops. Congress at first refused to allow any blacks to enlist in military service. But after the Emancipation Proclamation it was only logical to permit them to take part in the fight for their own freedom, and efforts were made to organize black regiments. Once the policy crystallized, recruiting was vigorously pushed and regiments were hastily formed; excepting only the 54th and 55th Massachusetts, the 29th Connecticut, and the 5th Massachusetts Cavalry, the new regiments were ultimately designated United States Colored Troops.

(See notes at end of chapter)

Most blacks who wore the Union uniform, however, served primarily in garrison and labor roles rather than as fighters. Officers for the units were usually white; federal policy was in general opposed to the commissioning of blacks except as surgeons and chaplains.[53] The 158 black regiments in the Union Army had 139 chaplains assigned to them, but only 12 were black.[54]

The blacks commissioned as chaplains were not given token appointments but were obligated to meet the requirements of the Act of 17 July 1862 and were as fully qualified as other chaplains. When Henry M. Turner, the first black chaplain commissioned, expressed the desire to become chaplain of the 1st Regiment, US Colored Troops, nearly a dozen Washington ministers wrote endorsements declaring him to be "fully qualified both in literary and theological point of view."[55] As a result of Turner's thorough training, President Andrew Johnson appointed him a chaplain in the Army after the Civil War and assigned him to the Freedman's Bureau in Georgia. Turner subsequently became a member of the Georgia legislature, a bishop in the African Methodist Episcopal Church, founder of several religious journals, and a college president.[56] Samuel Harrison, a Congregationalist, was highly recommended by the President of Williams College, Mark Hopkins, and by a professor, John Tatlock.[57] Garland White helped recruit the 28th Regiment, US Colored Troops, before becoming its chaplain; he was an outstanding theological student in Canada after escaping from his Georgia owner, Senator Robert Toombs, and was recommended for appointment by Secretary of State William Seward.[58] Black chaplains were especially required to be well trained, since one of the most important services they rendered was that of conducting schools for the soldiers, an estimated 90 percent of whom were illiterate former slaves.[59]

Blacks who entered the Army as chaplains were initially paid at the rate of $120 annually. When Congress authorized the employment of black persons for labor on fortifications and for similar tasks, it set a monthly wage of $10. With incredible meanness, the Army paymaster interpreted this to limit the pay of all blacks to that amount. When Samuel Harrison reported for duty on 12 November 1863, he refused to accept the amount offered and demanded the same pay as white chaplains got. He appealed to Massachusetts Governor John Andrew for assistance. Andrew wrote a fiery letter

---

(See notes at end of chapter)

to Lincoln excoriating the Federal Government because a "man in holy orders in the Christian Church has, by reason of his color .... been refused the rights, immunities and privileges pertaining to his office and character." After discoursing on the relative absence of discrimination in the early church, Andrew urged Lincoln to change the vexatious practice of unequal pay.[60] The President immediately asked the Attorney General for a ruling. On 23 April 1864 Edward Bates replied that Harrison was commissioned and mustered the same as other chaplains and was therefore entitled to the same pay, and that he belived the President should order the paymaster to conform to this decision.[61] When the matter later came before the Senate, the ruling of the Attorney General was considered to have settled the question.[62]

Early legislation and Army regulations did not prescribe duties for regimental chaplains; however, by the time laws providing for better quality and broader denominational and racial representation became effective, a pattern evolved. The dimensions of the pattern developed almost immediately as chaplains, relying on experience, attempted to provide ministerial leadership to regiments as though they were congregations in uniform. Other aspects emerged slowly as individual chaplains sensed needs and responded, regardless of the lack of precedents or directions. Chaplains who generally earned the respect of their men and were able to influence them religiously carried out the expected ministerial functions and at the same time undertook a multitude of tasks that eased the minds and bodies of the troops.[63]

From the very beginning the conduct of public worship was the most conspicuous function of a chaplain and became the chief means of fulfilling his duty. Most chaplains attempted to have at least one worship service each week, generally on Sunday. A manual prepared in 1863 to aid the chaplain in his work urged that a definite hour be fixed for the Sunday service. The period immediately following the customary morning inspection was recommended as the most desirable.[64] The majority of chaplains attempted to adhere to that recommendation. But when regiments were on reconnaissance or in combat, services were held erratically.

Places of worship varied according to the whim of the commander, the energy of the chaplain, the season, and the mobility of the regiments. In balmy weather outdoor assemblies

(See notes at end of chapter)

were common. Services were held at night around campfires when a unit was on the move. In winter months, during the relative deceleration of military operations, soldier worshipers built wooden chapels. A wave of chapel building began in 1861 when General George McClellan wired the Secretary of War; "Will you please authorize me to use boards to put up places of worship . . . Parties furnish nails and labor." The Secretary's reply, inaugurating the program, was classic: "The Lord's will be done."[65] Some chaplains were provided with large tents by friends, home congregations, benevolent organizations, or by men of the regiment.[66] The protable "tabernacle tent"—providing protection from the sun, rain, and cold—became a common sight and a source of pride for many regiments. As the Union forces penetrated into the Confederacy, southern church buildings were sometimes appropriated.

Whether the service was in the open or under shelter, it could be suddenly interrupted by a surprise attack or hasty preparation for battle. Chaplain John Adams once gathered a sizeable congregation for an evening meeting in the camp chapel, but just as he announced his subject, assembly was sounded, the cry "to pack up" was heard, and "within a minute not a man was in the house."[67] A Michigan chaplain who attempted to hold a service as his unit hurriedly prepared to march toward Gettysburg failed to secure the undivided attention of the congregation as cartridges and hardtack were distributed among them.[68]

Attendance at services was a primary consideration. The reputation of the chaplain sometimes accounted for the size of a congregation, but it was more likely determined by the attitude of the particular commander. Chaplains' efforts in many organizations were seriously hampered by uncooperative tactical leaders who deemed religious exercises ineffectual, if not a downright nuisance. Such officers were likely to make the chaplain's position intolerable by failing to allow time for services in the Sunday schedule.[69] Regimental commanders who concentrated totally on building disciplined organizations designed to destroy and kill felt threatened by ministers promulgating Christian ideals. At the other extreme were officers who, because of pious inclinations, belief in practical benefits, or both, entered wholeheartedly into the religious activities of their commands; they not only removed obstacles to attendance, but promoted religious services as vigorously as the chaplains.[70]

(See notes at end of chapter)

Some commanders in their enthusiasm made attendance compulsory, a practice most chaplains opposed. Commanders who were former ministers themselves were unusually supportive of all religious activities.

Forms of worship varied with denominational orientation and other circumstances, but the usual Sunday service consisted of Scripture reading, songs and a sermon. For chaplains from denominations which emphasized liturgical worship the general service presented difficulties. Episcopal and Lutheran chaplains normally observed the Sacrement of Communion and then conducted general worship. Catholic chaplains, in addition to celebrating the Mass, would conduct general worship if no Protestant chaplain was available. At times Catholic and Protestant chaplains shared in a worship service and in a common mission discovered a new sense of brotherhood during an era of more than a little friction between their churches. Chaplain H. Clay Trumbull and a Catholic priest arranged a joint service in which Trumbull conducted a simple worship and the priest gave an inspiring nonsectarian sermon.[71] Father B. F. Christy, writing of Protestants in his regiment who attended Mass, declared that a few years in the Army did more to allay bigotry than half a century in civil life.[72] Catholics as well as Protestants flocked to services conducted by Chaplain Arthur Fuller, a Unitarian.[73] Although sectarian differences occasionally hampered a chaplain in the conduct of worship, the close association of men who marched and fought together did much to remove prejudices and make general worship services successful.

In any service conducted by chaplains, the sermon was the preponderant element. Sermons constituted a major contribution to the spiritual well-being of the soldiers. Very few chaplains relegated preaching to a minor role. Many were judged by what and how they preached, and a few were pulpiteers of genuine talent who could fashion timely and well-reasoned discourses.

In the thousands of sermons preached, two general themes were prevalent. The first stressed loyalty to the cause of the Union as synonymous with service to God; in turn, God supported the righteous soldier. To be a Christian was to be a patriot, brave, reverent, strong, and righteous in the struggle against satanic attack. Chaplains strove both for a mood that would encompass the majesty of the cause and arouse the soldier's determination to fight valiantly

(See notes at end of chapter)

while maintaining good personal character. God would sustain the Northern cause only if its soldiers fought bravely and conducted themselves as Christians. The Lord's servants were not to become as debauched as the enemy was thought to be.[74] Convinced as they were of the righteousness of their cause, the chaplains became apostles. The spirit of the better ones was infectious, reviving patriotism when it languished, strengthening it when it blossomed.

As the war lengthened beyond the predictions of even the most pessimistic seers, patriots who entered service in high spirits found themselves campaigning for long, depressing months. When they saw friends slaughtered in battles directed by inept commanders, it eroded their feeling for the cause they were fighting to uphold. But chaplains' sermons responded to the trials and temptations by compounding strong mixtures of patriotism and piety as an antidote to despair. Chaplain Charles Humphreys assured his men that truth, goodness, and God endured through time. Chaplain James Caldwell urged each man in his unit to "endure hardships, as a good soldier"—a paraphrase of II Timothy 2:13. It was a useful text. He preached it again, later on. Other chaplains used it, too.[75] The preaching of both Catholics and Protestants did much to inspire courage in crisis after crisis.

Many sermons were admonitions against swearing, gambling, licentiousness, and drunkenness, but they were subsidiary to the larger theme of God and personal patriotism. Foremost was the chaplain's promise of God's support for the righteous soldier, and secondarily, the warning of divine wrath visited upon the irreligious.[76] Re-enlistment sermons and sermons for special days— Thanksgiving, prayer, fast—were all in accord with that general theme.

The second prevalent sermon theme of Protestant chaplains was the standard evangelistic one inherited from Edwards, Whitefield, and Finney. No matter how it was preached, it answered the gospel question, "What must I do to be saved?" The emphasis was on Paul's concept that all were sinners, subject at death to the wrath of a righteous God. Soldiers were told that wholehearted conversion was the only way to escape eternal confinement in hell. Procrastination was dangerous, for death could come at any time to soldiers caught up in battle; for them, salvation was especially urgent. The great Protestant aim was to "save" each man's soul prior

(See notes at end of chapter)

to physical death.[77] The preferred time for preaching evangelistic sermons was during the winter camping periods when the tempo of combat slowed enough to make nightly meetings possible. A few chaplains, capitalizing on the prevalence of fear, gave evangelistic discourses on the eve of battles.

Although chaplains received both praise and condemnation for their sermons, most were generally successful in their homiletical efforts. Chaplains who were respected by a regiment, sometimes because of extra-pulpit activities, were complimented even if they preached poorly. In each regiment there was a nucleus of devout Christians who thought every sermon commendable. Preachers with a canny ability for fitting sermons to the crucial situation and mood of the congregation were universally appreciated. Enthusiastic approval always greeted the sermons of a chaplain who spoke with conviction and authority to the immediate needs of a particular listener. When a regiment was made up primarily of men from a chaplain's former community—where a relationship of mutual trust and esteem prevailed, and war led pastor and people to share the same hardships and peril in support of a common cause—it was natural that mature and young alike held the chaplain in reverence and affection and believed him almost as they did the Bible.

Criticism was directed mainly at chaplains who attempted to inflict on soldier congregations ill-adapted sermons drawn from prewar storage. On one occasion, a chaplain "took an old piece of faded yellow manuscript and . . . discussed *infant baptism* and closed with an earnest appeal, touchingly eloquent, to *mothers. . . .*" The minister richly deserved the critical sarcasm of a lieutenant who was present: "I'm sure there wasn't a mother in the regiment and not more than two or three infants."[78] Some were condemned for lack of preparation, others for poor delivery, and a number for insincerity. Nearly always, chaplains who lacked rapport with their units, no matter how great their oratorical skill, were given poor marks on their discourses.

Worship services with sermons did not represent the full extent of the chaplains' religious activity. Some Protestants found that evening prayer meetings—consisting of singing, Bible reading, and testimonials—which varied in frequency were well supported, especially when soldiers could be persuaded to conduct them. Sessions for informal singing of sacred songs proved popular. Catholics were equally occupied with religious duties; one, Father William Corby, anticipating today's changes in the Catholic Church by more than a hundred years, created a new liturgy for the battlefield. He arranged a military Mass in which troops presented arms during the more solemn moments, bands played at appropriate intervals, and cannons were fired at the consecration.[79] Both Catholics and Protestants offered prayers at dress parades and officiated at weddings, baptisms, funerals and burials, sometimes hampered but not prevented by the exigencies of war.

Many Protestant chaplains felt the need for an organizational structure that would allow soldiers determined to lead a Christian life to band together, regardless of creed or denomination. The most common organization was the Regimental Christian Association. Requiring only good character and earnest purpose for membership, the objective was "to promote morality and religion among the members, and to persuade others to turn from the error of their ways."[80] Sometimes the organization took the form of a regimental congregation—complete with constitution, membership roll, officers, and frequently a broad creedal statement.[81] Converts were received into membership through baptism and members celebrated the communion service; the mode of baptism and frequency of communion were determined by the particular congregation. Many who belonged to the nondenominational regimental churches transferred their memberships to civilian congregations when they left the Army. One important function of the members of the Association and regimental churches, which assisted chaplains in promoting the spiritual welfare of all soldiers, was the dissemination of religious periodicals, testaments, and tracts. The tracts, especially those with a military slant, were quite popular; to meet the needs of foreign-nationality groups, some were printed in several languages.[82]

Chaplain counseling sessions were many and varied. Sometimes in the shade of trees or the shadows of night, chaplains and soldiers discussed theological issues that led to a sustaining faith. In the thick of battle, without thought for personal safety, chaplains attempted to bring comfort to the wounded and dying. Visiting from tent to tent, chaplains provided guidance that assisted in solving personal problems of the moment. As they successfully ministered to individuals—whether cowards or heroes, sinners or saints, generals

(See notes at end of chapter)

or privates—competent chaplains were often the most effective men in the regiments.

In upholding spiritual values within the Army, considerable energy was expended in fighting prevailing sins. Chaplains of all faiths fought human vices with a unanimity that transcended all sectarian lines, though they differed about the comparative serious-ness of each one. Many saw intemperance and gambling as the most pernicious evils. Drunkenness was a serious problem, and many chaplains fought it with temperance societies; men were urged to join and promise abstinence. Father Peter Cooney, a realist, asked his men to take an abstinence pledge for only six months a year. Chaplain James Dillion's efforts to sign up members were so successful that his unit, the 63rd New York, became known as the Temperance Regiment.[83] But securing members was an uphill fight, especially in areas like the Chickahominy Swamps, where the water was so bad that whisky was issued by the commissary. Even there some temperance men remained faithful, and others appropriated the share they would not touch.

The struggle against gambling was consistent but often in vain. Many chaplains worked tirelessly to persuade the men to avoid gambling, save their money, and send it home to their families. At times soldiers co-operated spectacularly. Once Father Thomas Scully was carrying $22,000 to the post office to send home for the soldiers; three ruffians tried to hold him up, but he whipped out a revolver and sent them scurrying. When co-operation was lacking, some chaplains took unusual action. Chaplain Scully, for example, frequently seized the gamblers' money in the midst of a game and later used it for the benefit of the church or an orphanage.[84] Late one night Chaplain Frederick Denison saw a light in a tent and approached, thinking someone was sick. Hesitating outside, he realized his mistake when he heard an excited voice saying, "Who'll go it?" Quietly Denison stepped inside the tent, laid a New Testament on the cards and said, "I've got it boys," and left.[85] There was very little gambling in the regiment for a long time afterward. During his tour Denison exposed a number of corrupt hustlers who were defrauding soldiers.

A few chaplains considered profanity the most outstanding evil. Chaplain H. Clay Trumbull used to tell his men that the colonel had detailed him to do all the necessary swearing and that they might send for him if some had to be done. They usually took it as a joke and rebuked each other for meddling with the chaplain's work, but the overall effect was good. Trumbull declared that less profanity was heard in the Army than on the streets of most Northern towns; he quoted the remark often heard in camp after some especially violent cursing, "You swear like a new recruit."[86]

As the concept of their role widened, most chaplains undertook duties over and above those associated with the ministry. While most argued that their chief purpose was to lead men to begin a religious life or to intensify devotion to its ideals, they felt there was a place for attention to the other aspects of soldiers' lives. The performance of chores unrelated to the clerical state brought chaplains into contact with every man in the regiment. In many instances military ministers were judged more by what they did in these areas than on their performance of traditional ministerial functions. Some harried, overworked fighting men tended to scorn chaplains who contributed only hymns, prayers, and sermons to their welfare; they were drawn to those who labored diligently at extra-ministerial activities. Some chaplains who undertook tasks that eased the minds and bodies of the troops were, in time, able to influence them spiritually.

Education had a place in the program of most chaplains. Operating elementary schools was one of the most important services provided by chaplains of black regiments; an estimated 90 percent of their men were illiterate. Many soldiers instructed by chaplains learned to read and write well enough to earn promotion. In one regiment it was reported that 200 men unable to write their names at enlistment could do so before their tours of duty ended.[87] Chaplain John Eaton, superintendent of schools in Toledo before the war, became responsible for the educational and physical needs of the large number of blacks who attached themselves to General Grant's army. When the Freedman's Bureau was organized, he was appointed an assistant commissioner. In 1865 he became a brigadier general by brevet, the one person whose advancement to that rank was a direct outgrowth of his service as a chaplain.[88] Chaplain Arthur Fuller organized a school with five instructors to teach the common branches, mostly to soldiers of foreign birth.[89] To support their educational endeavors, chaplains established regimental libraries and generally served as librarians.

(See notes at end of chapter)

In most regiments the chaplain acted as postmaster. He delivered incoming letters, collected outgoing mail, and franked all mail that was not stamped. He also delivered the sacks to the nearest railhead and received others in return. The mail handled was apt to be voluminous. For example, Chaplain Richard Eddy sorted 3,063 letters for his regiment in one month.[90] In the role of postmaster, some chaplains left themselves open to criticism. One soldier reported that the chaplain in his unit "hardly ever has an religious exercise and spends a great part of his time in New Orleans getting the mail, which generally takes longer than most of us think necessary." Another soldier was stronger in the denunciation of his chaplain. "I have lost all confidence in the chaplain; he lied to me about carrying the mail and does nothing at all but hang around his tent and sort the mail."[91] Universally disliked was the chaplain who was referred to as "one cent by God" because he collected a penny for each soldier's letter that he carried.[92]

Sometimes a sizeable portion of the letters sent was written by chaplains. They wrote them for wounded and dying soldiers, and for those who did not have the ability to write for themselves. Thousands of such letters passed homeward, and in time relatives and friends would write to chaplains asking for more information. Such requests were not just in response to a chaplain's letter. The regiments were recruited from relatively small towns, and the chaplain often knew many of the soldiers' families; he became a personal link between soldiers and their relatives. If the soldier was negligent in writing, the chaplain might receive an anxious inquiry. It was generally the chaplain's painful duty also to write the formal letter announcing the death of a soldier.[93] Since a number of chaplains served as regimental correspondents for hometown newspapers and religious periodicals, there was a steady flow of letters containing the most recent account of events from the field of battle. Through these letters the chaplains made known the needs of the men and made appeals for tents, literature, and other provisions and comforts.[94] It was not accidental that many regimental histories, published after the war, were written by chaplains; their letters, or correspondence, became primary source material.[95]

Many chaplains even functioned as bankers. When troops went for months without pay, and then suddenly received large lump sums, chaplains worked hard to persuade them to save their money and send it home to wives and parents. Trusting the chaplain, many soldiers handed their pay to him with the request that he get it to their families. When conditions permitted, the chaplain rode to the nearest city having an Adams Express office and sent the money to its destination. Sometimes he secured a leave of absence and delivered it personally. On one occasion Chaplain William Stevens personally carried $65,000 to Washington, where he expressed $20,000 that belonged to men from west of the Alleghenies; he then continued home with the remainder, in a satchel, for distribution there.[96] At least one officer had second thoughts about making a banker of the chaplain, but not because of untrustworthiness. At Chickamauga, a captain going into action, fearing he would be killed, asked Chaplain John Trecy to take care of his purse. A few hours later he found Trecy ministering to the wounded in the very front lines, with bullets flying all around him. "What brings you here, Father?" the captain shouted. "My duty, of course, Captain," Trecy replied. "Then, by Jupiter, hand me out my purse, for it is much safer with me than with you," sputtered the captain.[97]

Numbers of chaplains drove ambulances, assisted in gathering the wounded, and worked in camp hospitals. They were generally those detailed to duty in field hospitals. A few chaplains even acted as defense counselors in courts-martial, as recruiters, and as escort officers. One was commended for being a good wagon master.[98]

While soldiers may not have been prepared to see a chaplain shoulder a rifle, some clergymen took a hand in the fighting. Chaplain Frederick Denison insisted that it was as legitimate for a chaplain to fight as to exhort the men to do so.[99] Although considered noncombatants, it was inevitable that some chaplains, holding such firm convictions of the righteousness of their cause, felt that active combat was a part of their duty. But direct action was not expected, and some chaplains were specifically told to remain in the rear. Most confined themselves to peaceful pursuits. Nevertheless, in the heat of battle some found war a more compelling master than Jehovah.[100]

Chaplain Frederick Denison wore a captain's uniform and told with gusto how he captured six of Jackson's men who took him for a "real captain."[101] During the siege of Vicksburg, Nathan Baker noted in his diary that he had been out in the trenches popping away at the Rebels. "I got several shots," he reported, "five times I

(See notes at end of chapter)

fired deliberately, each time at a head which was incautiously exposed. . . ."[102] Chaplain R. B. Bennett was commended for fighting in the ranks all day with a musket at Atlanta, which was "his custom on all such occasions." Lorenzo Barber was praised for using his skill as a marksman with the skirmishers at Chancellorsville.[103] Milton Haney was awarded the Medal of Honor for conspicuous gallantry in a federal counterattack during fierce fighting outside Atlanta.[104]

Casualties were an inevitable consequence of the boldness with which some chaplains exposed themselves. When his regiment was hard pressed at Resaca, John Springer seized a musket and fought for four hours before he fell with a mortal wound. Chaplain Arthur Fuller was killed at Fredericksburg, rifle in hand, while participating in a skimish after he was officially discharged from the Army. Orlando Benton was killed at New Bern "while nobly encouraging the men to do their duty," and George W. Bartlett was struck by a shell and blown to pieces at Cold Harbor. Horatio S. Howell was shot during the retreat through Gettysburg and died on the steps of a church. Thomas Ambrose was killed in the trenches before Petersburg. Two weeks after leaving home, John Eddy was slain by a cannon ball at Hoover's Gap in Middle Tennessee. Out of the 66 Union Army chaplains who lost their lives, 11 were killed in action.[105]

Although chaplains appeared to use about all of their time ministering to the spiritual and temporal needs of the troops, they had opportunity for meetings among themselves. Professional organizations, called Chaplains' Associations in the east and Councils of Chaplains in the west, gave opportunity for pooling experiences and for discussion of common problems. The major problem areas—pay, rank, vacancies—received primary attention.

Pay was a legitimate concern. As a group, chaplains were discriminated against by paymasters. The law of 17 July 1862, providing that the pay of all chaplains should be "one hundred dollars per month and two rations a day when on duty," was interpreted in a way never contemplated by those who enacted it. Literalistic and timid paymasters construed the law to read that all compensation was to be withheld from chaplains not only while they were on leave but when sick, wounded, prisoners, or absent on special duty. Of all the military, only chaplains were treated in this

(See notes at end of chapter)

way. By the fall of 1862 it became official policy that any chaplain not physically present for duty was not entitled to pay, even though his absence was caused by sickness, wounds, or capture. Since many chaplains were absent for these and other legitimate reasons, chaplains' professional organizations, as well as individual chaplains, worked for correction of the injustice. In a decision on the matter, the Attorney General inserted a comma after *month*, showing that he had no doubt of its meaning. But for want of this comma, many chaplains were left wholly without pay for varying periods.

It was not until July 1864 that Congress dealt with the issue. An Act of 9 April 1864 specified in terms that could not be misunderstood that chaplains absent from duty should suffer no loss of pay and allowances different from that of other officers in the same situation, and the provision was made retroactive.[106] Some chaplains still continued to lose pay as paymasters made their individual interpretations of the law, and the issue was continually on the agenda of the Chaplains' Associations and Councils.

In the act attempting to straighten out the pay of chaplains, Congress also tried once more to establish the status of the chaplain and to explain to the Army that he was a commissioned officer and on the same footing as other officers. The first section of the law declared "that the rank of chaplain, without command . . . is hereby recognized." It added that chaplains were to be listed "on the field and staff rolls next after the surgeons" and were to wear the uniform "as is or may be prescribed by Army regulations."[107] (An insignia for chaplains was never authorized.)

This legislation was an effort to settle a concern with which the chaplains' organizations dealt. From the earliest days of the war the military clergymen in their gatherings discussed rank and its relationship to status. The chief purpose of the first meeting of chaplains in the Washington area was to consider a plan to give them the rank and pay of military grades from lieutenant to brigadier general with corresponding uniforms and insignia.[108] Although Congress considered chaplains to be officers, many amateur commanders doubted that, in spite of the commissions held. Chaplains felt the need for a positive statement that they were officers, because the term "chaplain" was generally taken to designate a title rather than grade. Even in payment procedures chaplains were treated differently. While officers were paid upon

(See notes at end of chapter)

their word, another regimental officer had to testify that a specific amount was due the chaplain; the officer accepted the difference as a sign that chaplains were not genuine officers.

Thus while Congress in two apparently forthright statements felt that chaplains received the official recognition requested, the cryptic phrase "rank of chaplain" proved to be confusing. Some held that it implied a new grade between those of captain and major. To clarify this issue, the Adjutant General, on 31 October 1864, proposed that the law be amended so "that the chaplains' rank shall be ... assimilated to that of captain, and that their names shall appear on the rolls and returns after those of the medical officers." Four months passed before Secretary Stanton forwarded this suggestion to the President, and the war ended without action by Congress.[109]

Another important item that chaplains considered when they assembled professionally was how to fill the numerous chaplaincy vacancies that always existed. Never was there a time when all positions were filled. Some were never occupied. Although over 2,500 clergymen served as regimental chaplains, no more than 600 were on duty at any given date.[110] On occasion over half of the regiments in the Army had no chaplains. The length of service with a regiment varied greatly. If some chaplains served four years, the service of many was limited to a few months. The average length of service was approximately one year. The reasons for so great a turnover are not altogether clear. Voluntary resignation, prompted by ill health or family exigencies, ended some careers. In an unusual case, Albert Wyatt resigned his chaplaincy because of ill health, only to have his father secure a commission and serve as chaplain of the regiment he left.[111] Changes in policy by Congress rightly forced others to discontinue their ministry. Capture by the enemy had the same effect, unless a release was obtained. Not infrequently a man served for a period, then dropped out of service but was recruited later. Approximately 100 chaplains transferred to staff positions or became line officers. Over 100 transferred to hospital chaplaincies. Vacancies were created, of course, when a chaplain died; one of the most uncalled for deaths occurred when Jesse James, a notorious outlaw, shot and killed Chaplain U. P. Gardner, after telling him to face forward so he would not be shot in the back.[112] Positions were also opened when 11 chaplains were dismissed, including one for

(See notes at end of chapter)

falsehood, one for disloyal correspondence, and two "for the good of the service."[113]

Sometimes the assembled chaplains discussed their problems and opportunities, considered their shortcomings and talents, and recognized their failures and successes. They became aware that, in spite of all, they were making a considerable contribution to the morale and combat efficiency of the Union Army through their service with the regiments.[114]

NOTES

[1] Richard Dupuy, *The Compact History of the United States Army* (New York: Hawthorn Books Inc., 1956), 115, 116.

[2] *Ibid.* 117. The Federal government did not grant clergy exemption from military conscription; protracted debate in Congress did nothing but confuse the issue with that of conscientious objection.

[3] *War of the Rebellion. A Compilation of the Official Records of the Union and Confederate Armies.* 130 Vols. (Washington: Government Printing Office, 1880–1901), Series III, 1: 154, 157. Hereinafter referred to as *Official Records*.

[4] *Ibid.*, 368,375

[5] *Statutes*, XII: 270

[6] *Congressional Globe*, 37th Congress, 1st session, 80.

[7] Rollin Quimby, "Congress and the Civil War Chaplaincy," *Civil War History*, X(1964), 250

[8] *Congressional Globe*, 37th Congress, 1st session, 100.

[9] *Statutes*, XII: 288.

[10] *Statutes*, XII: 170

[11] William Y. Brown, *The Army Chaplain: His Office, Duties, and Responsibilities* (Philadelphia: William S. and Alfred Martien, 1863), 90.

[12] Brown, *The Army Chaplain*, 91.

[13] Frank Bristol, *The Life of Chaplain McCabe* (New York: Fleming H. Revell Co., 1908), 137.

[14] Bell Irvin Wiley, "Holy Joes of the Sixties: A Study of Civil War Chaplains," *Huntington Library Quarterly*, XVI (1952–53), 291.

[15] A. M. Cudworth, *A Memorial of Rev. Warren H. Cudworth* (Boston: Lathrop and Co., 1884), 55

[16] *Army and Navy Journal*, 19 December 1863.

[17] *Ibid.*; H. Clay Trumbull, *War Memories of an Army Chaplain* (New York: Charles Scribner's Sons, 1898), 2.

[18] *Army and Navy Journal*, 24 January 1885.

[19] Roy P. Basler, ed., *The Collected Works of Abraham Lincoln*, 9 Vols (New Brunswick: Rutgers University Press, 1953–55), VIII: 102, 103.

[20] Wiley, "Holy Joes," 291

[21] *Ibid.*

[22] Bertram Korn, "Jewish Chaplains During the Civil War," *The Military Chaplain*, XIX (January-February 1949), 30.

[23] Wiley, "Holy Joes," 294.

[24] *Ibid.*

[25] Rollin Quimby, "The Chaplains Predicament," *Civil War History*, VIII (1962), 28.

[26] *Ibid.*, 29

[27] Quimby, "Congress and the Civil War Chaplaincy," *Civil War History*, X (1964), 251

[28] Carl Sandburg, *Abraham Lincoln, The War Years*, 4 Vols. (New York: Harcourt, Brace and Co., 1939), III: 326.

[29] *Official Records*, Series III, 1: 728.

(See notes at end of chapter)

[30] *Congressional Globe*, 37th Congress, 2nd session, 1080.

[31] *Ibid.*, 1082

[32] 37th Congress, 2nd session, Senate, *Miscellaneous Document No. 21.*

[33] 37th Congress, 2nd session, House of Representatives, *Executive Document No. 136.*

[34] *Statutes,* XII: 595.

[35] *Ibid.* In this legislation is the origin of ecclesiastical endorsing agencies.

[36] Quimby, "Congress and the Civil War Chaplaincy," 255.

[37] *Statutes,* XII: 595; *Official Records,* Series III, II: 278.

[38] *Official Records,* Series III, II: 651.

[39] Philip Howard, *The Life of Henry Clay Trumbull* (Philadelphia: The Sunday School Times Co., 1905), 183.

[40] This conclusion is based on an examination of over 400 diaries, journals, and letters.

[41] Records of the Office of the Secretary of War. Letters Received (Irregular series, 1861–1866), Record Group 107, National Archives.

[42] *Congressional Globe,* 37th Congress, 1st session, 100.

[43] Quimby, "Congress and the Civil War Chaplaincy," 252.

[44] Louis Barish, ed., *Rabbis in Uniform* (New York: Johathan David, 1962), 3

[45] Korn, "Jewish Chaplains," 31.

[46] *Statutes,* XIII: 595; Quimby, "Congress and the Civil War Chaplaincy," 254.

[47] Korn, "Jewish Chaplains," 31

[48] Barish, Rabbis in Uniform, 7.

[49] *Congressional Globe,* 27th Congress, 1st session, 100.

[50] Don Aidan Germain, *Catholic Military and Naval Chaplains, 1776–1917* (Washington: Privately Printed, 1929), 58–107.

[51] 37th Congress, 2nd session, House of Representatives, *Executive Document No. 84;* John Smith, "The Military Ordinariate," discusses in detail problems peculiar to Catholic chaplains and the efforts of the hierarchy to deal with them.

[52] Blied, *Catholics and the Civil War,* iii; John Smith, "The Military Ordinariate," 73

[53] Bell Irvin Wiley, *The Life of Billy Yank, The Common Soldier of the Union* (Indianapolis: Bobbs Merrill, 1952), 313.

[54] John Blassingame, "Negro Chaplains in the Civil War," *The Negro History Bulletin,* XXXI (1963), 23.

[55] *Ibid.,* 1.

[56] Ibid.; Cornelius Thorp, *Distinguished Negro Georgians* (Dallas: Royal Publishing Co., 1962), 180.

[57] *Blassingame,* "Negro Chaplains," 1.

[58] *Ibid.*

[59] *Ibid.,* 23

[60] 38th Congress, 1st session, Senate, *Executive Document No. 42.*

[61] Benjamin Quarles, *Lincoln and the Negro* (New York: Rinehart, 1959), 171–172.

[62] *Congressional Globe,* 38th Congress, 1st session, 2879.

[63] Quimby, "Chaplains Predicament," 33; It was not until 9 April 1864 that duties were prescribed. A Congressional act of that date merely stated that a chaplain was to hold appropriate burial services for a soldier who died in the command to which the chaplain was attached and that he was to conduct "public religious services at least once each Sabbath, when practicable." There is no other reference to duties in either Congressional acts or Army Regulations.

[64] Brown, *The Army Chaplain,* 96.

[65] Depuy, *Compact History of the United States Army,* 138.

[66] Richard Fuller, *Chaplain Fuller* (Boston: Walker, Wise, and Co., 1863), 181–182; H. Clay Trumbull, *War Memories,* 16; Bristol, *Life of Chaplain McCabe,* 123.

[67] Quimby, "Chaplains Predicament," 31.

[68] *Ibid.*

[69] Wiley, *Billy Yank,* 268

[70] *Ibid.*

[71] Trumbull, *War Memories,* 28

[72] Roy Honeywell, *Chaplains of the United States Army* (Washington: Government Printing Office, 1958), 134.

[73] *Ibid.*

[74] Rollin Quimby, "Recurrent Themes and Purposes in the Sermons of Union Army Chaplains," *Speech Monographs*, XXXI (1964), 428–432.

[75] *Ibid.*

[76] *Ibid.*

[77] *Ibid.*

[78] Wiley, *Billy Yank*, 270.

[79] Honeywell, *Chaplains*, 136.

[80] William McDonald and John Searles, *The Life of Rev. John S. Inskip* (Boston: McDonald and Gill, 1885), 141.

[81] John Evjen, *The Life of J. H. W. Stuckenberg* (Minneapolis: The Lutheran Free Church Publishing Co., 1938), 110.

[82] Wiley, *Billy Yank*, 272–273.

[83] Honeywell, *Chaplains*, 145

[84] *Ibid.*

[85] Frederick Denison, *A Chaplain's Experiences in the Union Army* (Providence: Rhode Island Soldiers and Sailors Historical Society, 1893), 37.

[86] Trumbull, *War Memories*, 106–107.

[87] Blassingame, "Negro Chaplains," 23

[88] Philip W. Alexander, "John Eaton, Jr., Preacher, Soldier, and Educator," (Unpublished Ph.D. dissertation, George Peabody College for Teachers, 1939), 168.

[89] Fuller, *Chaplain Fuller*, 187.

[90] Quimby, "Chaplains Predicament," 34.

[91] Wiley, *Billy Yank*, 264.

[92] Wiley, "Holy Joes," 297.

[93] Quimby, "Chaplains Predicament," 34.

[94] William W. Sweet, *The Methodist Episcopal Church and the Civil War* (Cincinnati: Methodist Book Concern Press, 1912), 111–132, 140; Margaret Brunham Macmillan, *The Methodist Church in Michigan* (Grand Rapids: W. B. Eerdman's Publishing Co., 1967), 217, 219, 220.

[95] Denison, *Chaplain's Experiences*, 14.

[96] Quimby, "Chaplains Predicament," 33.

[97] Honeywell, *Chaplains*, 128–129.

[98] H. D. Fisher, *The Gun and the Gospel: Early Kansas and Chaplain Fisher* (Chicago: Medical Publishing Co., 1897), 161–180.

[99] Denison, *Chaplain's Experiences*, 10.

[100] Wiley, "Holy Joes," 298.

[101] Denison, *Chaplain's Experiences*, 22. General Orders of both the Federal and Confederate governments specified that chaplains were not to be held prisoners of war. While there were exceptions, the principle was generally followed.

[102] Wiley, "Holy Joes," 299.

[103] Honeywell, *Chaplains*, 96.

[104] *The Medal of Honor of the United States* (Washington: 1948), 165. Two other chaplains received the award—John Whitehead and Francis Hall, both for carrying wounded to the rear under very heavy fire.

[105] William Fox, *Regimental Losses in the American Civil War* (Albany: Albany Publishing Co., 1889), 43. Of the 66 chaplains who died in service, one died in an institution for the insane and another was a suicide.

[106] *Statutes*, XIII: 46.

[107] *Ibid.*

[108] Honeywell, *Chaplains*, 143.

[109] *Official Records*, Series III, IV, 809, 1207. The Act of 9 April had one other implication: the written reports of chaplains were increased in frequency and re-directed. The quarterly reports—made since August 1861 to regimental commanders on the moral and religious conditions of the regiment—were to be made monthly and sent to the Adjutant General through military channels.

[110] Over a third of the 2,500 appear to have been Methodists. The next largest contingent was from the Presbyterians. Over one half came from New York, Illinois, Pennsylvania, Ohio, and Indiana. One southern state, Tennessee, contributed 15. The 11 Illinois chaplains who lost their lives was the greatest number given by any state.

[111] William Wyatt, *The Life and Sermons of Rev. William Wyatt* (Albany: Charles Van Benthuysen and Sons, 1878), 203.

[112] Honeywell, *Chaplains,* 124.

[113] *Ibid.*

[114] Wiley, "Holy Joes," 304.

VI

SPECIALIZED SERVICES

Spoiling for a fight, the Union Army came marching down from Washington into Virginia, seeking out the Confederate forces under General Beauregard, hero of the bloodless battle at Fort Sumter. Excited reporters and politicians urged the citizens of the nation's Capital to hurry out and witness the battle that would end the new war. A throng of sightseers on horseback and afoot, Congressmen, ladies, and others in their buggies, rushed to see the sport. Surrounded by flowers, songs, picnic baskets, and champagne, politicians made speeches to the musket boys; the soldiers in turn cheered the platitudes and speculated they would all be back home in a few weeks at most. Then, on 21 July 1861, the two armies clashed near a small stream called Bull Run, just northwest of Manassas Junction. With unbelievably varied uniforms and amazingly similar opposing flags, a scene of extraordinary confusion took place. After two major engagements in one day between the ill-trained forces, the Union Army was forced to withdraw; the withdrawal became panic-stricken flight by early evening. The Confederates failed to mount any organized pursuit, and the fleeing forces survived their defeat. The press and politicians, along with all who were so vociferous about action, became aware that the affair at Bull Run portended a long conflict.

It also foretold a high casualty rate. Facilities would be needed to care for the wounded and sick. Even barely adequate medical accommodations, however, were slow to materialize. At Bull Run the only places for treatment of the wounded were small regimental hospitals, staffed by regimental surgeons. Located at the very rear of the Army and giving immediate attention to the campaign casualties, the field hospitals fell far short of meeting the needs. As the Union Medical Department wheezed and coughed into action, additional hospitals, improvised from schools, churches, and other large buildings, were established in nearby cities and towns. Either directly from the field of action or by transfer from the regimental hospital, the battle-injured troops rode or walked to these makeshift facilities; once there, they found most of the beds already taken by those sick with woefully prevalent diseases. The scene changed but little as the war progressed.

Slowly it dawned on the largely inept leaders in the Medical Department that more and larger stationary hospitals were required to support field hospitals; the latter shifted with the armies and, at best, gave only perfunctory medical attention to the wounded, practically none to the sick. Gradually general hospitals appeared, and as each opened it was rapidly filled, usually more with the diseased than the injured. Because of the failure to reject unfit men at the time of induction, and the unsanitary conditions and lack of field experience, disease began its onslaught soon after a unit organized. For every bed occupied by a battle-injured soldier, there were at least seven filled by those with diseases such as measles, typhoid, malaria, and dysentery. As battle casualties grew in number and disease continued, more and more general hospitals were opened and their facilities were immediately overtaxed.

The initial reaction to Army medical service, administered in the crowded and ill-equipped hospitals, was predominately unfavorable. Staffed with insufficient professionals, many of whom drank heavily, and manned by soldier details and volunteer nurses, the hospitals hardly provided the medical treatment the troops deserved. Inattention went beyond physical needs. No provision was made to furnish hospitals with spiritual care, as was done for the Army in the field. Dying because of the backwardness of medical service was difficult enough to comprehend; the thought of men dying without benefit of sacraments, last rites, or opportunity to repent shocked devout parents and relatives.[1] Since no chaplaincy service was available to a soldier once he left his regiment and entered a hospital, religious people generally, and Washington ministers in particular, became agitated over the lack of chaplains in Army hospitals. The Washington ministers and "other pious people," to use Lincoln's phrase, sent petitions to the President to let him know that they felt chaplains were especially needed at the hospitals.[2]

Lincoln was well aware of the valuable ministry that could be performed among hospitalized young soldiers. He believed his hands were tied, however, because Congress in the Acts of 22 July

(See notes at end of chapter)

and 3 August provided only for regimental chaplains. Necessity became the mother of invention; Lincoln initiated a temporary expedient. Late in September he wrote three Washington clergymen urging them voluntarily to perform the duties of hospital chaplains. In return, Lincoln promised to "recommend that Congress make compensation therefor at the same rate as chaplains in the army are compensated."[3] In October letters of invitation were sent to two additional ministers, and in November two more received invitations. The seven "voluntary chaplains," five Protestants and two Catholics, served with distinction in the medical facilities in Washington, Georgetown, and Alexandria.[4]

On 3 December 1861, in a message to the second session of the 37th Congress, Lincoln reminded the legislature of its failure to provide chaplains for the hospitals; he told of his appointments, requested legislation to compensate them, and recommended that provision be made for regular hospital chaplains.[5] Congress thoroughly aired the President's proposals. The debate showed that some Congressmen felt Army chaplains should not be provided for hospitals, but that clergymen near the facilities ought to serve on a rotation schedule. Others were convinced that civilian clergy should do the chaplaincy work in addition to their regular parish duties. One Senator who recorded his estimate of the relative value of regimental chaplains and hospital chaplains declared that the latter rendered 10 times the service. That prompted still another Senator to assert that if hospital chaplains were appointed they should be paid more than regimental chaplains because, in addition to doing more, they were exposed constantly to infectious diseases and heavily burdened with the shared care and sufferings of the patients.[6]

By spring a majority of both Houses saw the validity of a military ministry in the hospitals. An act of 20 May 1862 legalized the actions already taken by the President, and provided for the appointment of a chaplain to each of the permanent hospitals. Appointments were to be made by the President. The act was expanded by further legislation on 17 July, which specified that the standards used for commissioning regimental chaplains were to apply. Compensation was set at $1,200 annually; in addition, there was a $300 allowance for quarters. The total was $100 more than that paid regimental chaplains, and it remained unchanged

(See notes at end of chapter)

throughout the war.[7] A General Order of 14 July 1862 placed hospital chaplains under the Surgeon General for purposes of administration, including assignments.[8] That made the Surgeon General in effect a chief of hospital chaplains; he took this aspect of his work seriously, and to guide chaplains under his supervision he formally issued an *Army Chaplain's Manual.*[9] The Manual, with an appended hymnal and service book, was compiled by Chaplain J. Pinkney Hammond, brother of the Surgeon General and chaplain for a hospital located at St. John's College, Annapolis.

Congress attempted to estimate the number of hospital chaplains that would be required and arrived at a figure of 15. That was but another of the miscalculations of the war. By August 1862 approximately 100 hospital chaplains were in service. At the same time there were 930 regimental and 21 post chaplains.[10]

Once established, the hospital chaplaincies were very attractive. The applications from civilian clergymen and chaplains already in service far exceeded the available positions. In awarding commissions, chaplains with regiments received preference, and throughout the war most of the posts were occupied by experienced chaplains who had transferred. Very few civilian clergymen received direct commissions. Over 500 different clergymen served as hospital ministers, but no more than 175 were in service at a given time; the peak was reached near the end of the war, when there were 173 on duty. The ideal goal of a military minister at each hospital was never reached; when Grant accepted Lee's surrender, 20 of the 192 general hospitals were without a resident chaplain.[11] Hospital chaplains, all Protestant except for 13 priests and 2 rabbis, led a somewhat charmed life; only a few were injured, and no hospital chaplain was wounded or taken prisoner. Chaplain Francis McNeill, however, barely escaped capture when General Nathan B. Forrest destroyed the general hospital at Paducah, Kentucky.

Transfer from a regimental to a hospital ministry was looked upon by many chaplains as a promotion. The pay was slightly more and the relatively settled conditions were appealing, especially when compared to the perils and rigors of duty with a regiment. Some felt that the hospital setting was more conducive to an effective ministry. A number desired to serve in the medical facilities, somewhat permanently located, so their families could be situated near them. A few chaplains had wives who were nurses in the

_____

(See notes at end of chapter)

hospitals, and a ministry at the same installation made it possible for husband and wife to be together. In the case of Chaplain Jeremiah Porter the position at Marietta, Georgia, provided not only the opportunity to be with his wife, a nurse, but also to be with two sons, both Union Army privates.[12] This aspect was sometimes abused. One chaplain, in order to secure a transfer, untruthfully reported his wife to be a nurse in a hospital for which he applied.[13]

There were some who saw the hospital chaplaincy as a means of supplementing income, primarily by preaching for civilian congregations and raising produce for sale. Chaplain William Meech, for example, preached frequently for outside congrega- tions—for which he received a small stipend—and raised a garden on land adjacent to hospitals at Louisville and Bowling Green, Kentucky. The vegetables were sold to the hospital. The money from these endeavors exceeded his Army salary.[14] Before he was transferred to Kentucky, Meech was chaplain at a hospital in Newport News, Virginia. While there, he arranged for a Washing- ton law firm to secure the back pay of soldiers who died in the hospital. While most of the money eventually reached the family of the deceased, Meech received a fee for each case the firm handled. He also worked out an agreement with an undertaker to remove deceased soldiers to locations where relatives wanted them interred. The chaplain arranged to have the family pay the undertaker a fee ranging from $50 to $60. After the first transaction, Meech said: "I do this (for you), what you think you ought to do for me I leave to your generosity."[15] Meech also loaned money at interest and sold milk from a herd of cows he owned.

Unfortunately, Meech was not an exception. Although more than 95 per cent of the hospital chaplains had the traits one looked for in a minister, there were others whose performance reflected badly on the chaplaincy as a whole. Five chaplains were dismissed from service for being absent without official leave, and five more were discharged because of inefficiency. Several othere were eliminated because of delinquencies such as fraud and stealing. Perhaps the worst episode concerned Chaplain C. W. Denison, who escaped to Europe after the newspaper in whose name he collected funds was found to be nonexistent.[16] But for every time a hospital chaplain was censured for misconduct, the vast majority were cited many times for devotion to duty and to their parishioners.

(See notes at end of chapter)

Hospitals were improvised from hotels, schools, and other large buildings, and expanded when necessary by the use of tents. By the time the chaplaincy program was launched, the pavillion type general hospitals were being constructed, all of them quite similar. Generally built in the shape of a triangle, two sides consisted of between 15 and 30 frame wards accommodating between 40 and 60 patients each; the base was made up of the headquarters, dining hall, and other service buildings. Board walks connected the structures.[17] Large ward-tents were added when demanded, and occasionally a general hospital was composed entirely of tents. On the rivers in eastern Virginia, large steamboats and barges were sometimes pressed into service as hospitals. The "permanent" hospitals were as close to the fighting as practical; when the field forces moved, hospitals were phased out, and one or more new ones were erected in different parts of the country.

In ministering to the sick and dying, both spiritual and secular duties were delineated in the manual prepared by J. Pinkney Hammond. The volume was not published until 1863, however, a year after the chaplaincy program had been started. From training and inclination most of the ministers on duty quickly learned how best to carry out their work, and their successful experiences became the basis for Hammond's manual. The book became a valuable guide.

The general worship service was the primary corporate means of ministering to the spiritual welfare of the patients and staff. It was held on Sunday in either a building set apart as a chapel or in a dining hall. Generally every effort was made to provide a suitable room, appropriately furnished, for exclusive use as a chapel. The service—consisting of hymns, Scripture, prayer, and a sermon—seldom extended beyond half an hour. The congregation was made up primarily of ambulatory patients who came voluntarily; only very infrequently did a surgeon in charge of a hospital order some patients to attend worship services. To provide worship opportunities for the bedridden, weekly services were usually held in each ward. Some surgeons were convinced that wards were improper places for religious services, and prohibited them. In most hospitals there was also a service for patients who were prisoners of war.

The plain, pointed, brief sermons preached in hospitals usually presented the same themes as those proclaimed by regimental

(See notes at end of chapter)

chaplains. The evangelistic emphasis was perhaps more emphatic in the 7-to-12-minute discourse the hospital chaplain delivered each week. The sight of wounded and ill men lying in hopeless pain while awaiting death led many military ministers to conclude that each sermon "was the *last time,* and the *last* warning to some of them, and that their salvation, under God, hung suspended upon the decision of the hour. . . ."[18] The chaplains were thus prompted to make a last dramatic plea to the scoffer and the backslider.

Nightly prayer meetings in a chapel, dining room, or ward, were an important facet of the hospital ministry. Somewhat unstructured, they provided opportunity for patients to recite religious experiences and incidents. These testimonial sessions were instrumental in igniting revivals of religious interest in several medical facilities. In a number of hospitals the religious enthusiasm was sufficiently high to lead to formation of a "Hospital Union Church." This type of organization was encouraged because, as one chaplain declared, "Soldiers of the cross, like soldiers of the army, do much better, and accomplish more, with . . . organization. . . . Exposed to the strong temptations and asperities of the army, a Christian needs all the prayer and restraints a church can throw around him."[19]

Of course there were vices to be fought. Chaplain Joseph Anderson reported: "Profanity is the glowing vice . . . and meets you everywhere." Most chaplains agreed with him. Gambling and card playing were considered widespread by Protestant chaplains, and one exclaimed: "The whole army must play cards!" The soldiers gave the reason that there was nothing else to do. Drunkenness in hospitals was not the problem it was in camps, simply because intoxicating beverages were harder to obtain.[20]

The duties in the wards—visiting among the sick, wounded, and dying—were among the most difficult to perform. But at the bedside the chaplain probably did his most effective work. About half of the chaplain's time was given to daily visits in the wards, where—amid the mopping of floors, dressing of wounds, dispersing of medication, receiving and transferring of patients, and the moans of suffering men—attempts were made at religious conversation, prayers were said, and responses were made to the requests of particular patients. On their visits to the wards, the chaplains carried New Testaments, tracts, devotional books, and religious newspapers

(See notes at end of chapter)

for free distribution. Their reports to the Surgeon General indicated that chaplains handed out a monthly average of 500 New Testaments, 10,000 tracts, 1500 devotional pieces, and 3,000 religious newspapers each month.[21] The objective was to put a devotional piece into the hands of every patient able to read, at least once a week.

The hospital chaplain usually began his day with the most unsought chore: conducting burial services for those who died during the night and whose remains were not to be shipped home. Even though an average of more than 10 patients died nightly in each general hospital, appropriate religious services at the burial of those interred in the hospital cemetery were not neglected. Since one of the basic arguments for the creation of the hospital chaplaincy had been to "afford to the sick and wounded soldiers of the nation, the consolation of religion in their sickness, and in the case of death, a Christian burial," every effort was made to see that this was accomplished.[22] The service on such occasions consisted of selected passages of Scripture, an address, and prayer at the grave, accompanied by the usual military honors. A number of chaplains superintended the burials themselves.

Generally considered a secular chore, writing letters for patients, often on their behalf, was an important part of the chaplain's work. It was frequently used to a religious advantage. Informing friends and relatives about the condition of a sick or wounded soldier was almost always an unpleasant task; at the close of many letters, however, chaplains found favorable opportunities to draw out the religious feelings, purposes, and prospects of the patient, and sent such information along to comfort the anxious. Dispatching the mournful news of the death of a soldier to bereaved parents, widowed wife, or orphaned children was a particularly sad and painful duty. Most chaplains endeavored to ascertain the spiritual condition of the critically wounded and dangerously diseased, not only for their own benefit, but also for inclusion in a "death letter" for the comfort and consolation of those at home. The reports to the Surgeon General indicate that chaplains wrote an average of about 500 letters a month.

The work of establishing and maintaining a library and supervising a reading room fell, as a general rule, to the chaplain. Most of the libraries were adequate and contained between 1,500 and 2,500 volumes. Complimentary books were obtained from denominational publishing houses, individuals, churches, and from the chaplains' own libraries. Only a few volumes were purchased. While religious volumes predominated, fiction, history, biography, and geography books could be found in every library. Many of them were used in the library, but most were circulated in the wards. Ambulatory patients went to the reading room to read, write letters, play games, and just visit. A variety of pamphlets, periodicals, tracts, and religious newspapers was ordinarily available, and attempts were made always to have current copies of *The Army and Navy Journal* and several newspapers. Such games as chess and checkers could be secured and played, but card games and dice, which chaplains felt "demoralized the mind," were prohibited.[23] Without exception, the reading room was the most popular place in the hospital.

Schools were also established in most of the hospitals under the auspices of the chaplains. Some gave individual instruction in the elementary branches of learning, while others conducted formal classes. A number of chaplains utilized to great effect the services of patients and staff who had been teachers before entering the Army. Reading and writing were the subject most in demand among black troops. Chaplain Henry Hill, who had a large permanship class, mentioned that those who lost their right hand learned to write with their left. Chaplain Chauncy Leonard reported that his pupils became "quite interested with the historical part of their lessons. . . ."[24]

A few chaplains were able to combine spiritual ministrations with skill in bandaging wounds and relieving physical suffering. Others were tempted to branch out into all sorts of secular work. Chaplain Brown cautioned such persons in his manual:

> A thousand and one matters, which are entirely foreign to the duties of this office, will be constantly pressed upon the attention of the chaplain, and which he will do well to avoid. He is not a common-carrier, an express-man, a post-boy, a claim-agent, a paymaster, a commissary, a quartermaster, an undertaker, a banker, a ward master, a hospital steward or a surgeon; and he must not assume the duties of these several officers, although they will be constantly urged upon him.[25]

(See notes at end of chapter)

Although coveted by many regimental chaplains, the position of hospital chaplain was not without its disadvantages. Like his regimental counterpart, the hospital minister encountered numerous obstacles. Two hindrances to the performance of his tasks were especially bothersome.

First, there was the almost universal absence of religious sentiment among medical officers. For every co-operative surgeon, there were 100 who were complacent, if not antagonistic. So general was the indifference of hospital commanders that the work of effectively bringing to soldier patients the great truths of religion was made more burdensome than it needed to be. Many surgeons never understood that to heal body, mind, and spirit took doctors, nurses, attendants, and ministers working together as teams; too many surgeons thought of chaplains as useless individuals who wasted time holding hands and praying when more important things needed to be done.[26]

Second was the prejudice against time taken for religious ministrations, which surgeons often regarded as an intrusion upon patients' periods of rest and relaxation. Unfortunately, the relationship between surgeon and chaplain was not well defined, and so offered points of conflict over spheres of operation and methods. But the conscientious chaplain, for whom relationships with hospital personnel ran the gamut from praise to scorn, worked against the odds and discovered far more successes than failures in his ministry. He instructed many of the ignorant, comforted a large number of the afflicted, reformed a few of the vicious, brought again some erring ones to the path of virtue, and proclaimed to all the gospel of peace.

Supporting the hospital chaplain in his endeavors was an impressive array of active Catholic female religious workers, and women from the United States Sanitary Commission. The war was only a few weeks old when the Sisters of Mercy and the Sisters of Charity in the archdiocese of New York offered to send approximately 75 members to the Army. At first, Archbishop John Hughes of New York did not think well of the idea, but his views did not prevail; by the end of the conflict about 600 sisters, mostly of foreign birth, had served among the soldiers. These self-sacrificing women represented the Sisters of Charity; Daughters of Charity of St. Vincent de Paul; Sisters of St. Dominic; Sisters of the Poor of St.

(See notes at end of chapter)

Francis; Sisters of the Holy Cross; Sisters of St. Joseph; Sisters of Mercy; Sisters of Our Lady of Mercy; Sisters of Our Lady of Mt. Carmel; Sisters of Providence; and Sisters of St. Ursula.[27]

The sisters who left the convents served both the physical and spiritual needs of the hospitalized soldiers. Exemplary in their work as nurses, they gave sympathetic attention to the patients under their care. Some soldiers in a Baltimore hospital, however, while appreciative of the concern they received, felt the Sisters of Charity were somewhat overzealous. A private wrote home to New York: "There is a lot of ladies comes here to the Hospital, but they have not rubbed the skin off of any patients' faces yet."[28] The Protestant chaplain at Philadelphia hospital, however, probably spoke for most when he singled out the Sisters of Charity and declared that no commendation was too great for their exemplary lives of "practical philanthropy."[29]

The sisters worked as diligently for the spiritual welfare of the soldiers as for the physical. It became a common sight to see them passing out religious literature, praying with the patients, and preparing those who made confessions for baptism. The baptismal registers at the hospitals where the sisters labored showed many entries, often probably the result of decisions based on observation of the gospel in action. In one hospital "it was reported that over 200 soldiers had been baptized there before death, owing to the work of the nuns."[30]

Women also had a major role in establishing the United States Sanitary Commission. Touched by patriotism, concerned for the sanitary security and relative comfort of the soldiers, and hoping to impart a touch of home to the military environment, a group of about 50 New York women met in late April 1861 to organize the "Women's Central Association of Relief." Immediately the female enthusiasts began to seek out the role they could perform, but Army officers, buried under urgent preparations for war, dashed cold water on their aspirations. The Association was told that the Medical Department could take care of its own, and the work which the women proposed to do, although generous, would be superfluous. The determined women were not to be denied, however, and went to Washington with a delegation from two other agencies to confer with War Department officials on the matter of volunteer aid to soldiers. The turmoil in Washington convinced the visitors more than ever of the need for an agency to safeguard the soldiers' well-being, particularly volunteers. The War Department and most of the Medical Department protested against the unnecessary intrusion of "petticoats and preachers prying and poking about" until Dr. Robert C. Wood, brother-in-law of Jefferson Davis and acting Surgeon General, commented favorably on the ladies' plans. On 7 July 1861 Secretary of War Simon Cameron approved the establishment of an organization that was to center its activities on the sanitary conditions of the volunteers and the general comfort and welfare of the troops. Labeled the United States Sanitary Commission, its policy-making board was headed by Dr. Henry Bellows, a prominent Unitarian minister; its first administrator was Frederick Law Olmstead, well known traveler, lecturer, and architect.[31]

Key men in the organization were associate and assistant secretaries, through whom all activity was channeled. But it was a battery of salaried employees—around 200 at peak strength—who carried out the best services of the Commission; they distributed shirts, socks, drawers, blankets, quilts, and towels for the soldiers' personal use, and supplemented Army rations with condensed milk, beefstock, canned meats, fruit, crackers, tea, sugar, wine, cordials, and hospital accessories.[32] Agents of the Commission were found in every hospital and ministered to the temporal needs of the sick and wounded. The Commission also equipped, staffed, and put into operation hospital boats and trains, and collected valuable data that kept the country informed on the needs and conditions of the sick and wounded. In appraising the role of the Sanitary Commission, Chaplain William Y. Brown wrote:

> It has saved thousands of valuable lives by the distribution of its stores; and thousands more by its influence upon the sanitary condition . . . and the efficiency of the hospitals. Its stores are always at the command of a judicious chaplain, who has an opportunity of properly distributing them.[33]

Support for the Commission's activities came from the charity and benevolence of the American people. As soon as organization took place, the Commission began to receive articles from all over the North for use in the hospitals. As the war increased in momentum and scope, so did the gifts, both in cash and supplies. The estimated value of supplies distributed to the Army during the war was $15,000,000 with at least 80 percent of the items received

(See notes at end of chapter)

from Northern homes; $5,003,982 in cash was received. The total value of the Commission's services has been placed at $25,000,000.[34]

The Sanitary Commission lost its volunteer status when a paid staff was acquired. Its original objective—guardian of the volunteer soldier—became overshadowed as the agency participated in virtually all wartime activities. Yet the Commission proved to be a very valuable institution to the sick, wounded, and exhausted soldiers who received its benevolence. It was certainly an important ally of hospital chaplains as they ministered to the temporal needs of soldiers.[35]

Several other organizations undergirded the work of hospital chaplains as well as that of chaplains in regiments. Among them were the United States Christian Commission, American Bible Society, and American Tract Society.

The Christian Commission, in some ways the forerunner of the United Services Organization, was formed on 14 November 1861 under the auspices of the YMCA, and for all practical purposes became the wartime battlefield expression of the YMCA.[36] From the first months of the war, the YMCA in the larger Northern cities was active in providing items of comfort to troops. The limited coverage given made it apparent that a single agency of national scope was needed to plan and provide services and aid to the soldiers; for this purpose, the Christian Commission came into being.

The work of the Christian Commission was done almost exclusively by about 5,000 nonsalaried volunteers, each of whom labored an average of 38 days. The delegates, as they were called, soon won acceptance throughout most of the Army, and usually had free access to the soldiers. However, there was one high ranking officer with whom they had difficulty. General William T. Sherman refused to allow some delegates admission to his command because he felt that civilians among the soldiers were already numerous enough to interfere with military operations.[37]

The services of the Christian Commission were performed in two areas. The first was its religious ministry, for which it was primarily intended; the second was that of physical ministry, particularly to sick and wounded in hospitals, camps, and on battlefields.[38] Probably a chaplain stated it best when he wrote: "It goes forth into the camp and the hospital, with delicacies in one

(See notes at end of chapter)

hand, the Bible in the other, and the voice of the living minister between them, and so endeavors to meet every want of the soldier, and to mitigate all his sufferings."[39]

The religious work of the delegates, the majority of whom were evangelical clergymen, was mainly to augment the activities of chaplains. Delegates assisted by visiting the sick, wounded and dying; they arranged for civilian ministers to come for short periods and preach in hospitals and to regiments; when necessary, they themselves preached. They attempted to discourage vice of every kind. Probably the most significant support the Commission rendered chaplains was the provision of large quantities of religious literature. Late in its existence, the Commission even undertook to furnish chapel tents to the regiments. In these two activities it took over and supplanted the concept and work of such organizations as the Chaplain's Aid Society.[40] In hospitals and regiments where there were no chaplains, the delegates usually assumed the role.

In serving the physical welfare of the soldiers, the Christian Commission to a large extent also supplemented the activities of the Sanitary Commission. The Christian Commission was perhaps more personal in its work, relying less on supplies than the Sanitary Commission. Without a doubt the most important services rendered by the delegates were aiding surgeons and ministering to the sick and wounded.[41] Also important were sustained and comprehensive efforts to provide libraries throughout the Army. Libraries of 125 volumes each, supplemented with magazines and periodicals, were compiled and placed on loan to hospitals and regiments. At least one chaplain felt this was the most important thing the Commission did.[42] In catering to physical needs, much attention was given to supplementing the dull Army diet. In addition to hot drinks from "coffee wagons," tasty food was constantly distributed. For example, items sent from England for troops in the area around City Point, Maryland, included 261 tons of ice, 125 barrels of potatoes, 78 barrels of onions, 10 barrels of turnips, 5 barrels of pickled limes, 10 barrels of pickles, 900 cabbages, 750 pounds of codfish, 70 boxes of lemons, 10 boxes of cocoa, and 40 boxes of chocolate.[43] "Like the 'locusts of Egypt,' delegates from the Christian Commission swarmed with pails of water, canteens of brandy and such simple appliances as Christianity or humanity dictates."[44] A number of the delegates came to the conclusion that the men they visited were interested only in the gifts distri-

(See notes at end of chapter)

buted; had they been aware of the high esteem in which most soldiers held the organization and its services, they would have been reassured concerning the value of their work.[45]

Unlike the Christian Commission, the American Bible Society did not originate with the conflict between the states; it was organized in 1816, and over the years made a systematic drive to place a Bible in every house throughout America. The opportunity of supplying Scriptures to patients in hospitals and soldiers in camps and regiments was early seized by the Society. In the summer of 1861, chaplains in Volunteer regiments alone received over 400,000 Bibles for distribution.[46] There was no letup in the number of Testaments and Bibles provided for distribution by chaplains and delegates of the Christian Commission. For the one year period beginning in April 1863, 994,473 Bibles were distributed to military personnel.[47] Not only did the American Bible Society contribute to the needs of the Union Army, but during the same period several large shipments were sent South. Since practically all publishers of Bibles, or portions, were in the North, Confederate chaplains had difficulty meeting the requests of their soldiers until the British and Foreign Bible Society and the American Bible Society came to the rescue of the Confederate Bible Society.

The volumes supplied by the Society were intended for Protestants, but many Protestant chaplains saw to it that soldiers of the Catholic faith were not overlooked. Chaplain Frederick Denison solicited funds from a wealthy New York Catholic layman to purchase 300 Douay New Testaments for Catholics in his regiment.[48] Soldiers unable to read English were not neglected; Chaplain J. J. Marks gave out Testaments in German, French, and Italian.[49]

The American Tract Society, formed in 1825, worked hard over the years at printing and dispersing its materials across the land. During the war, the Society, largest and best known of several similar agencies, produced a wide variety of religious publications for dissemination by chaplains and Christian Commission delegates. The Society's *The American Messenger,* published and distributed gratuitously, had the largest circulation of any religious newspaper and was eagerly received; probably no literature, however, was as popular among the soldiers as the tracts, which were an invaluable aid to every chaplain. Chaplain William Brown reported that men

(See notes at end of chapter)

begged for "tracts as starving men beg for bread," and that they "were read from beginning to end, and passed from hand to hand, quite worn out."[50]

The tracts that helped overcome the monotony of military life varied greatly in character, content, and size. Generally they were designed to prevent demoralization, inspire confidence, encourage partiotism, strengthen heroic resolve. But above everything else, they were meant to "present gospel truths in articles terse and attractive, and illustrate their benign powers by narratives of conversions, revivals, and hallowed Christian examples of holy living and happy dying."[51]

Soldiers showed a perference for tracts having a military slant, such as *Masked Batteries, A Greater Rebellion, Halt, The Grand Army,* and *The Widow's Son Enlisting.* Those that pointed to pious examples from the careers of great soldiers of former times were especially appealing. So anxious were some of the writers to use historical figures to convey a moral lesson that they were not above distortion of facts. *The Religious Character of Washington* was an example, and it probably shocked those who knew history. Tracts that warned against camp vices—*The Gambler's Balance Sheet, The Temperance Letter,* and *Satan's Baits*—were also appealing.[52] To meet the needs of foreign-nationality groups, some tracts were printed in several languages. Those in German had the widest circulation; German soldiers showed unusual diligence in reading.[53]

The large number of Protestant tracts circulated led some Catholic soldiers to complain that their Church was doing them a disservice in failing to place adequate literature in the hospitals, regiments and camps. A leading Catholic periodical agreed and declared that while the soldiers wanted "Catholic reading . . . nothing is offered them except tracts from Protestant sources, offensive at once to their faith, their reason, and their good taste."[54] Another periodical published a letter from Chaplain Francis Fusseder in which he lamented the ubiquitous Protestant material and pointed out that for lack of Catholic literature, Catholic soldiers read these and were influenced by them. Other journals took up the cry and eventually the suggestion came that a society be formed to provide Catholic literature to the soldiers. Cash began to trickle in to support a society, but not enough; the project was abandoned. If the Catholics read tracts, they were Protestant in tone and intent.

(See notes at end of chapter)

The hospital and regimental chaplain's role in the Union Army was difficult at best. He stood for truth, purity, and righteousness, and attempted to be a friend to every soldier, especially in the hour of need. Without the valuable aid provided by the Catholic Sisterhoods, Sanitary Commission, Christian Commission, American Bible Society, and the American Tract Society, his task would have been all but impossible. Many a chaplain found cause for profound gratitude in the generous aid rendered by these agencies; and justly so, for they had made the difference between an effective program and an inadequate one, no matter how talented and dedicated the individual chaplain.

NOTES

[1] Quimby, "Congress and the Civil War Chaplaincy," 251.

[2] *Official Records,* Series III, 1: 712.

[3] *Congressional Globe,* 37th Congress, 2nd session, 1085.

[4] *Ibid.*

[5] *Ibid.; Official Records,* Series III, 1: 712.

[6] *Congressional Globe,* 37th Congress, 2nd session, 1078–1085.

[7] *Statutes,* XII: 403, 404. 595.

[8] *Official Records,* Series III, II: 67, 222.

[9] J. Pinkney Hammond, *The Army Chaplain's Manual* (Philadelphia: J. B. Lippincott, 1863).

[10] *Army Register,* 1865, 66, 78. Army policy was to allow one chaplain to each hospital and there were only two exceptions to it—2 chaplains were on duty at the Madison, Indiana, hospital and 3 at the Dennison Hospital, Philadelphia.

[11] Charles B. Pfab, Jr., "American Hospital Chaplains During the Civil War, 1861–1865," (Unpublished M. A. Thesis, Catholic University of America, 1955), 16.

[12] Jeremiah Porter Papers, Earl F. Stover Collection, US Army Chaplain Center and School, Fort Wadsworth, NY.

[13] Richard K. Smith Papers, Stover Collection, US Army Chaplain Center and School. Blake was tried by court-martial on this and other charges. He was found guilty and sentenced to dismissal from service, but the sentence was revoked and he was honorably discharged. Blake later re-entered the Army as a Post Chaplain.

[14] William W. Meech Paper, Stover Collection, US Army Chaplain Center and School.

[15] *Ibid.*

[16] Pfab, "American Hospital Chaplains," 25.

[17] A. S. Billingsley, *From the Flag to the Cross; or Scenes and Incidents of Christianity in the War* (Philadelphia: New-World Publishing Co., 1872), 82.

[18] *Ibid.,* 104.

[19] *Ibid.,* 259, 260.

[20] Pfab, "American Hospital Chaplains," 38.

[21] This conclusion is based on an examination of over 2,000 reports—characterized by a meagerness of comment and plenty of statistics—deposited at the National Archives, Record Group 94. In addition to the literature dispersed, the reports recorded the number of visits made, services held, funerals conducted, confessions received, and letters written.

[22] William Y. Brown, *The Army Chaplain: His Office, Duties and Responsibilities* (Philadelphia: William S. and Alfred Martien, 1863), 68.

[23] *Ibid.,* 70.

[24] Pfab, "American Hospital Chaplains," 37; Warren Armstrong, "Union Chaplains and the Education of the Freedmen," *Journal of Negro History,* LIIC (1967), 107.

[25] Brown, *The Army Chaplain,* 82.

[26] Quimby, "The Chaplains Predicament," 36.

[27] Benjamin Blied, *Catholics and the Civil War* (Milwaukee: Privately Printed, 1945), 82.

[28] Wiley, *Billy Yank,* 149.

[29] Nathaniel West, *A Sketch of the General Hospital, U. S. Army, at West Philadelphia* (Philadelphia: Ringwalt and Brown, Book and Job Printers, 1862), 4.

[30] Blied, *Catholics and the Civil War,* 119.

[31] William Thompson, "The United States Sanitary Commission." *Civil War History,* 11(1956), 41–44.

[32] *Ibid.,* 54, 55. The benevolent mantle of the Sanitary Commission also extended to Confederate prisoners and wounded.

[33] Brown *The Army Chaplain,* 136.

[34] Thompson, "The United States Sanitary Commission," 53.

[35] Katherine Wormeley, *The Other Side of War* (Boston: Tichnor and Company, 1889), 182.

[36] United States Christian Commission, *First Annual Report* (Philadelphia: Privately printed, 1863), 5; Lemuel Moss and Edward Smith, *Christian Work on the Battlefield* (London: Hodder and Stoughton, 1902), 9.

[37] Lloyd Lewis, *Sherman: Fighting Prophet* (New York: Harcourt, Brace and Co., 1932), 352; S. S. Cummings, *Life and Work of Rev. S. S. Cummings* (Somerville, Mass.: Privately printed, 1898), 144.

[38] United States Christian Commission, *Second Annual Report* (New York: Privately printed, 1864), 15–21.

[39] Brown, *The Army Chaplain,* 137.

[40] Carroll Quenzel, "Books for the Boys in Blue," *Journal of the Illinois Historical Society,* XXXXIV(1951), 218, 219.

[41] James Henry, "The United States Christian Commission in the Civil War," *Civil War History,* VI(1960), 383; William Tucker, *My Generation* (Boston: Houghton Mifflin Co., 1919), 48.

[42] Quenzel, "Books for the Boys in Blue," 228. Funds and supplies to support the work of the Commission came from individuals, churches, businesses, and religious organizations. During its 4 years of existence, the Commission was entrusted with over $2,500,000 in cash and more that $3,000,000 worth of supplies and publications.

[43] Henry, "United States Christian Commission," 382.

[44] *Ibid.,* 387.

[45] Wiley, *Billy Yank,* 269; Martha Lowe, *Memoir of Charles Lowe* (Boston: Cuppler, Upham, and Co., 1884), 319.

[46] *Western Christian Advocate,* 23 October 1861.

[47] Sweet, *Methodist Episcopal Church,* 167. Funds for the purchase of Bibles and Testaments were raised by agents of the Society from individuals and churches. During the four years of war, over $2,000,000 was secured.

[48] Denison, *Chaplain's Experiences,* 26.

[49] Honeywell, *Chaplains,* 141.

[50] Brown, *The Army Chaplain,* 129, 131.

[51] *Ibid.,* 132.

[52] Wiley, *Billy Yank,* 273.

[53] *Ibid.*

[54] Blied, *Catholics and the Civil War,* 116.

VII

BEGINNING AND ENDING A TRADITION

Before the initial shots on Fort Sumter that heralded the Civil War, the Provisional Government of the Confederate States of America assembled in Montgomery, Alabama, and faced the difficult, complicated task of providing for and mustering a military force. Familiarity with the structure of the War Department and the composition of the Army of the United States expedited matters; on 21 February 1861 the Provisional Congress, not quite a month old, enacted legislation that created a Department of War.[1] On 14 March an act clearly designed for the contingency of war provided for the organization of an army, for manning the newly created force.[2] Besides the regular combat components there were support services, such as the Medical Department, Engineers, and Quarter-master Corps. The form of the Confederate military establishment was, in fact, virtually a duplication of the United States Army, with but one notable exception: unlike the Federal Army, the Confederate organization made no provision for chaplains.[3] It was a deliberate exclusion on the part of President Jefferson Davis and the legislators. It offered an insight into the importance the Provisional Congress attached to the office of chaplain, and reflected an attitude which changed only slightly with the passage of time.

In contrast to the sentiments of the first President of the United States, the attitude of the first and only President of the Confederacy toward the chaplaincy was, at best, lukewarm. Davis' attitude was possibly tempered by contact with mediocre chaplains at West Point and during the Mexican War.[4] Even after chaplains were authorized, the Confederate Chief Executive attempted to persuade a medically trained minister to become a surgeon instead.[5] But Davis did not typify extreme opposition, and he was by no means the sole antagonist. James Seddon, who eventually became

(See notes at end of chapter)

131

Secretary of War, appreciated chaplains even less than Davis. Under pressure of forming a new government and providing for its defense, some lawmakers looked upon military ministers as drones. Others thought that the various churches, not the government, should be responsible for the chaplaincy.[6]

When it became known that the Confederate Army was not to have chaplains, a loud cry arose across the South from many ministers, women, and editors. The first official proposal for the inclusion of chaplains came from the Secretary of War, Leroy P. Walker. In a letter to President Davis on 27 April 1861, he urged him to support legislation that would empower his "Department to appoint chaplains."[7] On the same day that Walker wrote his letter, the Virginia Convention for Secession went on record favoring army chaplains.[8]

With such agitation and prodding, the legislature moved expeditiously; on 2 May it passed a bill providing for the appointment of army chaplains. The new law consisted of two sentences that empowered the President to appoint chaplains for the duration of the war to as many regiments, brigades, and posts as he "deemed expedient"; and, provided a monthly pay of $85 for the new appointees, which was exactly midway between the pay of a first and second lieutenant.[9] When it came time for appointments, however, they were made only to regiments. This did not change until 17 June 1864, when Davis was authorized to commission chaplains for hospitals.

The legislation contained no stipulations regarding age, physical condition, or ecclesiastical status. Neither did it prescribe duties nor provide for rank, uniform, or insignia. Although available pictures show chaplains wearing the uniform of a captain, and they were commonly thought to have the rank of captain, all legislative efforts to confer rank were defeated.

The lack of law permitted a freedom in dress that ran the gamut, which in turn prompted soldiers to repeat a lot of funny stories. They told about the chaplain whose deep blue clothing made him look like a Yankee; about chaplains (wearing clerical robes) who dressed like women; about the rather theatrical chaplain who was conspicuous for his bearskin leggings, the only pair of their kind in *either* army; or about the beaver-hatted chaplain who elicited

---

(See notes at end of chapter)

such disrespectful comments as, "come down out of that hat!" "See your legs hanging out!" "Take that camp kettle home."[10]

Since the legislation did not mention insignia, many assumed it was not prohibited, and some devised insignia that distinguished their office. For those in the Army of Northern Virginia, there was "the letter C, with a half wreath of olive leaves, worked in gold bullion, on a ground of black velvet." Chaplains in the Army of Tennessee adopted as their identifying insignia the Maltese Cross, worn as a major's star on each side of the collar.[11]

Within two weeks following the initial legislation regarding chaplains, and after a bitter fight, the act was amended to reduce the stipend from $85 to $50 per month.[12] Like much of the legislation throughout the war, this reflected the bias against military ministers. A Mississippi judge, who ardently supported the amendment, claimed that chaplains were not entitled to as much pay as company officers, as the latter worked every day, while the chaplains preached once a week and were free the remainder of the time.[13] Some supported the pay-reduction legislation for religious reasons; they were opposed, as a matter of principle, to paying preachers. Not a few argued that low salaries would rid the office of its materialistic members.[14] Again, the reduction was publicized as an economy measure. That prompted one writer to inquire, "Have salaries of all other officers been reduced?" "No," he answered, "the economy began and ended with chaplains."[15]

Both the secular and religious journals blasted the lawmakers for what they did. Several newspaper editors in Virginia and North Carolina exclaimed that many clergymen, some of them eminent men in their vocation, were willing to give up much larger salaries and the comparative ease of ordinary ministerial duties for the hardships and labors of army life, but they did not expect the meager stipend to be reduced to a token payment. The editor of the Richmond *Times-Dispatch* cried that the action was nothing more than an "act to abolish the office of chaplain in the Confederate Army." He reported that it had "been followed by the resignation of some of the most valuable chaplains in the service."[16] The religious periodicals were equally pointed. Apparently quite provoked, one journalist declared that the chaplains' "corps was degraded and God insulted."[17]

(See notes at end of chapter)

After several abortive attempts by sympathetic legislators and an increase in outside pressure from ministers, churches, the "ladies of Richmond," and chaplains themselves, compensation was raised to $80 monthly on 19 April 1862.[18] The publicity about the issue of pay prompted the *Army Cathechism,* a comic production published in 1862, to ask, "What is the first duty of chaplains?" The answer: "To grumble about the pay and privileges."[19] Before the war was over, chaplains received fringe benefits in the form of rations, stationery, and forage for their horses;[20] that made the annual compensation $1,325 and forage, compared to a Union chaplain's stipend of $1,434 and forage. Given the vast difference in purchasing power, the Southerner was at an even greater disadvantage.

The forage bill was delayed until 1864 by those opposed to its passage. One legislator wanted it made absolutely clear that the law provided forage, not horses—with no forage if the chaplain had no horse—and proposed an amendment to that effect. He was doubtless prompted to make this suggestion by the chaplain who appropriated a Virginia farmer's horse and said his precedent was Jesus Christ who "took an ass from his owner, whereon to ride into Jerusalem." The chaplain in turn was squelched by an officer who summed up the matter thus: "You are not Jesus Christ; this is not an ass; you are not on your way to Jerusalem; and the sooner you restore that horse to its owner, the better it will be for you."[21]

The processes by which ministers came to receive their commissions and assignments were many and varied. The first chaplains came into Confederate service when the militia of their respective states reported for active duty. A well known citizen of Tennessee, Charles T. Quintard, was greatly honored by his election as chaplain of a military company stationed in Nashville, the "Rock City Guards."[22] When Tennessee joined the Confederacy, the company was expanded to regiment strength and within a month fought at Bull Run as part of the Confederate Army. Most state militia had unit-elected and governor-appointed chaplains like Quintard who shifted their allegiance to the Confederacy, their new commission merely a matter of form.

This transition was not always simple. John Bannon served Catholic troops for almost a year without recognition. He was finally commissioned, but only because the bishop of Mobile asked Navy Secretary Mallory to use his influence with the Secretary of War.

(See notes at end of chapter)

Bannon was chaplain of the Missouri militia and had followed his unit into General Price's army. Serving 1,800 Missouri Catholics as they fought under Price at Elkhorn, Farmington, and Corinth, the priest spent all his money and was $1,000 in debt when the bishop intervened. The commission was finally granted in 1863, but the bishop's influence was not quite strong enough to get Bannon paid retroactively.[23]

Despite trouble in getting commissioned, Bannon's talents did not go unrecognized. In September 1863 Secretary of State Judah P. Benjamin persuaded him to undertake an overseas propaganda mission. The Secretary was concerned by reports that Irishmen were promised railroad jobs if they would immigrate to New York; he believed the real motive of the United States was to secure Irish recruits for the Federal Army, and chose Bannon to enlighten his fellow countrymen.[24]

In October 1863 Bannon began spreading Confederate propaganda in Ireland. He told his countrymen that immediately upon arrival in America, immigrants were conscripted into the Federal Army and assigned to the most dangerous posts. As proof Bannon cited Northern newspapers favorable to the South. He also recounted Northern church burnings, outbreaks of native Americanism, and the rise of the Know-Nothing Party. His strategy was to show that the United States was never friendly to Catholicism. Because he was a Catholic, Bannon was well received and his mission produced results: the Roman Catholic clergy in Ireland protested to the Vatican that the North was "using up the Irish in the war like dogs."[25]

His job done in 1864, Bannon tried to return to the South, but the Federal blockade kept him abroad. While waiting for the war to end, he joined the Jesuit order and remained in Ireland until his death in 1913. He thus became the only Confederate chaplain to die beyond the borders of the American continent.[26]

Another way into the chaplaincy was through the ranks. Those who transferred from the ranks were generally young and able men, and their enthusiasm made them popular and effective. Transfers were frequently initiated by troop petition when a soldier showed unusual dedication to religious endeavors. Two of the most publicized Protestant chaplains, Randolph McKim and J. William Jones, came from the ranks.

(See notes at end of chapter)

McKim was a native of Maryland and graduate of the University of Virginia; he enlisted in time for the first battle at Bull Run, and by autumn 1863 was aide-de-camp to Brigadier General George H. Stewart. He resigned as a lieutenant to become a chaplain. After an alarming delay by the War Department, he received his chaplaincy commission and served with the 2nd Virginia Cavalry.[27]

After graduation from Southern Baptist Seminary at Greenville, J. William Jones enlisted as a private and fought at Harper's Ferry in 1861. He became chaplain of the 13th Virginia Infantry in November 1863 and was present for every battle in which the Army of Northern Virginia participated; he was among Lee's surrendered forces at Appomattox. Like several other chaplains, Jones doubled as a war correspondent. In his column for the *Religious Herald*, he used the pen name "Occasional," and attempted to cover the aspects of military life and activity. Jones was perhaps the most readable and reliable writer among chaplain correspondents.[28]

Still another route into the military ministry was through direct commission. Many ministers, especially during the early days of the war, entered military service that way; commanding officers sometimes helped them get appointed. Colonel Angus W. McDonald wrote the Secretary of War on behalf of James B. Averitt, a minister he persuaded to accompany his 7th Virginia Cavalry. McDonald was pleased with Averitt's work and was also interested in retaining him for another reason: with an official chaplain on his staff, charges that his troops were hardly more than land pirates could be somewhat mitigated. As a result of the colonel's letter, Averitt allegedly became the first chaplain commissioned by the Confederate government.[29] Other colonels made similar requests. One desired a Baptist chaplain; another pointed out the need to do a better job at denominational matching of chaplain and troops; still another, not so concerned about denomination, just wanted a chaplain.

Some ministers were so fired up with southern loyalties that they could not wait for formalities but applied directly. Emmeran Bliemel, a Pennsylvania Catholic serving a Tennessee parish when the war broke out, made such an on-the-spot application, and so did Abram Ryan.

(See notes at end of chapter)

Bliemel applied directly to Colonel William Grace, commanding officer of the 10th Tennessee Regiment, and was immediately nominated. He was officially attached to the Tennessee 10th throughout his short career, but like most Catholic chaplains he traveled from unit to unit. When a Yankee bullet caught him, he was praying for a wounded soldier of the 4th Kentucky Regiment. After Bliemel's death, the *Confederate Veteran* identified him with the 10th of Tennessee, but a protest letter from the Kentucky 4th bore loving witness that the young priest did a good job everywhere he served. "There will be trouble in Tennessee," the latter stated, "if you don't give up the gallant, glorious martyred priest."[30]

Abram Ryan survived the war and distinguished himself for his patriotic poetry. He died in Louisville in 1886; after his death, some citizens of Mobile erected a statue of him—the only Confederate chaplain so honored.[31]

Protestants also sought Confederate chaplaincy commissions by the direct approach. They "candidated" for commissions. Chaplain S. M. Cherry, 4th Tennessee Regiment, said the surest way for a minister to become a chaplain was for him to visit the army and become known to the troops.[32] That was very good advice, even though not all who tried out were commissioned.

Other ministers who sought chaplaincy appointments took the initiative but were more indirect. One aspirant informed General Leonidas S. Polk, a former Episcopal bishop, that he needed political influence to secure a commission. Polk helped him become chaplain of the 2nd Louisiana Regiment.[33] Another applicant called on Vice President Alexander Stephens for help.[34] Others asked editors of religious magazines to intercede for them. One aspirant got a politician to personally submit his application through regular channels.

In short, there was no fixed way to become a chaplain. While some ministers tried in vain for appointments, some commanding officers were advertising vacancies. Partly because of inadequate legislation, entering the chaplaincy was not an orderly procedure; nevertheless, certain "clearinghouses" developed to make the task easier.

A few chaplains represented the Presbyterian Board of Domestic Missions; referred to as Commissioners, they sought prospective chaplains and helped them secure commissions. The Presbyterians

(See notes at end of chapter)

proposed interdenominational action aimed at securing at least one suitable chaplain for each Confederate brigade, but no such action ever really materialized. [35]

The Methodists also had Commissioners. John C. Granbery and Joseph Cross were the most effective. Granbery, a future bishop, was chaplain at the University of Virginia when the war began. He worked diligently to help Methodist ministers become chaplains. Cross, a native of England, came to the United States in 1825. While a professor at Transylvania in Lexington, Kentucky, he became prominent in the southern branch of the Methodist church. [36]

The Baptists' clearinghouse was Chaplain J. William Jones, whose function was sometimes misunderstood. One Baptist minister wrote Jones a terse note which said, "Send me my commission at once." [37] He finally published a letter explaining that he did not actually have the power to make chaplaincy appointments, but only furnished his brethren the names of regiments that needed chaplains, and vice versa.

Like those who joined the Union forces, many of the first Confederate chaplains were egoists, promoters, incompetents, and imposters. They were all too often men who called themselves chaplains but served only their own selfish ends. The Confederate government did not make a sincere attempt to provide for the establishment of an adequate and competent chaplaincy; as a result, many with virtually no interest in their work secured appointments by playing the demagogue with the men and currying the favor of officers. [38] An anonymous Englishman who fought for the Confederacy declared categorically that chaplains who served before the big pay reduction were "long-jawed, loud mouthed ranters," ". . . termed for courtesy's sake ministers of the gospel." He also accused "most chaplains" of coming into the army because they thought the jobs were soft and the pay good. He said they neglected their duties—as they had with the churches that forced them out—and could be counted on only at mealtime. He also accused chaplains of winking at "trifles" and displaying an unusual proficiency at the gentleman's game of poker. [39]

While the opinions of the irritated Englishman might be taken lightly, examples of mediocrity were abundant. Stories were widely circulated about chaplains who devoted themselves almost entirely to

(See notes at end of chapter)

trading horses, collecting table delicacies, and participating in black market activities.

Some horse-trading chaplains probably argued that their low salaries entitled them to extra compensation. Such a rationale scarcely explained the antics of one "chaplain" who candidly confessed stealing several hundred dollars on his way to join an Arkansas regiment. When he attempted to get away, he forged a "leave of absence" and an order for "free transportation" to the sea. Upon being found out, he feigned illness and was sent to a hospital from which he soon escaped.[40]

Chaplains were often seen at festive affairs, dancing to the tune of "Sugar in the Gourd" and "All Around the Chicken Roost." On occasion some placed bets on "the old grey mare."[41] An army surgeon was amazed that some were in the daily and constant habit of drinking whiskey for their health.[42] The sordid, mercenary pursuits led a Mississippi correspondent to conclude that "some of the largest extortioners on a small scale" he ever saw were army chaplains "going over the country buying up eatables at low figures and peddling them out at famine prices."[43]

Fortunately, the majority of the early influx of low caliber preachers—guilty of indiscretions and dissipations that cast shadows over the chaplaincy as a whole—left the military service as rapidly as they entered it. The sizeable cut in pay—from $85 to $50—was more than the materialistically minded could take. Moreover, when the lower salary was coupled with the hardships and dreariness of army life, the uncommitted accelerated their search for more palatable food, a warmer bed, and a less regimented life. Enthusiasm wore thin, and patriotism waned. The heavy exodus of incompetents made something resembling prophets of the legislators who argued that the reduction-in-pay bill would eliminate those more interested in pecuniary gain than moral inspiration.[44] The English combatant recorded that the "bores and drones" resigned when the salary was reduced, and left the field to true men of character and intelligence.[45]

The drastically reduced pay coupled with the drudgery of military routine that caused a mass exodus of inferior chaplains also forced the resignation of some of the competent and well qualified. In a letter to the *Church Intelligencer,* one soldier wrote that if a colonel, major, or captain received a salary of $50 a month, he would soon leave the service; yet the Confederate government expected chaplains to remain. In the same issue of that publication, a clergyman informed the editors that because of the pay cut many able ministers would be forced to resign.[46] This prediction proved true.

With the chaplaincy ranks depleted, Congress made an insincere effort at amends for the salary cut. On 31 August 1861 it enacted legislation authorizing chaplains to draw the rations of a private.[47] Some worthy ministers considered the provisions of the act humiliating and gave that reason for resigning their commissions. The legislation was bold discrimination, and so were some other practices. Officers were permitted to draw extra rations and also to purchase supplies and food from the commissary, privileges denied chaplains.[48] Again, when chaplains went to collect their meager stipend, they were required to have their application for payment certified by the commanding officer, a procedure no other officer had to follow.[49] This combination of factors prompted the resignation of some good chaplains who simply would not submit to the snubs and ill-treatment of the government.

After the weeding out of undesirables, and the resignations of far too many capable chaplains, those who remained—and those who joined them by direct commission or transfer from the ranks—generally possessed the traits expected of a minister and required by the standards of the church. Early in 1862 the editor of the *Christian Index* stated: "Some of the best and most useful ministers in the whole country ... are chaplains."[50] The editor of the *Southern Churchman* commented that chaplains were "earnest men ... endeavoring to do their duty."[51] Elaborating on the quality of military ministers, the editor of the *South Western Baptist* wrote: "It takes the very best capacity in the line of ministerial duties to be a successful chaplain," and "so far as I have seen our chaplains are pious, devoted and successful preachers of the gospel."[52] A Methodist wrote that "chaplains were very uncommon men" and that his father, "who was in the ministry more than fifty years and had a wide experience with men, expressed the highest estimate of them."[53] A leading Presbyterian minister said that he "never saw a nobler body of men, earnest, devoted, consecrated, self-sacrificing for the welfare of the men."[54] An Episcopal historian added: "The church sent many of her best and ablest ... as chaplains to the

(See notes at end of chapter)

army."[55] After the early unfortunate experiences there was hardly a chaplain whose life and activities did not illustrate those generalizations.

Educationally, Confederate chaplains came from a moderately well-informed clergy. The majority received at least some formal training before ordination. Catholic, Episcopal, and Presbyterian clergymen came from religious bodies that believed strongly in an educated clergy; their academic preparation was extensive, and they made up a third of the Southern chaplaincy.

Catholic priests studied almost to a man in Northern institutions, with the exception of those who secured instruction abroad. Virginia Theological Seminary, Alexandria, Virginia, was the alma mater of practically all of the Episcopal chaplains.[56] There were two Presbyterian theological schools in the South—one at Richmond, Virginia, the other at Columbia, South Carolina—and the majority of the Presbyterian chaplains had received their theological education at one or the other.[57]

In contrast, the Baptists—definitely opposed to an educated clergy, even after the Civil War—faced a paradox during the early days of their Southern Convention. Their anti-education stand was inconsistent with the fact that a number of Baptist colleges had been founded in at least 10 southern states before Secession. The colleges, which offered both "literary and theological" education, were established specifically for the purpose of training ministers.[58] Strong Baptist feelings against education were emphasized by the short history of Southern Baptist Seminary in South Carolina. Opened with 26 students in 1859, it closed for good in 1862.[59] Records do not indicate how many Baptist chaplains took advantage of the meager academic opportunities, but chances are that highly educated Baptist chaplains were few indeed.

Methodist ministers in Civil War days were not opposed to education, but were suspicious of it. To some, theological education "manufactured preachers" and "cooled devotion."[60] As a result, the Methodists owned more than 100 colleges in 1858, but—until the Civil War—not a single seminary.[61] Their seminaries did not appear in the South until after the war. The Methodist *Discipline* of 1784, however, directed ministers to study five hours a day; the first General Conference of Methodism did not deem a college education essential, but it did indicate that a minister of the gospel should have

(See notes at end of chapter)

an "ardent desire for useful knowledge."[62] Thus, long before 1861 Methodist ministerial candidates followed a course of reading and study suggested by their General Conference. But Methodist chaplains in the Civil War were reported to be variously qualified. For instance, Thomas J. Eatman was said to be "an acceptable preacher," while John C. Granbery was "distinguished at once for his genius and education."[63] Reflecting a growing emphasis on education within Methodism, William H. Browning, a dutiful chaplain, wrote in 1864 that Tennessee chaplains long felt the need of literary supplies "with which to feed the flock."[64]

Occupationally and professionally, almost all Confederate chaplains entered the service with some previous ministerial experience. Less than 30 came to the chaplaincy from civilian occupations other than the ministry, and these—mainly teachers and editors of religious magazines—worked in allied fields. When the Southern Baptist Seminary at Greenville, South Carolina, ceased operation, one of its four professors entered the chaplaincy, along with a Virginia seminary professor of the Presbyterian faith.[65] Isaac Tichenor resigned his academy principalship to become chaplain of the 17th Alabama infantry regiment. John L. Johnson came to the chaplaincy from his position as Professor of English at the University of Mississippi.[66] Frederick Fitzgerald, editor of the *Church Intelligencer;* William Williams, editor of *The Army and Navy Messenger;* Joseph Walker, editor of the *Christian Index;* and William Carson, editor of the *Southern Baptist,* all resigned in favor of chaplaincy commissions.[67]

Two of the three major religious traditions were represented in the Confederate chaplaincy. Although there were an appreciable number of Jews in service and no legal barriers to the appointment of chaplains from the Jewish faith, no rabbi served as a chaplain in the Confederate Army.[68] The 123,860 Catholics in the Southern states, over a third of whom were in Louisiana, were represented by approximately 30 priests.[69] The largest group of chaplains was Protestant. About 670 represented a total Protestant membership of 5,159,679, enrolled in over 16,000 individual Protestant congregations.[70]

Methodists, the largest Southern denomination, with a membership of about 2,000,000, led among Protestants in total number of chaplains. Dominant in any group, they outnumbered Baptists 200

(See notes at end of chapter)

to 100, even though the two denominations were about the same size.[71] At the same time Presbyterians, with about 722,747 members, furnished as many chaplains as did Baptists.[72] The best proportionate representation came from Episcopalians, who, with a membership of 192,777, furnished 65 chaplains.[73] About 50 military ministers came from other Protestant groups, and the remainder had no denominational identification.

Although Baptist chaplains did not serve officially in proportion to their denominational strength, the prevailing religious sentiment in the armies appeared to be Baptist. Apparently the many Baptist preachers who fought in the ranks and the sizeable number of Baptist missionaries who evangelized among the troops influenced sentiment in their direction. During a revival in a Georgia unit, 120 out of 180 converts joined the Baptist Church. Ironically, it was a revival led by four Methodists—and no Baptists.[74] A similar story was told of an Alabama regiment where only one Baptist chaplain served; of 200 converts in that regiment, 120 became Baptists.[75]

Youthfulness characterized the Confederate chaplaincy. Over two-thirds of the military ministers were under 30 years of age, and the average age was 28. Several were only 21, including the well known poet-priest, Abram Ryan. Only a handful were over 30; the oldest, Aristides Smith, was 53.[76] Religious publications made quite a bit of the relative youth of the chaplains, and were inclined to say it was too bad more experienced men were not serving. Many editors believed young men were too mobile to give the chaplaincy the stability it needed.

Reasons for such a large number of young chaplains in the Confederacy were not hard to come by. There was a definite tendency—primarily during the first 18 months—to say that the war was not going to last long and that "anybody would do." In addition, young men—even though an unusual number under 35 resigned for reasons of health—were more able-bodied. Then, too, some older ministers undoubtedly took a dim view of the hardships and sacrifice of income; the youthful were less likely to have families to support.

Although fiercely loyal to the South, not all of the clergymen who served in the Confederate chaplaincy were natives of the region. That was especially true of the Catholics. The greater number of priests who entered the military service were born,

_____

(See notes at end of chapter)

reared, and trained north of the Potomac or in Europe and moved South upon assignment to a parish. A few Protestant chaplains were counted among the adopted sons. Chaplains James Taylor, T. O. Ozann, and A. D. Cohen were natives of England. Chaplain George Patterson, while possessing an Anglo-Saxon name, was a native of Greece. Chaplain Francis Johnston was born in Turkey. Other Protestants with outstanding records who were not native Southerners included Charles T. Quintard of Connecticut, and Lafred Watson and William Gray of New York, all Episcopalians. Methodist chaplain Collins D. Elliott was a native of Ohio; Samuel Hoyle, another Methodist, was allegedly a "New England refugee."[77] Where the chaplain was a native Southerner, chances were good that he came from Virginia, North Carolina, or Tennessee, in that order. Among those from North Carolina were some Cherokee Indians serving battalions of their own people, conducting services in the tribal tongue.[78]

The religious duties of Confederate chaplains were identical to those of their Union counterparts. Evidence indicates there was modification at one important point: Southern military ministers placed greater emphasis on preaching and their sermons accentuated traditional aspects of the Christian gospel more than those of Northern chaplains. Many judged the value of ministers in the Southern army largely by what they did outside the pulpit; chaplains themselves considered preaching the most important aspect of their ministry, and measured success by effectiveness as proclaimers of the Word of God.

The Confederate soldier took sermon content seriously. As a matter of fact, he considered it a sin not to be able to quote the chaplain's text. But when it came to writing about a chaplain in letters home, it was easier to describe style than evaluate content. One critic noted bad pronunciation and grammar (*parentual* instead of parental; *have came* instead of *have come,* but made no comment about his chaplain's subject).[79] Another reported a good chaplain in his unit by the name of Tracy, but said of him, "He can't preach much."[80] It was impossible to please everybody. Many soldiers liked to hear a chaplain who would let go and roar at them. If a chaplain did not roar, he was not really preaching. One lieutenant wrote that his chaplain would really be great "if he would only let go."[81] On the other hand, some soldiers preferred reserved discourses, and

_____

(See notes at end of chapter)

frowned on overly dramatic presentations. But in each group the chaplain's reputation depended on his oratorical skills.

The Confederate chaplain's prevailing style was evangelistic, and almost every worship service centered around preaching. Baptists, Methodists, and Presbyterians gave most emphasis to preaching, but Episcopalians, Lutherans, and Catholics also preached. Even when chaplains went into battle—some were criticized for not going often enough—they gathered small groups around them and preached the gospel. The Confederate soldier talked about "going to preaching," not about "attending a worship service"; [82] when there was no preaching, the soldier wrote home about his disappointment. The Confederate soldier's eagerness to listen cannot be underestimated. He listened with deep interest when he was allowed—as he usually was—to attend services voluntarily.

Not all congregations were large, especially during the early part of the war; as a general rule, however, it took only a few minutes to gather a crowd of men eager to hear the gospel preached.

Barring an occasional skirmish, Sunday in the Confederate army was officially holy. It was the chaplain's day to lead worship. Everybody understood that fact, even in the early days when chaplains were not so popular. Catholic worship on Sunday consisted of Mass and usually a sermon. The Protestants were more informal. They met at no appointed hour, sometimes in the morning, sometimes in the afternoon. But as religious interest grew, most units began having two services on Sunday, and some included an afternoon extra. During the final months of the war, most commands had daily worship.

Even though Sunday meetings became more and more popular, a few officers were markedly unsympathetic toward them. They did not come right out and say they disliked chaplains or religion. They just filled the day so full of busy work that there was no time left for religious services. "I went over to see Willie last Sunday," a soldier wrote his mother, "and they were drilling just the same as any other day." [83] In addition to drill and company dress parades on Sunday, unsympathetic officers staged inspections of arms and equipment, as well as cleanup campaigns. Things got so bad in 1862 that General Bragg quieted protesting chaplains with an order for

(See notes at end of chapter)

better observation of the holy day.[84] Generals Lee and Forrest issued similar orders.[85] As late as 1864, General Hood was petitioned on the same subject.[86]

Unsympathetic officers became the exception rather than the rule, but Sunday worshipers were distracted in other ways. There were picket firings and the enemy's long-range guns, for instance. The effect of the big guns was largely psychological. A soldier could listen intently to his chaplain near heavy action at the front lines, but an occasional shell in camp made him fidget. He was ready, if not willing, to die in battle, but the prospect of losing his life to a Sunday fluke made him uneasy.

Sunday worshipers were also distracted by general camp odors and noises: rotting meat, frying bacon, yells of adjoining regiments, oldtime fiddlers, and running horses. The weather was another frequent handicap. One group stood 30 minutes in a driving rainstorm to hear a sermon preached; another, 14 of them barefoot, stood for the same purpose in the snow.[87]

When soldiers went voluntarily to preaching, they were not easily distracted. They even listened politely to chaplains who preached poor sermons. Reporters felt that Confederate soldiers showed much deeper religious interest than they had ever shown as civilians. One was so impressed with how his companions flocked to meetings, he intimated that civilian ministers were wasting their time. Why should they preach to "little squads in the churches," he reasoned, when they could become chaplains and reach so many more souls?[88]

Sermons were usually simple, sometimes criticized as appealing only to the "lower class in the regiment."[89] Though quite elementary, they were unusually clear, logical, and earnest. In some instances the elementary nature was attributable to the military minister. Chaplains with the least education were from denominations that stressed the sermon. But as one Alabama soldier declared, "even the greatest preachers delivered ordinary sermons."[90] Undoubtedly it was recognition of the average soldier's low educational level that caused even highly trained chaplains to keep their thoughts simple. Private Sam Watkins criticized one sermon for being so "high larnt" that only generals could understand it. He said other officers perhaps caught a word now and then, but that the sermon merely dazzled the ordinary soldier.[91] Another man from

---

(See notes at end of chapter)

the ranks authenticated Watkins' testimony. He wrote his sister that plain and practical sermons were the only kind that did any good.[92]

Even the simplest of sermons was not always comprehended. On one occasion, a Methodist chaplain was reported to have addressed a regiment of Louisiana soldiers who knew but little English. At the close of the discourse, to which the troops listened attentively, the commander gave the men a short talk: ". . . boys, I want you to remember what the minister has told you. It is all for your good; take his advice; and follow it; for there is no knowing but than in less than six months every d—d one of you will be in h–ll!" At this point a voice from the ranks called out, "three cheers for h–ll," and they were enthusiastically given. The preacher asked for an explanation of this behavior, and the colonel responded, ". . . the boys don't know much about the scriptures. They think H–ll is somewhere between Montgomery and New Orleans, and they are d—d anxious to get down in that neighborhood."[93]

The average sermon was also brief, never more than a half hour, sometimes only 15 minutes long. Youth and inexperience may have been the reason; the weather was perhaps a better explanation. Chaplain Milton Kennedy once shortened his message to the 28th North Carolina Regiment because he could not bear to detain his congregation on the wet, cold ground.[94] Contrary to general opinion, war sermons did not characterize chaplain preaching. The civilian minister may have been so preoccupied, but not his military counterpart. Most Confederate chaplains were expository preachers; they examined biblical passages and expounded upon their current meanings. For some, that meant sermonizing on bad habits or particular systems and dogmas. For a very few, it meant applying the gospel to military and political questions.

Chaplains sometimes advanced the Deuteronomic idea that God protected those who served him and punished those who did not. Most seemed aware that the Christian interpretation of war was not at all that simple; that the God of the Confederacy was not the God of Joshua; that the Christian God was not a war God impressed mainly by tribal purification rituals. Furthermore, to suggest scriptural explanation for specific victories and defeats was to limit the gospel message.

The large majority of Confederate chaplains knew only Christ and Him crucified. They usually avoided war topics, and especially

(See notes at end of chapter)

the slavery question. According to Chaplain John Granbery, sermons preached to Confederate soldiers would ordinarily have suited any congregation. He said the prevailing style was not usually "controversial, speculative or curious," but "practical and direct." Above all, Granbery believed that very few chaplains preached malice toward the enemy.[95]

Chaplain J. William Jones supported Granbery in his evaluation of Confederate preaching. He said that when a chaplain was speaking, he could always expect the "long roll" of the drum to interrupt his message. Time was too short for analyses of the current military situation or discussions of the issues which divided South from North. The chaplain preached as "a dying man to dying men." He used the precious time at his disposal to tell the "old, old story of salvation."[96]

The average chaplain was neither inclined nor trained to deliver dissertations on government and the war. When he was astute enough to capitalize on events around him, he spoke more directly to the problems of military men. With proper compassion, he did not need to lecture; neither did he need to prophesy, like Jeremiah, about the boiling cauldron from the north.

The field chaplain could not sit down just any time and write out a new sermon. He often reached into his carpetbag for antebellum material, sometimes even for an outline used in a seminary homiletics class. When the carpetbag was empty, he spoke from his heart. As he plunged into extemporaneous gospel preaching, he somehow reversed the Deuteronomic formula. He no longer claimed that the Lord was on the side of the South. He asked, "Who is on the Lord's side?" That was the all-important question with intensely personal meaning for every veteran who tried to point himself toward things eternal. It took for granted that the kingdom of God was greater than any habit, formula, denomination, or government. It was an appropriate question for congregations everywhere, civilian or military; it set the tone for many a preaching service.

The impact of the sermons can best be measured, perhaps, by the part they played in the most publicized aspect of religion in the Confederate armies, the "Great Revival." Preaching was the dominant element in army revivalism; it was consonant with the long tradition of spiritual rekindling in the South that dated back to the

(See notes at end of chapter)

days of the religious outpouring on the Western frontier of Kentucky and Tennessee. Chaplains counseled the disturbed, visited the wounded, baptized the converted, solemnized marriages, distributed tracts and bibles, conducted prayer meetings and Bible classes, administered the sacraments, and undertook other general pastoral functions; they were best known, however, for their preaching activities in connection with the emergence, course, and consequences of the spiritual awakening among the military.[97]

Nothing like an evangelistic awakening appeared among Confederate troops during the first 18 months of war. But in the closing months of 1862, after the character of the chaplaincy had been tremendously improved, chaplains reported isolated revivals in army units throughout Virginia. Earliest reports came from Jackson's corps, which was the most successful in recruiting competent ministers to serve as chaplains.

Given the strong nondenominational support of Lee, Jackson, and William Pendleton, a former Episcopalian rector who was Lee's chief of artillery, it was only natural for revival to take hold first in the Army of Northern Virginia. The first group within Jackson's corps to be seriously affected was Trimble's brigade, including regiments from North Carolina, Georgia, and Alabama. The brigade that Jackson commanded before he became a corps leader also had a revival. There was a religious awakening in Early's brigade, with other reports coming from Pickett's division.[98]

Chaplain A. Mathias Marshall, promoted from the ranks to the chaplaincy, was the most conspicuous figure in this early movement. With Chaplain James Nelson, he began a series of meetings shortly after Lee's Army returned from its invasion of Maryland in September 1862. Sometimes such meetings lasted for 55 consecutive days, and veterans just emerged from bloody experiences attended in increasing numbers.

As the great revival began to catch on, soldiers pitched in to give it momentum. One of their major contributions was the construction of chapels for use in winter when fighting was at a standstill. Log chapels had been built as early as the winter of 1861–62; construction picked up considerably during 1863–64 when Southern tactics called for holding actions and revivalism was moving to a climax. When troops moved to a new location their axes rang continuously for a week or more, building for the glory of

(See notes at end of chapter)

God. As religious interest mounted, chapels required enlargement. Construction reached amazing proportions in the final winter of the war, and according to one estimate every brigade between the Appomattox and James Rivers had a house of worship.[99] Most accommodated from 300 to 500 persons and were ususally crowded. The area between the two rivers, however, was but a small sector of the whole front and was manned by only four brigades.

Early revivalism was confined to Confederate units in the east. Religious activity in that sector accelerated after the South shattered Burnside's forces at Fredericksburg on 3 December 1862. Between then and the inconclusive Southern victory at Chancellorsville on 1–6 May 1863, eastern action was confined to cavalry skirmishes. Chaplains took advantage of the relative inactivity to promote religion.

William B. Owen, chaplain of the 17th Mississippi regiment, began revivals in Fredericksburg. Owen was a Methodist, but a Baptist chaplain who helped him was moved to describe the thirty-first day of their religious awakening. He reported that about 75 penitent men confessed their sins that day, and 100 others were "still seeking the way of life." "It was a touching scene," the Baptist wrote, "to see the stern veterans of many a hard-fought field, who would not hesitate to enter the deadly breach or charge the heaviest battery, trembling under the pressure of Divine truth, and weeping tears of bitter penitence over a misspent life."[100]

Practically all who made the profession of faith wanted to be baptized immediately. Owen usually baptized by "pouring," but his associate practiced immersion. Special baptismal arrangements were sometimes made for converts who chose to join denominations not represented among cooperating revival leaders. Denominational papers carried regular reports on new baptisms, and most chaplains kept their own records. A Methodist reported baptizing five by pouring; a Baptist immersed 82 in a creek near Orange Court House.[101] Immersion usually attracted many witnesses. One chaplain cut a hole in the ice and immersed 14.[102] A soldier wrote home that he "quit restin' to go see them baptized."[103] Baptisms became such an everyday affair that they evoked a legend about two rival colonels who always tried to outdo one another. When one heard of a revival in the other's regiment, he ordered a revival of his own. Moreover, when he learned of the baptism of 15 men in the other

(See notes at end of chapter)

regiment, he formed a special detail of 20 men and ordered them immersed immediately.[104]

Another story was told about a soldier named Dock Knight. As Dock was about to be baptized, he saw a water moccasin in a tree. Unable to pronounce the name of the snake clearly, he said to the chaplain, "Don't you see that okerson?" The question failed to register with the chaplain, and he kept urging Dock to a deep spot in the stream, directly under the snake. Finally, Dock jerked away and yelled, "Oh, dammit, don't you see that okerson?" Dock was in greater need of baptism than his chaplain had thought.[105]

Revivalism spread from Fredericksburg to neighboring camps. Spiritual awakenings were soon reported in brigades commanded by Barksdale, Lawton, Walker, Paxton, Cobb, and Kershaw. Sermons and prayer meetings on the hour lasted from noon until late at night.

Converts from Jackson's corps numbered in the thousands, many being "saved" at great outdoor meetings. One of those meeting places was a large sloped clearing with log seats for some 2,000 and a platform at the lower end. Wire baskets were hung in a circle around the platform and placed in front of the seats. They held chunks of light wood which burned in the night.[106]

Those were quiet months, when death was not so close at hand. Catholic candles burned in the subdued daylight of a wild forest and Protestant fire lamps flickered on evening worshipers. Forest life chirped and croaked in a balmy night of early spring and a full moon hung behind the outdoor sanctuary. Everything seemed to say in unison, "There is no war."

Those were times when pleasant background noises of camp life were noticed—the chopping of wood, the rattling of military wagons, the neighing of horses, the playing of brass bands, the singing of devout men on their way to worship. A few taps of the drum, a few strains of the bugle brought the men together.

It was not unusual for Protestant meetings during that period to last three hours. Interest was so great that off-duty men came early in the afternoon to get a good seat. A soldier from Jackson's corps said of the meetings that the "order was perfect," that he knew of "no disturbance of any kind," and that attention to the words of the preacher "was never more faithful."[107]

(See notes at end of chapter)

The religious and secular press was quite excited about revivalism during the December 1862 to May 1863 period. A Richmond writer said such a movement had not been seen for years, and that his heart was gladdened by the list of converts. He thought that both men and angels could rejoice over the moral sublimity which converts reflected. He concluded: "Pentecostal fire lights the camp, and the hosts of armed men sleep beneath the wings of angels rejoicing over many sinners that have repented."[108]

Revivalism became even more intense after the victory at Chancellorsville; it began to subside after Gettysburg. During the winter of 1862–63, more than 15,000 soldiers confessed their sins— 300 during one meeting, 100 at another, 500 a week in the Army of Northern Virginia alone. Just after Chancellorsville, the chaplain of the 26th Alabama Regiment said his unit averaged 100 converts a week for several weeks.[109] Another chaplain declared: "Modern history presents no example of an army so nearly converted."[110] In addition to such reports, a marked improvement in moral conditions prevailed.

Gettysburg and Vicksburg dampened the martial ardor of the South, but not the spirit of the revival movement. Revivals lost steam during active campaigning, but regained momentum when the units paused for rest and reorganization. Even when battles interfered with regular meetings, many soldiers were converted on marches and in battle positions. Scattered reports of evangelistic campaigns in the trenches appeared throughout the summer of 1863, and revivals continued unabated in hospitals. In midsummer of 1863, a Richmond hospital chaplain reported the greatest revival he had ever witnessed.[111]

Spiritual enthusiasm reached a climax in camps along the Rapidan during the winter of 1863–64. During the fall, winter, and spring preceding Grant's attack in May 1864, the revival reached its greatest heights in the Army of Northern Virginia. It spread from company to regiment, regiment to brigade, brigade to division, division to corps. Soldiers were converted by the thousands every week. A Virginia chaplain reported almost universal interest in the preaching meetings; he estimated 500 converts a week and voiced the need for more experienced chaplains.[112]

Revivalism was not confined in 1863–64 to the Army of Northern Virginia. It moved west. Both secular and religious

(See notes at end of chapter)

newspapers carried accounts of conversions in units of the Army of Tennessee, and a jubilant Presbyterian exclaimed that the whole area was under a spirit of awakening quite unlike that of the Army of Northern Virginia.[113]

The western theater movement began late. Western troops were not encouraged to participate in religious services. The supply of chaplains was not as great, and the generals, including Polk, were not as attentive to religious matters as were Lee, Jackson, and Pendleton. With a little time in camp and an increase in chaplains, however, revivalism began to stir. Some of its leaders west of the Appalachians were: S. M. Cherry, 4th Tennessee regiment; N. B. DeWitt, 8th Tennessee; James H. McNeilly, 49th Tennessee; Tilman Page, 52nd Tennessee; and P. A. Johnson, 38th Mississippi Volunteers.

The Western revival reached its climax at Dalton, Georgia, when the army, then under General Joseph E. Johnston, went into winter quarters in 1863. Meetings at Dalton grew until May 1864, and there were large and appreciative crowds who prayed for great things. Chaplain A. D. McVoy said he had never seen a better field for preaching the gospel. Evangelist John B. McFerrin reported that in all his life he had never witnessed more "displays of God's power in the awakening and conversion of sinners."[114] Chaplains of all denominations participated in the Dalton revivals. They lived, ate, marched, and suffered beside the soldiers to whom they preached. They were aided by missionaries who helped them visit the wounded and distribute religious literature. Doing their part to support the movement, soldiers erected stands, improvised seats, and built log churches where they "worshipped God in spirit and in truth." These facilities went unused only four nights during the long Dalton encampment.

Results at Dalton were "glorious." Thousands were "happily converted" and "prepared for the future that awaited them." Dalton revivals touched officers and enlisted men alike. One chaplain said work there had no parallel. "In the coldest and darkest nights of the winter," he reported, "the crude chapels were crowded and at the call for penitents, hundreds would come down in sorrow and tears." He said that Dalton "was the spiritual birthplace of thousands."[115] Even though Western reports were enthusiastic, they fell short of

(See notes at end of chapter)

those from Lee's Army. Western units did not have nearly as many chaplains, and that made the difference.

When the flanking movements of Grant against Lee and Sherman against Johnston began in May, 1864, the action slackened revival activity in the East and subdued it in the West. As the desperate Petersburg struggle drew to a close, Pickett's division reported an unusual number of conversions. One soldier said a stranger would have no trouble concluding that the Confederate army was very religious.[116] There were log churches every six or eight hundred yards and revivals in Lee's Army continued until the very end of the war. But by the time a Yankee bullet strayed across the lines in the summer of 1864 and found the spot where Chaplain James McNeilly was holding a meeting, Dalton had come and gone. As one observer put it, the Western revival began and ended with the Dalton meetings.[117]

Results of the revival were quite evident. Religious publications agreed that there were between 125,000 and 140,000 conversions. Their observations were supported by a Baptist tract distributor who wrote: "Modern history presents no example of armies so nearly converted into churches as the armies for southern defense."[118] The spiritual about-face of Confederate soldiers was so marked that one chaplain said the awakening caused the army to begin praying on behalf of churches. An Alabama chaplain added: "Talk about the army demoralizing the church—I don't know of any church that wouldn't demoralize my regiment."[119]

More respect for women and children; more honesty; less card playing, swearing, and drinking were improvements attributed to revivalism. During the "Great Revival" Generals Bragg, Ewell, Hood, and Joseph E. Johnston entered the church, and soldiers made decisions to enter the ministry. There were tangible effects like meetings, baptisms, and log chapels; various organizations—army churches, Christian societies or associations, Bible study and prayer groups, and Sunday Schools—also reflected deep spiritual progress among Confederate troops. A final effect of the spiritual awakening was implied in the way soldiers returned to their home churches after the war "more religious than when they went away." Some historians even argued that Confederate veterans patiently endured postwar indignities and hardships largely because of wartime religious experiences.[120]

(See notes at end of chapter)

After spending most of their considerable energy in a spiritual ministry to the troops, many Confederate chaplains—like their conscientious counterparts in the North—found time to perform a variety of other chores. These were not entirely unrelated to ministry but were considered beyond the normal call of duty. They were sometimes burdensome activities that generally added to the stature of chaplains who engaged in them. Quite a number attempted to establish libraries, with space for reading and writing. Supporters throughout the Confederacy supplied a large assortment of papers, magazines, and pamphlets; special efforts were made to provide reading matter for the sick and wounded. Because many soldiers could not read or write, teaching became an extra-duty chore for some chaplains; basic subjects were taught when men had time on their hands. Even though chaplains were often men of academic and literary ability, and a number were qualified teachers, their basic-level schools enjoyed only moderate success. Advanced courses, especially languages, were somewhat more successful; advanced students had high interest plus proven ability. Among the most distinguished teachers of advanced courses was Chaplain Crawford H. Troy, whose specialties at the time were Greek and theology. After the war, he taught Greek at the University of Virginia, later moved to Harvard to teach Hebrew and oriental languages.[121]

In addition to operating libraries and teaching, many chaplains took up the pen, and a few distinguished themselves. Chaplain Abram Ryan had a marked ability to express himself in writing, and coupled a fierce patriotism with his art. Chaplains like J. William Jones, who served as correspondents for various religious publications, may have been clear and reliable, but they were all outclassed by Ryan.

Chaplain Kensey Stewart served in an unusual "literary" way. An Episcopalian, he was hired by a Richmond bookseller, John W. Randolph, to get a Southern Episcopal Prayer Book published in London. He completed his printing mission, but the prayer books were captured by the Federal blockade and thrown into the ocean. Stewart, however, returned on a different vessel and reached Richmond with a few of the books in his baggage; these he delivered to Mr. Randolph, who gave copies to Mrs. Robert E. Lee and President Davis. A second attempt to have a prayer book

(See notes at end of chapter)

published was successful; no chaplain, however, was involved in that effort.[122]

Other special tasks were undertaken by various chaplains. B. S. Dunn was sent abroad to buy arms. Darius Hubert and William Gwaltney served as lawyers and administrators for soldiers killed in action. John Bannon's propaganda mission to Ireland has already been considered.[123] Thomas Caskey administered the hospital in his unit; he had a hand in almost everything except prescription of medicines and surgery.[124] Charles T. Quintard, who possessed a medical degree from the University of the City of New York, performed as both chaplain and surgeon throughout the war.[125]

Another unusual chore was undertaken by Chaplain Stephen Cameron. He delivered certification to neutral Canada that six men who carried out a raid in Vermont and fled across the border were actually Confederate soldiers, a fact Federal authorities were unwilling to concede. Involved in the plot was a mysterious widow who showed up unexpectedly with a duplicate set of papers; Cameron's document proved more acceptable, and the men were released to his custody. His success spared them from return to the United States and trial in a civilian court for arson, robbery, and felony.[126]

Chaplain William Crocker did far more than was expected of him when he formed the Army Intelligence Office in Richmond. What he actually organized was a missing persons bureau. He got the idea in May 1863 while a convalescent from a severe fever; he made a search for members of his outfit in Richmond hospitals, and found only a few. His instincts were aroused by the confused situation, and he soon devised a plan: a service that would reestablish communication between wounded soldiers and their families. The plan was immediately approved by the Secretary of War. Crocker was detailed to secure office space, muster clerical help from among disabled veterans, and supervise operation of the bureau, which was instrumental in locating over 30,000 individuals during its existence.[127]

Some chaplains were not content to minister to the spiritual and physical needs of the troops but felt obligated also to take a hand in the fighting. Although the official position of both governments was that chaplains were noncombatants, there were Confederate chap-

(See notes at end of chapter)

lains who bore arms and were combatants. No corps was without its
"fighting parson."

Chaplain Isaac Tichenor, 17th Alabama regiment, killed a
Federal colonel, a major, and four privates during the battle at
Shiloh. After the battle he wrote: "I feel in my heart I have served
the cause of God and my country."[128] W. D. Chadick, 4th Alabama
regiment, was another who entered the fighting with gusto. Chadick
bought a rifle at Harper's Ferry, a gun that once belonged to John
Brown, invader of Virginia. Like Tichenor, Chadick seemed pleased
that he was a freelance fighter. He enjoyed choosing his own battle
station and "fighting the rascals" with one of their own weapons.[129]

Among other rough and tumble chaplains was a young minister
who, when criticized for not preaching a single sermon during six
months of service, replied that his business was to kill Yankees, not
to preach the gospel. Another exhorted soldiers to be brave, aim
low, and kill Yankees as if they were wild beasts. Near Columbus,
Kentucky, one chaplain allegedly shot two Union soldiers, slashed
the throat of a third, and barbarously yelled after the routed foe,
"Go to hell, you damned sons of bitches."[130]

There were others: A. A. Lomax, 16th Mississippi regiment,
siad his rightful place was on the firing line. Thomas Duke, 19th
Mississippi, fought in the lines and helped direct skirmishes. John
Sinclair, 5th North Carolina, acted as a lieutenant colonel at
Manassas, led a number of charges, and was commended by
General Longstreet. Thomas Witherspoon, 42nd Mississippi, accepted his chaplaincy commission only on the condition that he was
allowed to carry a gun. John Andrews, 3rd North Carolina, raised a
company of volunteers to avenge the capture of his brother.[131]

Some who fought paid a high price. B. F. Ellison, 6th Virginia
Cavalry, was mortally wounded, as was William Vanderhurst,
chaplain of the 6th Texas Cavalry.[132] Some lost their lives because
they were not battlewise. Often "fighting parsons" got in the way
and were ordered off the field. An unidentifed Presbyterian
chaplain who belonged in the rear ran before his regiment in a
foolhardy charge and lost his life in a "rash and needless
manner."[133] Other chaplains were wounded while fighting. Chaplain
John Granbery was hit at least twice, as was Edward Hudson and L.
H. Jones.[134]

News of the exploits of "fighting parsons" spread, and the
proper duties and place of a chaplain during battle became a

(See notes at end of chapter)

sensitive issue. A few chaplains solved the problem of where they should be during fighting by simply staying in camp, but most accompanied the surgeon or his assistant. The discussions, however, centered on fighting chaplains rather than those who helped the medical staff. Opposition to chaplains in battle was first voiced after action near Richmond in the spring of 1862, when one was killed, another wounded, and a third captured. The *Religious Herald* compared chaplains with surgeons and argued that for either to plunge thoughtlessly into battle was to impair his special function. The *Herald* conceded that under certain conditions—if his Christian courage was in doubt, or if the troops wavered—the chaplain might be justified in fighting; however, army preachers were scarce, and it was only good sense for them to remain safely in the rear.[135] The chaplain who was wounded near Richmond countered with the argument that those remaining behind lost influence with the troops. The *Herald* called self-sacrifice a mistaken virtue and reiterated its stand that the chaplain's first concern was with soldiers as sinners, not as fighters. It argued that the chaplain's function should be thought of as "distinctively spiritual," and other publications echoed that sentiment.[136]

Even though William Owen came from the ranks and was eventually killed in action, he agreed with what the religious press said. He stopped carrying a rifle after he was commissioned a chaplain, and never fired another shot. The more distinguished chaplains did not bear arms. Quintard never carried a weapon. Randolph McKim, after he became a chaplain, never shouldered a rifle. General Jackson strongly opposed the "fighting parson" and said his business was prayer, not combat.[137]

The dilemma Southern chaplains faced was a sacred calling on the one hand, and on the other, commitment to the Southern cause. Some took up arms because they could see no other way. They believed what they did was right. Their unequivocal answer was clear, dramatic, and in most cases, selfless. These ingredients made their answer popular, and in a sense, natural and easy. Some even enjoyed being called "fighting parsons."

The large majority of Confederate chaplains simply could not reconcile prospects of maiming and killing enemy troops with their sacred calling to render comfort and blessed assurance. They chose

(See notes at end of chapter)

the dilemma's traditional horn, but—sensitive to the situation— seldom criticized their fighting brethren.

Chaplain Thomas Caskey made an attempt to solve the problem for some. He had a theory about how to win the war without killing any Union soldiers. Aiming for the legs, he advocated, was more humane than aiming for the heart. His idea was simple. He thought it was poor planning to kill the enemy, because dead soldiers were no trouble to anybody until after the battle. Caskey figured the enemy should be wounded so he would need immediate help. Shooting him in the arm was not enough, because a man with a broken arm could go to the rear unaided. Caskey believed in aiming for the legs, because a crippled soldier needed two men to carry him off the field; one bullet in the right place would take three men out of action. Furthermore, the wounded man's two helpers would surely find some excuse for not returning to the battle. At least that was what Caskey thought.[138]

Where to be in time of battle, however, was but one of several problems that plagued chaplains. Confederate military ministers were beset with considerable difficulty because they lacked adequate official recognition. Many felt they could serve with much less confusion, misunderstanding, and hardship if they enjoyed some kind of rank.

As things stood, chaplains were neither officers nor enlisted men; they were given commissions but allotted the rations of noncommissioned officers. They were entitled to the quarters of a second lieutenant, but were not permitted his commissary privileges. They received pay equal to that of second lieutenant, were generally thought of as captains, and on some regimental rosters were listed just above enlisted men. In addition, some chaplains who entered service through North Carolina and Virginia militia units were accustomed to the rank of major, and were surprised to learn—too late—that the situation in the Confederate Army was decidely confused. Attempts to clarify the rank of chaplains failed in Congress.

Confused rank naturally resulted in confused dress. Quite a few chaplains had their pictures taken in the uniform of captain; they actually wore anything from beaver hats to clerical regalia. Chaplains in the Army of Tennessee made some attempt at uniformity by adopting buttons worn by other staff officers and dressed sometimes

---

(See notes at end of chapter)

like the surgeon, in gray cloth with black facing and trimming. Some chaplains felt these things were important because they generated respect from officers and men. But the matter of rank— along with confused uniform—was not a serious problem to those who felt the chaplain needed no other recognition than that which came from doing a good job. However, the confusion worried many, caused some resignations, and kept a few well-qualified ministers from becoming chaplains.

A more serious problem was the pay situation. Chaplains hurt most by that were family men who formerly served with the rank and pay of major in North Carolina and Virginia militia units. Those men were quite naturally dismayed when they found their pay drastically reduced; their only out was resignation, a step they took only after the burden proved too heavy. Religious publications made quite an issue of low salaries paid chaplains and tended to say that because of meager pay only young men fresh out of seminary were attracted to the chaplaincy. Numerous letters of resignation attest to the fact that many chaplains found it impossible to survive on the money they were paid by the government.

Among attempts to supplement salaries were special funds contributed by enlisted men and officers. One unit, still without a chaplain in July 1863, offered to supplement the salary and promised to furnish a horse—provided the minister who came to them was a Presbyterian. Assistance also came from some home churches—one minister's church continued to pay him a full salary during his army service.

On a denominational basis, Presbyterians began to supplement their chaplains' salaries as early as May 1861. Southern Methodists began in September 1863. By February 1864, The Baptist Sunday School and Publications Board was undergirding salaries of needy Baptist chaplains, and a month later the Domestic Board of Missions was also helping.[139] Except for those programs, no other communion added to its chaplains' pay. Salary was not considered a problem among Catholics, because they were not married. Church bodies like the Disciples of Christ virtually opposed any pay for ministers, military or civilian. It was not accidental that denominations concerned about pay were the ones best represented in the chaplaincy; their supplements to salaries kept the army supplied with at least some military ministers.

(See notes at end of chapter)

The obstacles of low pay and confusion about rank took their places beside undelineated responsibilities and government negligence as special problems of military ministers. The problems were never solved and that caused many chaplains to give up their jobs as hopeless, long before Appomattox. In turn, that produced the chaplains' greatest problem—his own depleted ranks.

Although about 700 chaplains served in the Confederate Army, no more than 250 were available at any one time to fill the approximately 800 regimental and hospital positions. The largest number present for duty was in early 1864, the height of army revivalism. There was a decline in numbers after that and the shortage grew steadily worse until Lee's surrender at Appomattox, when there were no more than 75 chaplains in all of the Confederate forces.

Turnover was extremely high, and only about 50 remained in service from the date of their commission to the cessation of hostilities. While the turnover and shortage of chaplains was a source of much concern throughout the war, the Southern civilian clergy during the period were estimated at between 5,000 and 6,000; one Methodist conference in 1863 even reported that preachers outnumbered available appointments.[140]

General "Stonewall" Jackson took special pains to have his corps provided with military ministers; yet in March 1863, almost two years after hostilities began, he stated in a communication to the Adjutant General that more than half his regiments were unsupplied.[141] At the time of the letter, chaplains in Jackson's corps estimated that no more than 200 chaplains were serving the Confederacy and appealed to denominational officials to urge clergymen to become chaplains.[142] The appeal from Jackson's corps caused other units to take stock. Someone noted that in Bragg's army there was scarcely a chaplain for each brigade. One correspondent reported 16 North Carolina units in one command without any religious guidance. Testimony of this "lamentable deficiency" was abundant.[143]

The situation in the West was even more critical. Speaking to a Presbyterian assembly, Chaplain J. N. Brinson pointed out the scarcity in Tennessee, and named several brigades without any chaplains. He even said some divisions heard no sermons for months.[144] On 18 June 1863 the *South Western Baptist* carried an

(See notes at end of chapter)

appeal—on behalf of Polk's corps—similar to the one by Jackson's chaplains. On 30 July the *Southern Christian Advocate* printed a similar plea for chaplains in the Army of Tennessee. Accelerated evangelistic efforts during the winter of 1863–64 accentuated chaplaincy needs, and denominational leaders as well as chaplains intensified their efforts to get more clergymen into the military ministry. Taking the lead, some Presbyterian ministers formulated a detailed plan for recruiting chaplains. The idea was for denominations to accept total responsibility for all aspects of the military ministry. In a letter to William Miles, Chairman of the Committee on Military Affairs, which outlined the plan, Moses D. Hodge termed it a scheme for increasing the number and efficiency of chaplains without expense to the Confederate government.[145] While the Presbyterians apparently made the greatest effort, a few other denominations were also active in recruitment of chaplains. The Methodists had fair response and the Baptists, in a campaign to secure 25 additional chaplains, also experienced some success.[146]

Chaplains used sessions of their Associations—generally an organization composed of the chaplains in a corps—to consider ways of adding to their number. At practically every meeting of the Associations reports were made on progress in procuring military ministers. The 1 May 1863 business meeting of Polk's chaplains heard a pessimistic report on efforts to secure more chaplains. The chaplains in the Army of Tennessee had a committee "to supply destitute regiments with religious privileges." The members of the Richmond Chaplains Association and the chaplains in Hindman's corps, Army of Tennessee, appointed standing committees to aid ministers in obtaining chaplaincy commissions. Even when the war ended, the Associations were still considering proposals designed to interest more clergymen in the military ministry.[147]

The problems of filling depleted ranks and the many other difficulties of Confederate chaplains' were never solved. They simply were lived with, adjusted to, taken in stride, or transcended. The chaplain unable to deal with his own problems was not good at his main job, which was to help men resolve, as Christians, the perplexities of hardship, death, and defeat. The chaplain anxious about himself—the type who often stumbled and fell on the long, hard road to Appomattox—was not effective in conveying the essential features of Christianity.

(See notes at end of chapter)

Frustrated and anxious persons could not explain eternal matters to losing soldiers. But there were chaplains who tried to do so, like Quintard and McNeilly of the Army of Tennessee, and Jones and McKim of Lee's Army. They rose above their special disturbances and transcended their own frustrations. As they comforted the men who followed Lee to Appomattox, and inspired them along the way to face eternal truths, they exemplified to the bitter end the very best in the tradition of the military chaplaincy.

NOTES

[1] *Official Records,* Series IV, 1, 252.

[2] *Ibid.,* 163.

[3] *Ibid.,* xxx.

[4] "The Religion of Jefferson Davis," *Confederate Veteran,* XXXV (1927), 374.

[5] "Surgeons of the Confederacy," *Confederate Veteran,* XL(1932), 172.

[6] Herman Norton, *Rebel Religion,* (St. Louis: Bethany Press, 1961), 23.

[7] *Official Records,* Series IV, 1, 252.

[8] *Religious Herald,* 2 May 1861.

[9] J. W. Matthews (ed.), *Acts and Resolutions of the Second Session of the Provisional Congress of the Confederate States, Held at Montgomery* (Richmond: R. M. Smith, 1861), 3. The monthly pay scale in effect at the time the Congress authorized the appointment of army chaplains was as follows: brigadier general, $301; colonel, $195; lieutenant colonel, $170; major, $150; captain, $130; first lieutenant, $90; second lieutenant $80; sergeant major, $21; first sergeant, $20; sergeant, $17; corporal, $13; private, $11.

[10] Chaplain Oscar Addison to Secretary of War George Randolph, MS War Department Office Files, National Archives; Fred C. Foard Papers, North Carolina Department of Archives and History; James McNeilly, "Reminiscences of a Confederate Soldier," *Nashville Banner,* 17 June 1911; George Harper Papers, Southern Historical Collection.

[11] *Religious Herald,* 25 June 1863; *The Army and Navy Messenger,* 1 May 1863.

[12] *Confederate Statutes,* 32.

[13] *Church Intelligencer,* 20 December 1861.

[14] *Southern Presbyterian,* 16 November 1861.

[15] *Southern Churchman,* 13 December 1861.

[16] *Religious Herald,* 26 December 1861 quoting the Richmond *Times Dispatch.*

[17] *Southern Churchman,* 13 December 1861.

[18] *Journal of the Congress of the Confederate States of America* (Washington: 1904–1905), I, 361, 341, 450, 709; II, 79, 92; V, 77, 190; *Official Records,* Series IV, I, 1076.

[19] *Religious Herald,* 25 June 1864.

[20] *Official Records,* Series IV, III, 194.

[21] Felix G. DeFontaine (compiler), *Marginalia; or Gleanings from an Army Note Book* (Columbia: F. G. DeFontaine and Co., 1864), 57.

[22] Arthur Noll (ed.), *Doctor Quintard, Chaplain, C. S. A.* (Sewanee: The University Press of Sewanee, 1905), 10–12.

[23] Germain, *Catholic Military and Naval Chaplains,* 107–109.

[24] James D. Robertson, *A Compilation of the Messages and Papers of the Confederacy* (Nashville: U.S. Publishing Co., 1906), II, 562–563; Albert Danner, "Father Bannon's Secret Mission," *Confederate Veteran,* XXVII (1919), 180.

[25] Leo Francis Stock, "The United States at the Court of Pius IX," *The Catholic Historical Review,* III(1923), 120.

[26] Danner, *"Father Bannon's Secret Mission,"* 180.

[27] Randolph McKim, *A Soldier's Recollections. Leaves from the Diary of a Young Confederate* (New York: Longmans Greene and Co., 1911), 26, 110, 209, 210, 216.

[28] *"Our Leaders: Surgeons and Chaplains," Historical Records of the United Daughters of the Confederacy,* XX, No. 7, Confederate Museum.

[29] *Official Records,* Series I, II, 954.

[30] Norton, *Rebel Religion,* 81.

[31] *Confederate Veteran,* XXXVII(1929), 61.

[32] *Southern Christian Advocate,* 21 May 1863.

[33] *Confederate Veteran,* XII (1904), 543.

[34] Thomas Conn Bryan, *Confederate Georgia* (Athens: University of Georgia Press, 1953), 235.

[35] *Presbyterian Historical Almanac for 1865,* 252, 253.

[36] *Southern Christian Advocate,* 21 May and 11 June 1863.

[37] *Religious Herald,* 31 December 1863.

[38] Wiley, "Holy Joes," 291.

[39] *"An English Combatant," Battle-Fields of the South* (New York: John Bradburn, 1864), 194, 277, 278.

[40] O. P. Fitzgerald, *John B. McFerrin, A Biography* (Nashville: Publishing House of the M. E. Church South, 1888), 348.

[41] George Baylor, *Bull Run to Bull Run* (Richmond: Johnson Printing Co., 1904), 318–320.

[42] *Religious Herald,* 13 February 1862

[43] *Ibid.,* 5 January 1863.

[44] *Southern Presbyterian,* 16 November 1861.

[45] "An English Combatant," *Battle-Fields of the South,* 194.

[46] *Church Intelligencer,* 27 September 1861.

[47] *Acts and Resolutions of the Third Session of the Provisional Congress of the Confederate States* (Richmond: Enquirer Book and Job Press, 1861), 72.

[48] *Church Intelligencer,* 3 April 1863.

[49] *Regulations of the Army of the Confederate States,* 1862, 111. Union chaplains at the time also had to have countersigned applications.

[50] *Christian Index,* 2 March 1862.

[51] *Southern Churchman,* 1 July 1864.

[52] *South Western Baptist,* 25 December 1862; Ibid., 29 October 1863.

[53] Robert Stiles, *Four Years Under Marse Robert* (New York: Neale Publishing Co., 1903), 143.

[54] James H. McNeilly, "Religion in the Confederate Armies," *Confederate Veteran,* XXIII(1915), 29.

[55] Joseph Cheshire, *The Church in the Confederate States* (New York: Longmans, Green and Co., 1912), 79

[56] James Addison, *The Episcopal Church in the United States* (New York: Scribners, 1951), 223.

[57] *Memorial Volume of the Semi-Centennial of the Theological Seminary at Columbia, South Carolina* (Columbia: Presbyterian Publishing House, 1884), contains biographical sketches of alumni who served as chaplains. *Southern Historical Society Papers,* XXIV (1914), 102–103 lists the graduates of Union Theological Seminary who served as chaplains.

[58] William Barnes, *The Southern Baptist Convention,* 1845–1953 Nashville: Broadman Press, 1954), 120.

[59] *Ibid.,* 133–134.

[60] Ezra Tipple, "Methodism and Theological Education," The New York *Christian Advocate,* CI(1926), 1156–1159.

[61] Gross Alexander, *History of the Methodist Episcopal Church, South* (New York: The Christian Literature Co., 1894), 134.

[62] Walter Brownlow Posey, *The Development of Methodism in the Old Southwest, 1783–1824* (Nashville: Privately Printed, 1933), 67.

[63] *Religious Herald,* 1 October 1863; Southern Christian Advocate, 14 August 1864.

[64] *Southern Christian Advocate,* 4 February 1864.

[65] *South Western Baptist,* 12 June 1862; *Presbyterian Historical Almanac for 1866,* 321.

[66] Issac Tichenor Papers, Alabama Department of Archives and History; J. Williams Jones, "The Morale of the Confederate Armies," *Confederate Military History* (Atlanta: Confederate Publishing Co., 1899), XII, 160.

[67] *Religious Herald,* 6 June 1861; P. J. Odle, *Lives of Christian Ministers* (Richmond: The Central Publishing Co., 1909), 254; *Christian Index,* 20 May 1862; *Religious Herald,* 17 September 1863.

[68] Bertram W. Korn, *American Jewry and the Civil War* (Philadelphia: The Jewish Publication Society of America, 1951), 57; Bertram W. Korn, "Jewish Chaplains During the Civil War," *American Jewish Archives*, I(1946), 6; Ella Lonn, *Foreigners In the Confederacy* (Chapel Hill: University of North Carolina Press, 1940), 265 erroneously refers to the Reverend Jacob Frankel as a Confederate chaplain. Mrs. Townes Leigh, "The Jews in the Confederacy," *Southern Historical Society Papers*, XXXIX(1914), 178, is also in error at this point.

[69] *Eighth Census of the United States: 1860. Statistics of the United States*, Book IV, 479–501, hereinafter cited as *United States Census: 1860*; Germain, *Op. Cit.*, 107–134.

[70] *United States Census: 1860*, 497–501.

[71] *Ibid.*; Sweet, *Methodist Episcopal Church and Civil War*, 222; *Religious Herald*, 24 September 1863 and 1 October 1863.

[72] *United States Census: 1860*, 497–501; *Southern Presbyterian*, 23 April 1863.

[73] *United States Census: 1860*, 497–501; Cheshire, *Church in Confederate States*, 79.

[74] *South Western Baptist*, 13 October 1863.

[75] *Ibid.*

[76] These conclusions are based on a study of approximately 200 biographical sketches.

[77] Lonn, *Foreigners in Confederacy*, 264, 616; *Southern Churchman*, 26 February 1864.

[78] *Religious Herald*, 15 May 1862.

[79] Bell I. Wiley, *The Life of Johnny Reb* (Indianapolis: The Bobbs-Merrill Co., 1943), 189.

[80] William R. Stillwell to Mrs. Stillwell, 13 May 1863, in "Letters of Confederate Soldiers," V, Georgia Department of Archives and History.

[81] Dr. E. P. Becton to his wife, 23 October 1863, in "Letters of Confederate Soldiers," V, Georgia Department of Archives and History.

[82] Henry Beveridge diary, entry of 17 April 1864, MS in Manuscript Collection, Duke University Library.

[83] H. M. Wagstaff (ed), "The James A. Graham Papers, 1861–1884," *The James Sprunt Historical Publications* (Chapel Hill: University of North Carolina Press, 1928), XX, No. 2, 112.

[84] *Southern Churchman*, 20 February 1863.

[85] *Christian Index*, 3 June 1863.

[86] *Southern Churchman*, 18 March 1864.

[87] J. William Jones, *Christ in the Camp or Religion in the Confederate Army* (Atlanta: The Martin and Hoyte Co., 1887), 248, 249.

[88] *Southern Christian Advocate*, 30 July 1863.

[89] George Wills to his brother, 16 November 1862, MS. in Southern Historical Collection.

[90] Robert Parks diary, entries of 6, 7, 8 January 1865, *Southern Historical Society Papers*, I(1876).

[91] Sam Watkins, *Company Aytch* (Nashville: Cumberland Publishing House, 1882), 90.

[92] Mary Gay, *Life in Dixie During the War* (Atlanta: The Foote and Davies Co., 1894), 67.

[93] *The Daily Journal*, 3 June 1861.

[94] Francis Kennedy diary, entry of 11 June 1963. MS. in Southern Historical Collection.

[95] Jones, *Christ in the Camp*, 14.

[96] *Ibid.*, 151.

[97] Herman Norton, "Revivalism in the Confederate Armies," *Civil War History*, VI(1960), 410.

[98] Jones, *Christ in the Camp*, 289; Benjamin Lacy, Jr., *Revivals in the Midst of the Years* (Richmond: Knox Press, 1943), 116.

[99] *Christian Index*, 2 February 1965.

[100] Jones, *Christ in the Camp*, 297.

[101] William Betts (ed.) *Experiences of a Confederate Chaplain* (Greenville, South Carolina: Privately Printed, 1904), 38; Jones, *Christ in the Camp*, 246.

[102] Jones, *Christ in the Camp*, 224.

[103] John Hartman to his wife, 28 March 1864, MS. in Manuscripts Collection, Duke University Library.

[104] *Southern Field and Fireside*, 2 May 1863.

[105] Stephen Moon to his mother, typescript copy in "Reminiscences of Confederate Soldiers," III, 107, in Georgia Department of Archives and History.

[106] John Worsham, *One of Jackson's Foot Cavalry* (New York: Neale Publishing Co., 1912), 181.

[107] *Ibid.*

[108] William Bennett, *A Narrative of the Great Revival* (Philadelphia: Claxton, Remsen and Haffelfinger, 1877), 323.

[109] *Southern Churchman,* 5 June 1863.

[110] *Religious Herald,* 11 June 1863.

[111] Bennett, *Narrative of the Great Revival,* 178.

[112] *Ibid.,* 324.

[113] *Ibid.,* 338.

[114] *Ibid.,* 359–369; Fitzgerald, *John B. McFerrin,* 276.

[115] Bennett, *Narrative of the Great Revival,* 366.

[116] *Christian Observer,* 26 January 1865.

[117] Jones, *Christ in the Camp,* 589.

[118] *Religious Herald,* 11 June 1863.

[119] *Ibid.,* 29 October 1863.

[120] John Shepard, "Religion in the Army of Northern Virginia," *North Carolina Historical Review,* XXV(1948), 365.

[121] Jones, *Christ in the Camp,* 132–133.

[122] G. MacLaren Brydon, "The Confederate Prayer Book," *Historical Magazine of the Protestant Episcopal Church,* XVII(1948), 339.

[123] Germain, *Catholic Military and Naval Chaplains,* 113, 119; Chaplain A. S. Worrel to Secretary of War George Randolph, 19 November 1862, War Department Office File, National Archives.

[124] Manire, *Caskey's Last Book,* 30–34.

[125] Noll, *Doctor Quintard,* 18, 60, 91, 118, 155.

[126] James Aldridge, "The Confederate Invasion of Vermont," *The National Guardsman,* IX(1955), 3.

[127] W. A. Crocker, "Army Intelligence Office," *Confederate Veteran,* VIII(1900), 118–119.

[128] Isaac Tichenor diary, in Tichenor Papers, Southern Baptist Historical Commission.

[129] *South Western Baptist,* 29 August 1961.

[130] Wiley, *Life of Johnny Reb,* 188.

[131] *Confederate Veteran,* XVIII(1919), 80; *Official Records,* Series I, XXV, Part 1, 873; *Southern Presbyterian,* 10 August 1861; *The Christian Instructor and Western United Presbyterian,* 20 November 1861.

[132] *Confederate Veterans,* XXIII(1915), 205.

[133] Fitzgerald, *John B. McFerrin,* 278.

[134] W. H. Morgan, *Personal Reminiscences of the War of 1861–65* (Lynchburg: J. P. Bell Co., 1911), 137; *Confederate Veteran,* XXIII(1915), 205; *Church Intelligencer,* 13 June 1862.

[135] *Religious Herald,* 10 July 1862.

[136] *Ibid.,* 17 July 1862.

[137] *Southern Presbyterian,* 8 August 1862.

[138] *Southern Presbyterian,* 1 June 1861 and 29 January 1863.

[139] *North Carolina Presbyterian,* 4 May 1861; *North Carolina Christian Advocate,* 23 September 1863; *Christian Index,* 19 February and 11 March 1862.

[140] *Southern Christian Advocate,* 15 October 1863.

[141] General Thomas J. Jackson to General Samuel Cooper, Adjutant General, Confederate States of America, 10 March 1863, MS. in the Confederate Museum.

[142] "An Address of the Chaplains of the Second Corps ("Stonewall" Jackson's Army of Northern Virgiria, to the Churches of the Confederate States," *Southern Historical Society Papers,* XIV (1886), 348–356.

[143] *Religious Herald,* 12 March 1863; *Southern Christian Advocate,* 2 April 1863; *North Carolina Presbyterian,* 11 April 1863.

[144] *Southern Churchman,* 29 May 1863.

[145] Moses D. Hodge to W. P. Miles, Chairman of the Committee on Military Affairs, 7 May 1862, Moses D. Hodge Papers, University of Virginia Library.

[146] *Religious Herald,* 11 February 1864; *Christian Index,* 6 and 19 February 1864.

[147] *The Army and Navy Messenger,* 1 May 1863; *Southern Presbyterian* 3 March 1864; The Soldiers Paper, 1 March 1865; *Southern Christian Advocate,* 11 February 1864.

EPILOGUE

Although the chaplaincy as an institution was legally established by Congress on 29 July 1775, it virtually disintegrated after the Revoluntionary War, along with the rest of the Army. Reconstituted in 1791 with a single appointment, its existence for the next four score years was marked by uncertainty and uneasiness. For chaplains themselves the years involved struggle for recognition, appreciation, and acceptance.

The reconstitution came when religion was at a lower state of vitality than at any other time in American history. The process of decline was hastened by the loss of church leadership, ecclesiastical divisions, and widespread apathy in regard to religious faith. Church membership dropped both relatively and absolutely until in 1790, when the first census was taken, it was estimated that less than ten percent of the population was affiliated with a church. There are no documents to indicate the religious composition of the Army during the period, but it is reasonable to assume that the percentage of church affiliations was about the same as that of the general population.

It was not long before the religious climate improved. Church membership substantially increased as a result of the Great Revival in the West and the work of western ministers and missionaries. Immigrants, especially in the two decades before mid-century, accounted for a marked growth in Catholic membership. On the eve of the War between the States, almost half of the population was at least nominally acquainted with institutionalized religion. Interestingly, as religious membership grew, so did the authorized number of peacetime chaplains, from one in 1791 to thirty in 1849. No extraordinary circumstances were at work: as the percentage of church members in the country increased, there was an increase in the Army as well; as the number of clergymen who served in the civilian communities grew, there was an increase in the number of chaplains. The friendlier religious atmosphere won a wider acceptance of the chaplaincy by soldiers and clergymen.

The first Regular Army chaplains not only began their activities in an unpropitious religious environment, they were also plagued by professional and military problems. While their successors witnessed an improvement in the religious climate, progress in overcoming difficulties was not as evident. Two areas were especially troublesome—the role of the chaplain and his military status.

Most chaplains thought their primary tasks were to lead religious worship, foster moral behavior, and contribute to a good state of individual and collective morale. Some commanders did not agree, and thought of a chaplain as a flunky, available for various peripheral jobs. Those were the two concepts between which understanding of the chaplain's role ran the gamut by chaplains and commanders alike.

Without defining statute or directive, the activities covered a wide range. Some chaplains emphasized social services; some became cheerleaders for patriotism; others served mainly as morale officers, or charismatic mascots; not a few betrayed strong leanings toward either officers or enlisted men, rather than both; and a few felt most at home as fighting men, participants in combat actions. The most talented and committed, however, always seemed to have a remarkably free hand to follow their calling and undertook ancillary duties only as a secondary obligation. Men of that stripe, who embodied a more spiritual type of ministry, slowly won recognition for the position of chaplain until, during the War Between the States—when the term chaplain was first commonly used—the role was generally viewed as that of a clergyman doing spiritual work in a military context to which he was closely related.

If many were confused about their role, all were uncertain about their military status, which was associated primarily with rank but also involved issues of pay and uniform. From 1791 until the War Between the States, chaplains were appointed without rank, whether the assignment was to a unit, a post, or to the Military Academy. As a matter of protocol, they were generally recognized as holding the rank that paralleled their military pay. Except for the War of 1812, when chaplains were paid the salary of a major, compensation was fixed at the level of captain, and a parallel rank of captain was generally presumed. During the Civil War, ministers were *commissioned as chaplains* in both the Confederate and Federal forces; chaplain was regarded as equivalent to captain in the Confederate Army, while it was thought of as a special new grade between captain and major in the Union Army. Uniforms did not clarify the issue; when chaplains were authorized to wear them, they were worn without the epaulets indicative of rank.

Because the majority of chaplains considered themselves primarily ministers and secondarily officers, they were able to transcend the frustrations that surrounded their role and status. In a very taxing ministry, both during the drudgery of peace and the hazards of war, they tried to be faithful and conspicuous representatives of another way, loyal subjects of a kingdom not totally of this world.

Over the period, some soldiers and officers expressed resentment of clerical presence in the Army. Debates in the House and Senate over the issue of government chaplaincies, which revealed a wide range of attitudes, regularly surfaced opposition. But it was not until the War with Mexico that the opposition became a ground swell and posed a serious threat to the chaplaincy as an institution. Speaking articulately from diverse convictions, critics pointed to the chaplaincy as unconstitutional on the ground that it effected a mingling of the functions of church and state. The arguments, however, were characterized more by prejudice than by insight into principle; they reflected in varying degrees sharpening sectional animosities within most denominations, and the fears and hostilities of larger denominations over the impact of Catholic immigration.

In response to widespread and sharp criticism, the Judiciary Committees of the Senate and House argued in several reports that chaplaincies did not contravene the First Amendment; and, that the government should continue to provide facilities for worship and religious activities. Opposition continued to be heard. Two years before the outbreak of the War Between the States the House Judiciary Committee declared that while religion was unable to prevent war, it tended to mitigate the rigors of war; abolishment of that mitigating influence would reverse rather than advance the course of civilization; the military chaplaincy was a constitutional necessity to provide for free exercise of religion. It would continue.

Even though chaplains were not fully accepted into the framework of military organization, not fully understood or appreciated, they were nevertheless the most important representatives of institutionalized religion in the Army. Because they were present, religion played a role in the regiments, brigades, posts, hospitals, and at the Military Academy. During the period, religious work in the Army centered in the presence and influence of chaplains, and nearly all organized religious action was due to their endeavors.

Although there were some unqualified and unworthy men, the final verdict on the chaplaincy for these years was generally positive. A large number of chaplains were held in high esteem by commanding officers; even irreligious officers, disposed to discount their contributions, admitted that chaplains performed a necessary function. Religious publications registered an affirmative vote. Civilian ministers voiced praise for their military counterparts. Perhaps the most meaningful evaluation came from the troops; given half a chance to know their chaplain, they usually said some complimentary things.

The wars of the period—War of 1812, War with Mexico, War Between the States—threatened to brutalize the nation. The fact that it did not happen was partially because those who fought the battles were accompanied by ministers who carried no weapons, and whose primary purpose was propagation of a gospel of personal forgiveness, peace, and reconciliation with God.

SELECTED BIBLIOGRAPHY

PRIMARY MATERIALS

MANUSCRIPTS

Alabama Department of Archives and History, Montgomery, Alabama
    Newton Davis Letters
    Francis Hanson Diary
    Isaac Tichenor Papers
    Official Records of the 16th
    Alabama Infantry Regiment

American Baptist Historical Society, Rochester, New York
    David Jones Papers

Confederate Museum, Richmond, Virginia
    Miscellaneous Letters Collection
    William H. Routt Papers
    Cornelius Walker Diary

Georgia Department of Archives and History, Atlanta, Georgia
    Letters of Confederate Soldiers
    Reminiscences of Confederate Soldiers

Manuscript Collection, Duke University, Durham, North Carolina
    James H. Alexander Diary
    Charles Andrews Letters
    William H. Arehart Diary
    J. J. Bell Diary
    Henry Beveridge Diary
    John D. Harris Papers
    John H. Hartman Papers
    John B. Magruder Papers

Bessie N. Mason Papers
Dudley Pendleton Papers
Charles T. Quintard Papers
C. L. Refo Letters
Irby H. Scott Papers
James Wilson Letters

Manuscript Collection, United States Army Chaplain Center and School, Fort Wadsworth, New York
William W. Meech Papers
Earl F. Stover Collection
Richard K. Smith Collection

Manuscript Collection, United States Military Academy, West Point, New York
Jasper Adams Papers
John French Papers
Thomas Picton Papers
Thomas Warner Papers

Microfilm Collection, Joint University Libraries, Nashville, Tennessee
H. S. Archer Diary

North Carolina Historical Commission, Raleigh, North Carolina
Milton Carter Papers
Henry A. Chambers Diary
J. B. Clifton Diary
DeRossett Papers
Fred D. Foard Papers
John C. Garman Diary
J. E. Green Diary
R. C. Mabry Letters
Frank M. Parker Letters
Adolph Pitcher Diary
Stephen Reed Letters
Colin Shaw Papers
A. S. Webb Papers

Southern Historical Collection, University of North Carolina, Chapel Hill, North Carolina
James W. Albright Diary
Isaac Alexander's Letters

John W. Beckwith Papers
Alexander Betts Papers
Thomas P. Boatwright Papers
Gratz Cohen Collection
Joseph A. Cotton Papers
William Gale Collection
James A. Graham Letters
Charles F. James Papers
Francis Kennedy Diary
D. M. Key Letters
Bishop H. C. Lay Papers
Mackay-Stiles Papers
Basil Manley Papers
Frank Nash Papers
John Paris Collection
W. D. Pender Papers
W. S. Pettigrew Papers
Ruffin-Roulhas-Hamilton Papers
Cary Whitaker Papers
Henry F. Williams Letters
W. H. Wills Papers

Virginia State Library, Richmond, Virginia
George M. Neese Diary
John F. Sale Collection

NATIONAL ARCHIVES COLLECTIONS

Records of the Confederate Adjutant General's Office, Confederate
    Chaplains' Letters
Records of the Confederate War Department, Chaplains' Letters
Records of the Office of the Secretary of War, Letters Received
    (irregular series, 1861–1866)
Records of the United States Army Command, Department of the
    West, Letters Received.

PUBLIC DOCUMENTS

*Acts and Resolutions of the 2nd, 3rd, and the 4th Sessions of the
    Provisional Congress of the Confederate States.* Held at Montgo-
    mery, Alabama, Richmond, 1861, 1862.

American State Papers: Documents Legislative and Executive of the Congress of the United States. Military Affairs, Vols. I–IV, Washington, 1832–1861.

Army Regulations Adopted for the Use of the Army of the Confederate States, Richmond, 1861.

Congressional Globe, Washington, 1833–1865.

General Regulations of the Army of the United States, Washington, 1841–1863.

Heitman, Francis (comp.). *Historical Register and Directory of the United States Army.* 2 Vols., Washington, 1903.

Journal of the Congress of the Confederate States of America, 1861–1865. 58th Congress of the United States, 2nd Session. Senate Document No. 234. 7 Vols., Washington, 1904–1905.

Matthew, J. M. (Ed.). *Statutes at Large of the Provisional Government of the Confederate States.* Richmond, 1864.

Ramsdell, Charles W. (Ed.). *Laws and Joint Resolutions of the Last Session of the Confederate Congress.* Durham, 1941.

Regulations for the Army of the Confederate States. Richmond, 1863.

The Public Statutes at Large of the United States of America, Vols. I–XII, 1827–1865. Titles, dates and publishers vary.

War of the Rebellion. A Compilation of the Official Records of the Union and Confederate Armies. 130 vols. Washington, 1880–1901.

NEWSPAPERS

Augusta *Southern Christian Advocate,* 1861–1865.

Baltimore *Niles Weekly Register,* 1811–1849. Title varies.

Columbia *Southern Presbyterian,* 1861–1865.

Fayetteville *North Carolina Presbyterian,* 1862.

Louisville *Western Recorder,* 1863.

Macon *Christian Index,* 1861–1865.

Nashville *Banner,* 1911.

Petersburg *The Army and Navy Messenger,* 1863–1864.

Raleigh *Church Intelligencer,* 1863.

Richmond *Religious Herald.*

Richmond *Southern Churchman,* 1861–1865.

Tuskegee *South Western Baptist,* 1861–1863.

Washington *Army and Navy Journal,* 1863–1887.

PUBLISHED DIARIES, LETTER COLLECTIONS, MEMOIRS, REPORTS AND BIOGRAPHIES

"An Address of the Chaplains of the Second Corps

('Stonewall' Jackson's) Army of Northern Virginia, to the Churches of the Confederate States." *Southern Historical Society Papers,* XIV (1886), 348–356.

Anderson, Charles (ed.). "Frontier Mackinac Island, 1823–1834, Letters of William Montague and Amanda White Ferry." *Journal of the Presbyterian Historical Society,* XXV (1947), 192–222.

Barbiere, Joe. *Scraps from the Prison Table at Camp Chase and Johnson's Island.* Doyleston, Pennsylvania: Privately printed, 1863.

Barringer, Graham. "The Mexican War Journal of Henry S. Lane." *Indiana Magazine of History,* LIII (1957), 383–436.

Bassett, John S. (ed.). *Correspondence of Andrew Jackson.* Washington: Carnegie Institute, 1926–1935.

Battle-fields of the South, from Bull Run to Fredericksburg, with Sketches of Confederate Commanders, and Gossip of the Camps. New York: John Bradburn, 1864.

Baylor, George. *Bull Run to Bull Run; or, Four Years in the Army of Northern Virginia, containing a detailed account of the Career and Adventures of the Baylor Light Horse Company B, Twelfth Virginia Cavalry, C.S.A.* Richmond: Johnson Printing Company, 1900.

Bennett, William A. *A Narrative of the Great Revival which Prevailed in the Southern Armies during the late Civil War Between the States of the Federal Union.* Philadelphia: Claxton, Remsen and Haffelfinger, 1877.

Betts, William A. (Ed.). *Experience of a Confederate Chaplain.* Greenville, South Carolina: Privately printed, 1904.

Blackford, Susan Leigh (Comp.). *Letters from Lee's Army, or Memoirs of Life in and out of the Army of Virginia During the War Between the States.* Chapel Hill: The University of North Carolina Press, 1938.

Blackwood, Emma. *To Mexico With Scottt; Letters of Captain E. Kirby Smith to His Wife.* Cambridge: Harvard University Press, 1917.

Brown, William Y. *The Army Chaplain: His Office, Duties, and Responsibilities.* Philadelphia: William S. and Alfred Martien, 1863.

Carus, William. *Memorials of the Right Reverend Charles Pettit McLLvaine.* New York: Thomas Whittaker, 1882.

Cate, Wirt Armistead (Ed.). *Two Soldiers; The Campaign Diaries of Thomas J. Key, C.S.A. and Robert J. Campbell, U.S.A.* Chapel Hill: The University of North Carolina Press, 1938.

Commanger, Henry Steele (Ed.). *The Blue and the Gray; the Story of the Civil War as Told by Participants.* 2 vols. Indianapolis: The Bobbs-Merrill Company, Inc., 1950.

Cullom, Jeremiah. *Pastoral Sketches, 1851–1907.* Nashville: Publishing House of the Methodist Episcopal Church, South, 1907.

Cumming, Kate. *A Journal of Hospital Life in the Confederate Army of Tennessee from the Battle of Shiloh to the End of the War: With Sketches of Life and Character, and Brief Accounts of Current Events During the Period.* Louisville: John P. Morton and Company, 1866.

Davis, Nicholas A. *The Campaign from Texas to Maryland.* Richmond: Presbyterian Committee of Publication of the Confederate States, 1863.

DeFontaine, Felix G. *Marginalia; or, Gleanings from an Army Note-Book.* Columbia: F. G. DeFontaine and Co., 1864.

Denison, Frederick. *A Chaplain's Experiences in the Union Army.* Providence: Rhode Island Soldiers and Sailors Historical Society, 1893.

"Diary of Lieutenant Colonel John G. Pressley," *Southern Historical Society Papers,* XIV (1886), 35–62.

Durkin, Joseph T. (Ed.). *John Dooley, Confederate Soldier, His War Journal.* Washington: Georgetown University Press, 1945.

Ellis, Albert G. "Fifty-four Years Recollections of Men and Events in Wisconsin." *Collections of the State Historical Society of Wisconsin,* VII (1873–1876), 210–268.

Fitzgerald, O. P. *John B. McFerrin, A Bibography.* Nashville: Publishing House of the Methodist Episcopal Church, South, 1888.

Flourney, Henry W. (Ed.). *Calendar of Virginia State Papers and Other Manuscripts.* 2 vols. Richmond: Printed under the Direction of the State Librarian, 1893.

Furber, George. *The Twelve Months Volunteer or, The Journal of a Private in the Tennessee Regiment of Cavalry.* Cincinnati: A. J. and U. P. James, 1850.

Gay, Mary A. H. *Life in Dixie During the War*. Atlanta: The Foote and Davis Company, 1894.

Goodloe, Albert Theodore. *Confederate Echoes: A Voice from the South in the Days of Secession and of the Southern Confederacy*. Nashville: Smith and Lamar, 1907.

Gordon, John Brown. *Reminiscences of the Civil War*. New York: Charles Scribner's Sons, 1903.

Hall, W. T. "Religion in the Army of Tennessee." *The Land We Love*, IV (1867), 129–131.

Hammond, J. Pinkney, *The Army Chaplain's Manual*. Philadelphia: J. B. Lippencott, 1863.

Hancock, Robert R. *Hancock's Diary; or, A History of the Second Tennessee Confederate Cavalry, With Sketches of First and Second Battalions, also, Portraits and Biographical Sketches*. Nashville: Brandon Printing Company, 1887.

Hudson, H. N. *A Chaplain's Campaign with General Butler*. New York: Privately printed, 1965.

Hurt, John. "An Address to the Virginia Brigade." *Virginia Magazine of History*, XVII (1909), 213–214.

Jones, J. William. *Christ in the Camp or Religion in the Confederate Army*. Atlanta: The Martin and Hoyte Company, 1887.

Lane, James H. "Glimpses of Army Life in 1864." *Southern Historical Society Papers*, XVIII (1890), 406–422.

Law, John G. "Diary of a Confederate Soldier." *Southern Historical Society Papers*, X (1882), 378–381, 564–568.

Lewis, Richard. *Camp Life of a Confederate Boy of Bratton's Brigade, Longstreets Corps, C.S.A.* Charleston: The News and Courier Book Press, 1883.

Manire, Benjamin F. (Ed.). *Caskey's Last Book, Containing an Autobiographical Sketch of His Ministerial Life, with Essays and Sermons*. Nashville: The Messenger Publishing Company, 1896.

McCarthy, Carlton, *Soldier Life in the Army of Northern Virginia 1861–1965*. Atlanta: B. F. Johnson Publishing Company, 1908.

McElroy, John. "Chaplains For the Mexican War—1846." *Woodstock Letters*, XV (1886), 198–202; XVI (1887), 33–39.

McFerrin, John B. "Religion in the Army of Tennessee," *The*

Home Monthly, IV (April–June, 1868), 161–162, 211–213, 281–285.

McKim, Randolph. *A Soldier's Recollections: Leaves from the Diary of a Young Confederate, With an Oration on the Motives and Aims of the Soldiers of the South.* New York: Longmans, Green and Company, 1910.

Mooney, Chase (Ed.). "A Union Chaplain's Diary." *Proceedings of the New Jersey Historical Society,* LXXV (1957), 1–17.

Moore, Edward A. *The Story of a Cannoneer under Stonewall Jackson; in Which Is Told the Part Taken by the Rockbridge Artillery in the Army of Northern Virginia.* New York: The Neale Publishing Company, 1907.

Morgan, William H. *Personal Reminiscences of the War of 1861– 1865; In Camp—in Bivouac—on the March—on Picket—on the Skirmish Line—on the Battlefield—and in Prison.* Lynchburg: J. P. Bell and Company, 1911.

Noll, Arthur (Ed.). *Dr. Quintard. Chaplain C.S.A. and Second Bishop of Tennessee; Being His Story of the War (1861–1865).* Sewanee: The University Press of Sewanee, Tennessee, 1905.

Phelps, Dawson (Ed.). "The Diary of a Chaplain In Andrew Jackson's Army: The Journal of the Reverend Blackman— December 28, 1812—April 4, 1813." *Tennessee Historical Quarterly,* XII (1953), 264–281.

Pierson, William W. (Ed.). "The Diary of Bartlett Yancey Malone." Vol. XVI, No. 2 of *The James Sprunt Historical Publications.* Chapel Hill: The University of North Carolina Press, 1919.

Pleasants, J. Hall (Ed.). "Memoirs of the Rev. James Jones Wiler." *Maryland Historical Magazine,* XIX (1924), 220–246.

"Proceedings of the First Confederate Congress, 2nd Session," *Southern Historical Society Papers,* XLVII (1930), 1–463.

Quaife, Milo (Ed.). *The Diary of James K. Polk.* Chicago: A. C. McClurg Company, 1910.

Rowland, Cunbar (Ed.). "My Journal: The Story of a Soldier's Life as Told by Himself," by William Pitt Chambers. Publications of the "Robert E. Parks Diary," *Southern Historical Society Papers,* I. (1976), 370–386, 430–437.

Srygley, Fletcher D. *Seventy Years in Dixie: Recollections and*

Sayings of T. W. Caskey and Others. Nashville: Gospel Advocate Company, 1891.

Stephenson, Wendell Holmes, and Edwin Adam Davis. "The Civil War Diary of Willie Micajah Barrow." *Louisiana Historical Quarterly,* XVII (1934), 436–451, 712–731.

Stewart, A. M. *Camp, March and Battlefield; or Three Years and a Half In the Army of the Potomac.* Philadelphia: James B. Rodgers, 1865.

Stiles, Robert. *Four Years Under Marse Robert.* New York: Neale Publishing Company, 1903.

Sullins, David. *Recollections of an Old Man: Seventy Years in Dixie, 1827–1897.* Bristol: The King Printing Company, 1910.

Tanner, George. "History of Fort Ripley, 1849–1859. Based on the Diary of Rev. Solon W. Manney, D.D., Chaplain at the Post from 1851 to 1859." *Collections of the Minnesota Historical Society,* X. Part I (1905), 179–202.

Trumbull, H. Clay. *War Memories of an Army Chaplain.* New York: Charles Scribner's Sons, 1898.

United States Christian Commission. *First Annual Report.* Philadelphia: Privately printed, 1863.

United States Christian Commission. *Second Annual Report.* New York: Privately printed, 1864.

"Vinson Confederate Letters," *North Carolina Historical Review,* XXV (January, 1948), 100–110.

Wagstaff, Henry H. (Ed.). "The James A Graham Papers, 1861–1884." Vol. XX, No. 2 of the *James Sprunt Historical Publications.* Chapel Hill: The University of North Carolina Press, 1928.

Watkins, Sam R. *Company Aytch, Maury Grays First Tennessee Regiment; or, A Side Show of the Big Show.* Nashville, Cumberland Publishing House, 1882.

Welch, Spencer Glasglow. *A Confederate Surgeon's Letters to His Wife.* Marietta, Georgia, Continental Book Company, 1954.

Wright, Marcus. *Tennessee in the War, 1861–65.* New York: Ambrose Lee Publishing Company, 1908.

Secondary Material

Alexander, Philip W. "John Eaton, Jr., Preacher Soldier, and Educator." Unpublished Ph.D. dissertation, George Peabody College for Teachers, 1939.

Ambrose, Stephen E. *Duty, Honor, Country, A History of West Point.* Baltimore: The Johns Hopkins Press, 1966.

Armstrong, Warren. "Union Chaplains and the Education of the Freedman." *Journal of Negro History,* LIIC (1967), 104–115.

Barish, Louis (Ed.). *Rabbis in Uniform.* New York: Johnathan David, 1962.

Blassingame, John. "Negro Chaplains in the Civil War." *The Negro History Bulletin,* XXXVII (1963), 1, 23.

Bearss, Ed & Gibson, Arrell. *Fort Smith; Little Gibraltar on the Arkansas.* Norman: University of Oklahoma Press, 1969.

Blied, Benjamin J. *Catholics and the Civil War.* Milwaukee: Privately printed, 1945.

Bristol, Frank. *The Life of Chaplain McCabe.* New York: Fleming H. Revell Company, 1908.

Billingsley, A. S. *From the Flag to the Cross; or Scenes and Incidents of Christianity in the War.* Philadelphia: New-World Publishing Company, 1872.

Bryden, G. MacLaren. "The Confederate Prayer Book." *Historical Magazine of the Protestant Episcopal Church,* XVII (1948), 339–344.

Capers, Walter B. *The Soldier-Bishop Ellison Capers.* New York: Neal Publishing Company, 1912.

Cheshire, Joseph B. *The Church in the Confederate States; a History of the Protestant Episcopal Church in the Confederate States.* New York: Longmans, Green & Company, 1912.

Clark, Dwight & Ruhlen, George. "The Final Roster of the Army of the West, 1846–1847." *California Historical Society Quarterly,* XL (1964), 37–43.

Clark, Walter (Ed.). *Histories of the Several Regiments and Battalions from North Carolina in the Great War, 1861–65.* 5 vols. Raleigh: Published by the State of North Carolina, 1901.

Confederate Veteran. Vols. I–XXXIX. Nashville, 1893–1932.

Conyngham, D. P. "Soldiers of the Cross—Heroism of the Cross or Nuns and Priests on the Battlefield." Unpublished manuscript in the Archives of Notre Dame University, n.d.

Cudworth, A. M. *A Memorial of Rev. Warren H. Cudworth.* Boston: Lathrop & Company, 1884.

Cullum, George W. *Biographical Register of the Officers and Graduates of the U.S. Military Academy.* New York: James Miller, 1879.

Daniel, W. Harrison. "The Southern Baptists in the Confederacy." *Civil War History*, VI (1960), 389–401.

Davis, Mrs. Charles. *Reminiscences of West Point*. East Saginaw: Evening News Printing and Binding House, 1886.

Edsall, Samuel. "Rev. Ezekiel Gilbert Gear, D. D. Chaplain at Fort Snelling, 1838–1858." *Collections of the Minnesota Historical Society*, XII (1908), 691–696.

Ellsworth, Clayton. "American Churches and the Mexican War." *American Historical Society Review*, XLV (1940), 301–326.

Evjen, John. *The Life of J.H.W. Stuckenberg*. Minneapolis: The Lutheran Free Church Publishing Company, 1938.

Fisher, H. D. *The Gun and the Gospel: Early Kansas and Chaplain Fisher*. Chicago: Medical Publishing Company, 1897.

Fleming, Thomas. *West Point, The Men and Times of the United States Military Academy*. New York: William Morrow & Company, 1969.

Fleming, Walter L. "The Churches of Alabama During the Civil War and Reconstruction," *Gulf States Historical Magazine*. I (1902), 105–127.

Forman, Sidney. *Cadet Life Before the Mexican War*. West Point: United States Military Academy Printing Office, 1945.

Fox, William. *Regimental Losses in the American Civil War*. Albany: Albany Publishing Company, 1889.

Fuller, Richard. *Chaplain Fuller*. Boston: Walker, Wise, & Company, 1863.

Gamble, Richard, "Army Chaplains at Frontier Posts, 1830–1860." *Historical Magazine of the Protestant Episcopal Church*, XXVII (1958), 285–306.

Germain, Aiden Henry. *Catholic Military and Naval Chaplains, 1776–1917*. Washington: Catholic University of America, 1929.

Greene, Howard. *The Reverend Richard Fish Cadle*. Waukesha: Privately Printed, 1936.

Heathcote, Charles W. *The Lutheran Church and the Civil War*. New York: Fleming H. Revell Company, 1919.

Henry, James O. "The United States Christian Commission in the Civil War." *Civil War History*, VI (1960), 374–388.

Hinckley, Thomas. "American Anti-Catholicism during the Mexican War." *Pacific Historical Review*, XXXIC (1962), 121–137.

Honeywell, Roy. "John Hurt, First Regular Army Chaplain." *The Army and Navy Chaplain*, XVI (1954), 7.

————. *Chaplains of the United States Army.* Washington: Government Printing Office, 1958.

Howard, Philip. *The Life of Henry Clay Trumbull.* Philadelphia: The Sunday School Times Company, 1905.

Hughes, William J. "The Methodist Ministry to American Military Personnel to 1900." Unpublished M.A. thesis, New Mexico State University, 1974.

Johnson, Lorenzo D. *Chaplains of the General Government.* New York: Sheldon, Blakeman and Company, 1856.

Johnson, Richard. "Fort Snelling from its Foundation to the Present Time." *Collections of the Minnesota Historical Society,* VIII (1898), 427–448.

Kenny, Michael. *Catholic Culture in Alabama; Centenary Story of Spring Hill College, 1830–1930.* New York: American Press, 1931.

Kernodle, Peter J. *Lives of Christian Ministers.* Richmond: The Central Publishing Company, 1909.

Keyes, E. D. *Fifty Years Observation of Men and Events.* New York: Charles Scribner's Sons, 1884.

Korn, Bertram W. "Jewish Chaplains During the Civil War." *American Jewish Archives* I (1948), 6–22.

Knox, Henry. "A Plan for the General Arrangement of the Militia of the United States." *Proceedings of the Massachusetts Historical Society,* Series I, VI (1862–1863), 364–403.

Lacy, Benjamin Rice: *Revivals in the Midst of the Years.* Richmond: John Knox Press, 1943.

Leigh, Mrs. Townes R. "The Jews In the Confederacy." *Southern Historical Society Papers,* XXXIX (1914), 177–180.

Livermore, Thomas L. *Numbers and Losses in the Civil War in America, 1861–65.* Boston: Houghton Mifflin and Company, 1900.

London, Lawrence. "The Literature of the Church in the Confederate States." *Historical Magazine of the Episcopal Church,* XVII (1948), 343–355.

Lonn, Ella. *Foreigners in the Confederacy.* Chapel Hill: University of North Carolina Press, 1940.

Lockwood, James. "Early Times and Events in Wisconsin." *Collections of The State Historical Society of Wisconsin.* II (1856), 98–196.

Lucey, William L. (Ed.). "The Diary of Joseph B. O'Hagan, S. J.,

Chaplain of the Excelsior Birgade." *Civil War History*, VI (1960), 402–409.

McDonald, William and Searles, John. *The Life of Rev. John S. Inskip*. Boston: McDonald & Gill, 1885.

McEniry, Blanch. *American Catholics in the War with Mexico*. Washington: Privately printed, 1937.

Mahan, Bruce. *Old Fort Crawford and the Frontier*. Iowa City: University of Iowa Press, 1926.

Moss, Lemuel and Smith, Edward. *Christian Work on the Battlefield*. London: Hodder & Stoughton, 1902.

Neill, Edward. "Fort Snelling Echoes." *Magazine of Western History*, X (1889), 604–612.

Norton, Herman. *Rebel Religion*. St. Louis: Bethany Press, 1961.

―――. "Revivalism in the Confederate Armies." *Civil War History*, VI (1960), 410–424.

O'Reilly, Isabel. "One of Philadelphia's Soldiers in the Mexican War." *American Catholic Historical Society Records*, XIII (1902), 257–284.

"Our Leaders: Surgeons and Chaplains," *Historical Records of the United Daughters of the Confederacy*, Vol XX No. 7. (This is a miscellaneous collection of newspaper clippings and magazine articles in the Confederate Museum.)

Payne, Darwin. "Camp Life in the Army of Occupation." *Southwestern Historical Quarterly*, LXXXIII (1969–1970), 326–342.

Pennington, Edgar P. "The Church and the Soldiers," *Historical Magazine of the Protestant Episcopal Church*, XVII (1948), 356–383.

Pitts, Charles. *Chaplains in Gray*. Nashville: Broadman Press, 1957.

Pfab, Charles B. "American Hospital Chaplains During the Civil War, 1861–1865." Unpublished M.A. thesis, Catholic University of America, 1955

Pride, Woodbury F. *The History of Fort Riley*. Fort Riley: The Cavalry School, 1926.

Quenzel, Carroll. "Books for the Boys in Blue." *Journal of the Illinois Historical Society*, XXXIV (1951), 218–230.

Quimby, Rollin. "Congress and the Civil War Chaplaincy." *Civil War History*, X (1964), 246–259.

―――. "The Chaplains Predicament." *Civil War History*, VIII (1962), 25–37.

―――. "Recurrent Themes and Purposes in the Sermons of Union Army Chaplains." *Speech Monographs*, XXXI (1964), 425–436.

Romero, Sidney. "The Confederate Chaplain." *Civil War History*, I (1955), 127–140.

Ryan, Abram J. *Poems: Patriotic, Religious, Miscellaneous.* New York: P. J. Kennedy, 1896.

Shepard, John. "Religion in the Army of Northern Virginia." *North Carolina Historical Review*, XXV (1948), 341–376.

Shindler, Henry. *Public Worship at Fort Leavenworth, Kansas, 1827–1907.* Fort Leavenworth, 1907.

Smith, John. "The Military Ordinoriate of the United States of America." Unpublished J.C.D. thesis, The Catholic University of America, 1966.

Sprague, William B. *Annals of the American Pulpit.* 9 vols. New York: Carter & Brothers, 1857–1865.

Stapleton, Ernest S. "The History of Baptist Missions in New Mexico, 1849–1866." Unpublished M.A. thesis, University of New Mexico, 1954.

Stock, Leo Francis. "The United States at the Court of Pius IX," *The Catholic Historical Review*, III (1923), 103–122.

Sweet, William W. *The Methodist Episcopal Church and the Civil War.* Cincinnati: Methodist Book Concern, 1912.

Tanner, George. "Early Episcopal Churches and Missions in Minnesota." *Collections of the Minnesota Historical Society*, X, Part I (1905), 203–231.

Thompson, William. "The United States Sanitary Commission." *Civil War History*, II (1956), 46–63.

Waugh, E. D. *West Point.* New York: The MacMillan Company, 1944.

Weigley, Russell F. *History of the United States Army.* New York: The Macmillan Company, 1967.

Wesley, Edgar B. "Life at a Frontier Post." *American Military Institute Journal.* III (1939), 203–209.

White, Henry A. *Southern Presbyterian Leaders.* New York: Neale Publishing Company, 1911.

Whitford, W. C. "Early Education in Wisconsin." *Collections of the States Historical Society of Wisconsin*, V. Part 3 (1869), 321–351.

Wiley, Bell I. "Holy Joes of the Sixties: A Study of Civil War Chaplains." *The Huntington Library Quarterly*, XVI (1953), 287–304.

———. *The Life of Johnny Reb, the Common Soldier of the Confederacy.* Indianapolis: The Bobbs-Merrill Company, 1943.

————. *The Life of Billy Yank, the Common Soldier of the Union.*
    Indianapolis: The Bobbs-Merrill Company, 1952.
Wyatt, William. *The Life and Sermons of Rev. William Wyatt.* Albany:
    Charles Van Benthuysen & Sons, 1878.

INDEX